# Snap to Grid

# Snap to Grid

A User's Guide to Digital Arts, Media, and Cultures

*Peter Lunenfeld*

The MIT Press  Cambridge, Massachusetts  London, England

This book was set in Janson Text and Rotis Semi Sans by Wellington Graphics and was printed and bound in the United States of America.

Library of Congress Cataloging-in-Publication Data

Lunenfeld, Peter.
  Snap to grid: a user's guide to digital arts, media, and cultures / Peter Lunenfeld.
    p. cm.
  Includes bibliographical references and index.
  ISBN 0-262-12226-X (hc: alk. paper)
  1. Computers and civilization.  2. Art, Modern—20th century.  3. Digital media.  4. Multimedia systems.
QA76.9.C66L86   2000
006.7—dc21                                                              99-040216

The three part dividers are illustrated with paintings by Miltos Manetas: I. *Untitled (Big Glass)*, 1998; II. *Untitled (Zip Drive and Legs)*, 1998; III. *Untitled (Levi's with Cables)*, 1999. Courtesy of Postmasters Gallery, New York.

To Susan
for everything

# Contents

# Foreword

Imagine a city colonized by its own economy, where power is diffuse but highly centralized. This city is wrapped as smooth as a vinyl texture map. The class structure and day-to-day business are highly ergonomic. They rely on easy listening surveillance, nothing more threatening—at first glance—than a beep from a remote control. The weather and the architecture offer no immediate threat, no sense of rifle sights aimed by lunatics at innocents on the street. In fact, at a glance, there is nothing more than the risk of a bad sunburn or an occasional mudslide. We can drive or navigate its "streets" without getting crushed by biker assassins from a Japanese animé. So we can assume that this site is by no means a dark cyberpunk world. You do not jack up sour memories like shooting with dirty needles. Nor is it an electrotopia, where everyone loves to talk digital and sleep near the warmth of their monitors. None of the easy tropes will serve here. Instead, a very different place emerges out of Peter Lunenfeld's encyclopedic journey in *Snap to Grid*.

When I say place, I suspect that the reader immediately assumes that I speak metaphorically, or "virtually," something about snapping into a grid along a $z$ axis. But I refer more to the geopolitical culture, the background to Lunenfeld's survey, what makes *Snap to Grid* very much a look into where the next few decades will have to go. Peter Lunenfeld is one of the leading figures in an emerging digital theory in Southern California. He understands very well how the digital has already married into trillions of dollars of investment capital. He sees every day how this marriage has advanced into real space and into social imaginaries, like the global Los Angeles that is spread like a grand

Los Angeles by night evokes the grid. This image conjures up the Web and the digital city and the real spaces, all so obviously infected by something infinitely larger than any single medium or technology.

Doug Aitken, *rise* (1998). Courtesy of 303 Gallery, New York.

catholicity across the world; in other words, into the transnational export of cinema and the new urban structures that fit so easily with the digitized corporation.

In Southern California, the long-term effects are already at work. There is very little need for post-structural theory to locate the political text hidden inside the inscrutable. This mess is as evident as a train roaring through a feudal village in 1880. In LA, one can see the epistemic sprawl as clearly as smog lifting every morning toward the San Gabriel Mountains. Media now have become the principal employer in LA—for the first time in the city's history. New systems for urban planning are full speed ahead, the "metropolitan suburb" bringing the same standard of latte to every town within two hundred miles.

This place is as clear to read, and as hypertextual as the Internet itself. Sometimes when I drive through LA, I think I am watching a gigantic autopsy, every incision a mile long. Every stage of digitally related production into real space, from design to final product, is incontestably noticeable. And Lunenfeld has made a point of studying each of these with boundless enthusiasm. I know, because I have tried to keep up with him through hours of conversation, ranging from urban history to film studies to graphic design, contemporary art, even the subcultures of local politics, from neighborhood to neighborhood—always returning to the digital world as well.

So what city am I referring to? It is the conjunction of the Web and digital city and the real spaces so obviously infected by something infinitely larger than any single medium or technology. It is the city that suits all these places at once, the city behind vapor theory, for digital dialecticians, for artists in every area. In Southern California, there is no art form imaginable that is not epistemically under shock from this new economy.

And yet, if you simply play the *flâneur* and try to read the surfaces themselves, they are just as elusively transparent as that vinyl texture map I mentioned earlier. You have to restore paradox to the discourse as much as possible, and invite all modes of visual and architectural production to invent new approaches. In short, this city is the "virtual" and the metro-suburban tourist chat world. The real space and the sim-space have met. We are witnessing a massive institution-building, not simply global capital accumulation. So indeed, it is time to integrate all the arts into any discussion of the digital. The "vapor" has spread beyond any of the older notions of digital theory.

This book takes the reader through dozens of sites informed by this highly expanded, advanced digital civilization. We are introduced to artists, technologies, and sites of production where much of the more advanced theory and work is being done. The paradoxes are emphasized, the older debates let go. Indeed, Lunenfeld has taken stock of what we find here in Southern California, in relation to the transnational culture. *Snap to Grid* goes from algorithm to architecture, from installation art to photography, to the process that must turn into praxis. It is something of an activist manual for art inside the city that

is both digital and in real space, highly internalized, but utterly global-
ized, Lunenfeld points to the site behind the crisis of "vapor" theory,
toward what certainly is needed in its place.

Norman M. Klein
*Los Angeles, CA*

Norman Klein, a faculty member at the California Institute of the Arts, is the
author of *Seven Minutes: The Life and Death of the American Animated Cartoon, The
History of Forgetting: Los Angeles and Erasure of Memory,* and the forthcoming *The
Vatican to Vegas: The History of Special Effects.*

# Acknowledgments

This book would not have been possible without the years of conversations, gigabytes of emails, and endless rounds of conference-going, paper-reading, exhibition-making, and companionship offered by brilliant friends and colleagues Florian Brody, Coco Conn, Ken Goldberg, Dan Harries, N. Katherine Hayles, Paul Harris, Michael Heim, Erkki Huhtamo, Norman Klein, Brenda Laurel, Lev Manovich, Steve Mamber, Vivian Sobchack, Bob Stein, Jennifer Steinkamp, and Diana Thater.

I have had the good fortune to able to establish a context in Los Angeles for my interests through organizing *mediawork: The Southern California New Media Working Group*, leading my *Digital Dialogues* graduate seminar at Art Center, and finding support for various conferences, panels, publishing projects, and public programming. This has allowed me interact with a huge group of artists, scientists, critics, and thinkers. I want to thank just few of them here: Phil Agre, Rosanna Albertini, Jim Blinn, Anne Bray, Jillian Burt, Ben Caldwell, Erik Davis, Steve Davis, Nick DeMartino, Timothy Durfee, Bob Flanagan, Robbert Flick, Peter Frank, Kit Galloway, Steve Gibson, Todd Gray, Paul Haberli, David Hunt, Jon Ippolito, Carole Ann Klonarides, George P. Landow, Paul Lee, T. Kelly Mason, Michael Masucci, Chris Miller, William J. Mitchell, Michael Naimark, A. Michael Noll, Marcos Novak, Eric Paulos, Mark Pesce, Patric Prince, Sherry Rabinowitz, Sheree Rose, Steve Ricci, Joyce Cutler Shaw, Vibecke Sorensen, Maja Thomas, and Pae White. I want to offer special thanks to the artists with whom I spoke prior to writing about their work in these pages: Bill Barminski and Webster Lewin, Andrew Bucksbarg, Char Davies, Gary Hill, Perry Hoberman, George

Legrady, Christian Möller, Sara Roberts, Adam Ross, Stelarc, Victoria Vesna, David Wilson, and as noted above, Jennifer Steinkamp and Diana Thater. All of the preceding names and more constitute my real world communities, but those who enable my virtual relationships and make cyberspace a more interesting place to think also deserve thanks: Armin Medosch, editor of *Telepolis*, Geert Lovink, cofounder of <nettime>, and Alex Galloway, Rachel Greene, and Mark Tribe from *Rhizome*.

From Art Center College of Design, I first want to acknowledge the core faculty of the Graduate Program in Communication and New Media Design. Over the years, this mutual aid society has consisted of John Brumfield, Andrew Davidson, Fred Fehlau, Robert Hennigar, Richard Hertz, Ramon Muñoz, Linda Norlen, and Laura Robin. Other Art Center faculty from whom I drew insights that then found their way into this book include John Chambers, Jay Chapman, Ming Chen, Steve Diskin, Eva Forgacs, Jeremy Gilbert-Rolfe, Chris Kraus, David Mocarski, Terry Pendelbury, Patti Podesta, Bruce Yonemoto and David Young. As for my graduate students, there have been so many from whom I learned more than I taught that it would be embarrassing to list them all. Through Art Center, I came to admire and interact with a group of Los Angeles's remarkable designers. Anne Burdick, Denise Gonzales Crisp, April Greiman, Somi Kim, Lisa Krohn, Rebeca Méndez, and Petrula Vrontikis have shown me new ways to think with and through images and objects. I still find it almost inconceivable that I have been able to make a living as a new media theorist. I have the inestimable and indomitable Richard Hertz to thank for hiring me in the first place, for creating a remarkable environment for teaching and writing, and for extending his generous friendship.

I could always count on the expertise of old friends: David Gow on cognitive psychology and kayaking, Douglas Hepworth on finance and the Imp of the Perverse, Seth Tamrowski on special effects and the "Fellowship of the Yellow Duck," and Suzy Kerr on art practice and the proper way to mix a *Cuarenta y Tres*. For the absolutely vital time I spent at Lyon Lamb Video Animation Systems, I thank Bruce Lyon and Sheldon Pines, and the two most generous engineers I ever had the good luck to spend time with, Phil Wangenheim and Pierre

Yenokian. I remain indebted to Wim Smit at Columbia and Brian Henderson and Gerald O'Grady from my studies at SUNY/Buffalo. Tristin Tzimoulis was more help than she will ever know. Thanks to the staff at Buzz Coffee for never begrudging my laptop so much as a watt of electricity.

Although all the previously published materials have been significantly revised, I list their original venues: "Commodity Camaraderie and the TechnoVolksgiest," *Frame-Work*, v. 6, n. 2 (Summer 1993); "Demo or Die," *Afterimage* v. 25, n. 2 (October/November 1997); "Theorizing in Real Time: Hyperaesthetics for the Technoculture," *Afterimage*, v. 23, n. 4 (January/February 1996); portions of "The Alphanumeric Phoenix" and "*Camera Rasa*" were published in "Digital Dialectics: A Hybrid Theory of New Media," *Afterimage*, v. 21, n. 4 (November 1993); an earlier version of "Dubitative Images" was published as "Art Post-History: Digital Photography & Electronic Semiotics" in Hubertus von Amelunxen, Stefan Inglhaut, Florian Rötzer, eds., *Photography after Photography: Memory and Representation in the Digital Age* (Sydney: G+B Arts, 1996); "In Search of the Telephone Opera: From Communications to Art," *Afterimage* v. 25, n. 1 (July/August 1997); portions of "Hardscapes and Imagescapes" were published as "Hybrid Architectures & the Paradox of Unfolding," in Peter Droege, ed., *Intelligent Environments: Spatial Aspects of the Information Revolution* (Amsterdam: Elsevier Science, 1997); "Diana Thater: Constraint Decree," *art/text* 62 (August–October 1998); "Jennifer Steinkamp: Light in Space," *art/text* 58 (August-October 1997); "Click: Imagescape As Ruin," in Astrid Sommer, ed., *Artintact* 3 (Karlsruhe: Zentrum für Kunst und Medientechnologie, 1996).

Special thanks to Michael Starenko, who edited *Afterimage* while I was writing for it regularly, and the *art/text* team of editor Susan Kandel and publisher Paul Foss.

Doug Sery, my editor at the MIT Press, is committed to his authors. He listens and he pushes; his dialogues always extend beyond the book at hand. My parents, Katharine Daly and Marvin Lunenfeld, need to be reminded every once in a while of my boundless thanks for their support and love. My children, Kyra and Maud, would wander in and out of the office in the back of our house, say or do something silly and sweet, and pull their father away from the sterility of the screen back into the happy, messy world. Acknowledgments are often written in reverse, with the most important person listed last. So it is here. Susan Kandel encouraged me to expand out from film studies to new media theory, convinced me to write my first art review, commissioned my column for *art/text*, and did far more than her fair share taking care of our daughters (especially as the deadline for this manuscript loomed). She listened patiently to every idea and sharpened the good ones with an editor's practiced eye. There can never be adequate thanks for such labor, only delirious appreciation.

# Introduction:
## Snap to Grid

Futurity invades our here and now, erecting beachheads in our language,
in our architecture, 'til at last we're under occupation, and tomorrow's
coups depose the rule of history.
*Alan Moore*[1]

### Suspicious Seductions

These are the textual tracings of a drawn-out seduction. Like all interesting affairs, it was never entirely clear whether I was the pursued or
the pursuer. All I know is that I woke up over a decade later and still
felt the compulsion to write about my ambivalent affections for the
computer. Entranced as I was and remain, though, I never fell into a
technological swoon as deserving of an evocative name as the Stendhal
Syndrome (the nineteenth-century term for aesthetic experiences that
overwhelm the senses). Instead, memories of analog pleasures dis-
rupted my days and untethered guilt about technophilia haunted my
nights. But here I move from metaphor to hysteria, and as this is intended to be a reminiscence of a seduction rather than a symptom of
one, I should pull back to the technological discourses that generated
them.

Consider the command "snap to grid." It instructs the computer
to take hand-drawn lines and plot them precisely in Cartesian space.
Snap a freehand sketch of a rectangular shape to a grid and it immediately becomes a flawless, Euclidean rectangle. Artists regularly disable
the snap to grid function the moment they open an application because the gains in predictability and accuracy are balanced against the
losses of ambiguity and expressiveness. This trade-off resonates beyond computer graphics, of course, as the very act of writing about art

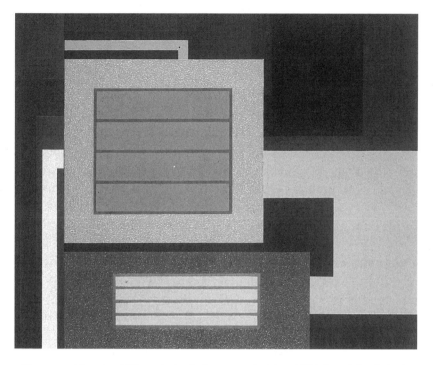

The command "snap to grid" is a metaphor for how we manipulate and think through the electronic culture that enfolds us. For two decades, Peter Halley has been making abstract paintings of cells and conduits, creating what can be seen as computer-inflected, rather than computer-generated objects.

Peter Halley, *The Negotiator* (1998). Courtesy of the artist.

and culture tends towards directing the unruly and categorizing the ineffable. I have come to think of the command "snap to grid," however, as a metaphor for how we manipulate and think through the electronic culture that enfolds us. This book is the result of snapping my seduction by the machine to the grid of critical theory. Skew enough grids, one atop the other at odd angles, though, and their angularity begins to slide back into the curvaceous and the unruly.

The arguments in *Snap to Grid* confound their grids as they erect them, shifting from, between, and around the discourses of technology, aesthetics, and cultural theory, rebuilding complexity in the process of categorizing it. These chapters overlap both within and outside their boundaries. The first way in which they overlap is the very way they have been grouped: as discussions of culture, as systemic analyses of different media, and as close readings of artists and their works. Yet, now more than ever, we know that media make cultures, that artists reconfigure media, and that cultures are having more and more trouble defining what art is, much less who their artists are.

So many grids sit uneasily atop each other. The grid that lays bare the workings of digital media technologies confronts the one that maps out Martin Heidegger's observation that "the essence of technology is by no means anything technological."[2] In turn, this critical grid overlaps a metacritical one, in which I analyze how others discuss these same phenomena (never forgetting that we love to correct those who tread closest to our own path, for who else would listen?). The desire to categorize cultural production after it goes digital juts up sharply against the obvious need to map out the historical precedents that support and subvert our contemporary cult of the new. These two grids explain why it is that I spend as much time discussing computer-inflected films, videos, installations, and paintings as I do computer-generated interactive, telematic, or immersive electronic artworks. I refer here to computer-inflected media in the interest of including the widest variety of objects influenced by digital technologies, even if they are not necessarily produced with, or consumed via, a computer.

### The Media of Attractions

In chronicling contemporary cultural phenomena, it is difficult for critics and theorists to avoid writing the life out of that which evoked their interest in the first place. Film theorist Christian Metz refers to an "epistemophilic sadism" that infiltrates serious discourse on the cinema and, like Susan Sontag, sees the act of criticism as somehow assaulting the object of study.[3] How much more intense the batterings when the critic is ambiguously enthralled? Still, I hope to explore the mysteries of the seduction even as I pose some of the questions that do not get asked enough. In what state do we find our new media? How, at this particular moment, can we compare them to established media? Have these new media reached a stage where we can evaluate them as successes or failures? Must we revert to a default dichotomy between utopia and desolation, that farcical notion that media, even digital media, by themselves can redeem or damn us?

This is not the first time in the history of media technologies that such questions have arisen. During the cinema's earliest decades, film exhibitions attracted audiences for the primary reason that they wanted to see a new technology up close and to experience the world in a different and mediated way. Customers would line up in front of Edison's Kinetographs for a half minute of juggling, dancing, and mugging, or for snippets of natural wonders and world events. "Fred Ott's Sneeze" (1891) is just such a snippet (as well as one of the great conjunctions of title and content in the history of imaging technologies). Historians now categorize films of that era as "the cinema of attractions."[4] It was only later that strips of celluloid faced with silver nitrate became the "movies"—the formally organized narratives of a certain style and length that have become integral to the imagination of our culture.

Potted histories of film date the "movies" from the release of *Birth of a Nation* in 1915, crediting this one film and its director, D. W. Griffith, with codifying a particular language of narrative cinema—creating a cinematic vocabulary that, was assimilated by the culture at large.[5] I would argue that, for all their stunning successes, the artifacts of digital culture are too often "media of attractions."[6] There is nothing wrong with media of attractions, of course, but their appeal is generally limited to their perceived novelty. In his lyric poem *Don Juan*, Byron notes that "novelties please less than they impress."[7] Too often, we marvel at the products of new media not for what they mean, but merely for the fact that they are.

## Tide Pools

The media of attractions impress in part because they are often in advance of other technological and even aesthetic developments. Yet it is difficult to categorize them as an avant-garde. In fact, I would like to rework what the idea of an avant-garde could mean in the context of digital media production. Too often, the avant-garde is thought to move as a vector: a central focus of energy projecting forward, supported far behind by phalanxes of the like-minded. This image makes for sturdy and often involving histories, a progression of daring moves that first suffer ignominy, only to garner universal acclaim in time. This teleological approach appeals to us both narratively and emotionally because it weaves a coherent story about a select few artists who agonized only to be redeemed in the light of history (it is only human, after all, to admire those who have been proven right in the end). But history as it develops is never history as it is written.

The unwritable histories of media are littered with artists, works, and movements that cannot be plugged into this accepted teleology (perhaps to be referred to as the "agony and the ecstasy" mode in honor of the culture's continued obsession with tortured genius). The early eras of a medium confuse the issue even further because in its first decades, virtually all important work pushes the edge, both creatively and technically. This was as true of photography as it was of the cinema, played itself out in the early years of video practice, and even more so today with digital media. In hindsight, some of these works will be seen as the definitive steps towards the dominant operating paradigm, others will be classified within the vector of the avant-garde, and huge amounts of interesting work will simply be ignored because it slots into none of the official narratives.

Rather than a single flying wedge, *Snap to Grid* proposes as a model the ebb and flow of the surf, with small tide pools, often separated and quite short-lived. This accounts for the attention to both computer-generated and computer-inflected media and the wide range of reference across disciplines and discourses. In other words, special effects blockbusters, music videos, and advertisements may not have the staying power of some of the art work I discuss in this book, but this does not mean that these commercial forms are not relevant, even determinative of that art. This is not the same as saying that these commercial forms constitute the "new" digital avant-garde, or that all cultural production has been leveled in the wake of the computer, but rather that one should take into account different modes of production, reception, and even intent.

Nor is this to fall into the hype of concentrating only on the technologists and the marketers, leaving artists at the margins of the discussion. The aesthetic imagination spurs technological progress as much as wired wonders inspire new art. Ezra Pound described artists as the antennae of the race, and Marshall McLuhan took this to mean that we should look to art as the harbinger of "things to come" (to lift language from that other great futurist, H.G. Wells). Yet the obverse is also sustainable, that our antennae themselves have become art, that the systems and software of engineers not only make possible, but in fact anticipate the art that follows them.[8] There is no distinct answer to these issues, and the grid of art will always overlap the grid of technology. One of the central questions of our time is to investigate how these two skew against each other, and how they abut against still more grids to create the field we call culture.

For any occasional harshness, this book strives for a redemptive criticality, a sense that the period that saw the emergence of the digital from the fringe to the center was an extraordinary period to have lived through. Kodwo Eshun, who writes about electronic music, captures this spirit quite well in talking about a writing practice that is "omni-directional rather than non-linear." Eshun rejects "this sense that we've been born too late and that all we can do is cite and quote in this classic postmodern way;" like Eshun, *Snap to Grid* takes the perspective "that everything's still to be done."[9]

### Overlapping Grids

The attention to the overlapping grid accounts for the variety of genres combined here: academic articles jostling against magazine criticism, catalogue essays interspersed with virulent polemics. I claim that this book constitutes a user's manual for digital arts, media, and cultures, but should admit that it really constitutes a guide to "this" user's experiences. Another of the underlying and only partly visible grids here charts the course of my own movements, from film studies to working in the computer graphics business to ending up on the faculty of an art, design and new media school. A more visible grid defines my ongoing efforts to bridge the divide between analyses of technological systems on the one side and the object-based criticism we inherit from art history on the other. Finally, there is the grid that maps my own specific interests. It has been said that poets are constrained to sing from their own family tree. My tree is kinesthetic and dynamic, more videographic than textual, more aesthetic than doctrinal. All these grids combine and diffuse in the face of the technological and artistic practices that have emerged in the computer's wake.

Part I deals directly with the way these technological and artistic practices have coalesced into "cultures." Each of the three chapters in this section offers operating paradigms for dealing with the closer readings of the media and artists that follow. Chapter 1, "Commodity Camaraderie," proposes an archaeology of technocultures, lays out the politico-economic context in which the new media develop, and suggests the scope of the debt these new formations owe to the market economy. These technocultures are intricately structured around the commerce of cybernetic tools, commodities that are not simply consumed but that in turn generate new commodities and new work. This creates a model of cultural production in which the reciprocity between producers and consumers is intensified to the extent that the distinction between these two rigid categories is blurred. All of this is contextualized within a theoretical framework that takes as its benchmark the dissolution of the rigid Cold War dichotomies of East and West in the post-1989 period. Chapter 2, "Demo or Die," offers a lesson in cyborg economics for artists and designers in this post '89 environment. As the stable technologies of the slide and the portfolio are giving way to the computer-based presentation, new questions arise: What is it to put work out to the world using such an inherently unstable platform? How do people enter into a synergy with their machines? After offering a history of the demo as performance and marketing tool and relating the demo to the practice of the studio "crit," this chapter introduces the notion that even the most expert of computer users are engaged in an ongoing battle with techno-anxiety. This is the anxiety engendered by the relationship between the human mind—in both its conscious and the unconscious modes—and the computer's dynamic nonconsciousness. It is in the demo that the digitally inflected artist encounters, and may even become, a cyborganic being. Chapter 3, "Real-Time Theory," lays out a hyperaesthetics to account for these questions and others, acknowledging that artists and theorists are drawn to the computer because it offers an end to the end-games of the postmodern era—that tendency to make final pronouncements about the end of authorship, the end of metanarratives, the end of progress, the end of the real, the end of scientific rationalism, even the end of history itself. The trick is to oscillate between temporalities, never privileging the past, present, or future in theorizing these media. While the realm of the digital entices because it is novel, this does not mean that it is entirely new. One way to historicize it is to practice a digital dialectic, grounding the insights of theory in the constraints of production, drawing from the histories of these media with an eye towards shaping their present.

Part II goes through these "media" in depth and constitutes the bulk of the collection. Chapter 4, "The Alphanumeric Phoenix," outlines the mechanics and meanings of hypertext, examining the shift away from the stable Gutenberg Galaxy of print into the realms of nonlinear reading and writing. Going beyond this technicist discourse, however, the chapter also investigates the very rebirth of textuality in digital environments after its near death during the cinematic and televisual era. Chapter 5, "Dubitative Images," engages with the digitization of the photographic image. The distinction between the digital image and its analog ancestors is now well understood, but this chapter concentrates on what the move from the discrete photograph to the embedded digital photoimage means to the very semiotics of representation. This confrontation between two forms of media transformed the very hierarchy of representation: whereas photography used to be the first among equals, now all is subsumed to the "graphic." The photograph as "photo-graphic" will have a profound impact on the development of the sciences of the signs for the next century. Chapter 6, "In Search of the Telephone Opera," raises an issue for the World Wide Web: just because a medium allows people to communicate, it does not necessarily follow that that medium will be capable of supporting artistic practice. By gridding out a number of the "default" uses of the WWW as an art, the chapter grapples with both the hype and the promise of the medium. Chapter 7, "*Camera Rasa*," continues in this vein, using virtual reality (VR) as an "object to think with." Rather than another encomium to the "possibilities" of a medium still in its infancy, the chapter questions what VR's explosion onto the mediasphere meant. Was VR ever as important a working set of technologies as it was a new environment for us to fill with our dreams, fears, and fetishes? Chapter 8, "Hardscapes and Imagescapes," returns to the world around us, with an investigation of the mutual influences of new media and architecture. Here are hybrid architectures that demonstrate the obvious incorporations of architectural metaphors in the development of cyber "space" and the more subtle infiltration of intelligent "imagescapes" into the realm of building technologies.

Part III concerns individual "Makers," but the choices may be surprising. The late Hollis Frampton is best-known for his structuralist films of the 1960s and 1970s, while Diana Thater and Jennifer Steinkamp have emerged as two of the most significant video and installation artists of our time. That the works of all three engage with but are not defined by the digital corresponds directly to what I mean by computer-inflected culture. Chapter 9, "The Perfect Machine," puts Frampton forth as an emblematic figure for the digital arts. His career moved through and combined photography, filmmaking, video and electronic imaging. The chapter offers a detailed analysis of his last great unfinished and unfinishable suite of films, the *Magellan Cycle*, and poses the question of whether digital arts are the totalizing *gesamtkunstmedium* of the age. Chapter 10, "Constraint Decree," looks at Diana Thater's powerful investigation of the first post-cinematic apparatus—video. Her lush imagescapes resonate with acculturated meanings, but she tweaks them regularly through the application of digital imaging techniques. Her work demonstrates that it is often only after a technology's utopian moment that artists can do their best work with it, freed from the pressure to save the world through media. "Chapter 11, "Light in Space," addresses the way that Jennifer Steinkamp's animated, computer-generated, enveloping image environments bear the weight of the culture's millenarian hopes (and concurrent fears as well, of course). Steinkamp battles this pressure by concentrating on the phenomenological importance of "being in" her pieces, foregrounding the presence of the spectator's body as a precursor to interaction. Chapter 12, "Click/Focus/Dream," is more specific, looking not at bodies of work but rather at three separate objects by three different artists. For all the technological innovations of the past two decades, our visual culture can seem trapped in a relentless present. These three art works are unified only in suggesting how to create a contemporary aesthetic imaginary that breaks free of our permanent present. While Perry Hoberman's interactive CD-ROM *The Sub-Division of the Electric Light* and Gary Hill's video *Site Recite (a prologue)* are sufficiently "techno" to pass without special mention, Edgar Allan Poe's Imp of the Perverse moved me to close with Adam Ross's *Unti-*

*tled* (*AT 7*), which distills our contemporary technological imaginary into one crystalline painting, an ambivalent image suited to an ambivalent age.

### Erasmus's Grid

In 1995, the artist Liam Gillick published a small project entitled *Erasmus is Late*, which dramatized a trans-temporal dinner party: moving from the home of Erasmus Darwin, the opium eating brother of Charles Darwin, in 1810 to the year 1997 (two years in Gillick's then future, now his—and our—imagined past).[10] This fiction allowed Gillick to thread a vast range of characters and opinions through the text, for his own perverse purposes. The seating chart for a formal dinner is its own grid, of course, and in surveying this book, I'm both reassured and somewhat surprised at who has been dining at my table. There are the usual suspects, Walter Benjamin and Marshall McLuhan, without whom a media theory house is not a home. There are visitors from the nineteenth century, Karl Marx and Sigmund Freud; and twentieth-century critical theorists like Roland Barthes and Michel Foucault. From farther afield come George Perec and his OuLiPo cohorts, the visionary science fiction author Philip K. Dick, and digital gurus like Brenda Laurel, Sherry Turkle and Ted Nelson. A good dinner party should include not just visiting luminaries, but also regulars. For some years now, I have been coordinating *media-work:* The Southern California New Media Working Group, and, with any luck, this book shows the influence of those artists, scientists and thinkers who have presented at and participated in *mediawork.* This is the final grid, the one that grows with every conversation about art, technology and culture. This is the grid to which this project hopes to contribute, in its own way.

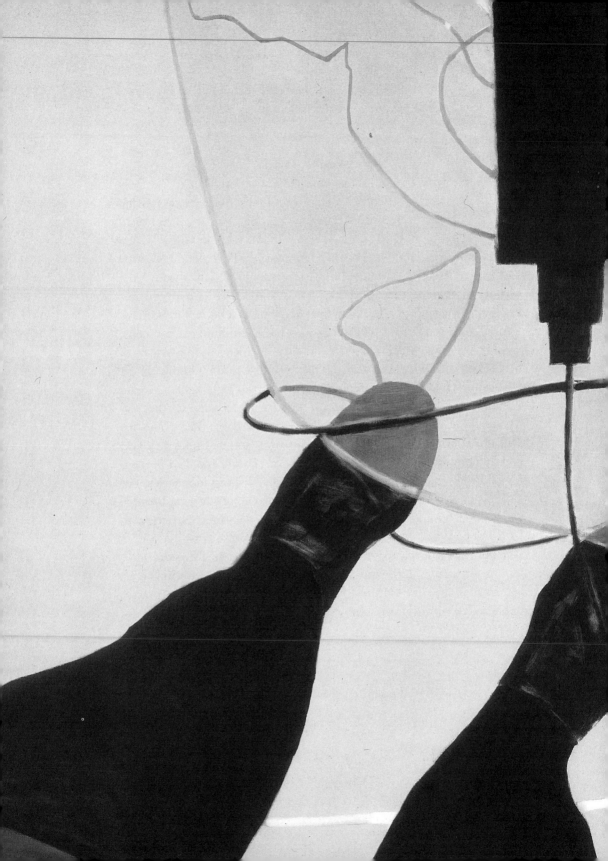

Part I

# Cultures

# TECHNOCULTURES:
# COMMODITY CAMARADERIE

There is a world where galleries overflow with new work, films and videos play non-stop, Web sites blossom, everyone has at least one acquaintance in common, learned discourse alternates with witty gossip, and every third conversation ends with optimistic projections about the future.

*This is not* the world of politics. Our politics are haunted by millennial exhaustion: control economies have imploded, their ruling apparatchiks tumbling into the void; postindustrial capitalism eschews most forms of leadership, pitting the dispossessed one against the other over the rinds left in all but empty pork barrels.

There is a world of technological wonder, where the equipment has such sheen that the aura of art pales in comparison. All is clean and new, things work, and if they don't, some extraordinarily competent neighbor will be able to help you out. For those lucky enough to be part of this world, barter is as effective as cash, and information flows like wine. There is even a common faith. Its axiom: your life *will be better*.

This is not the world of art. With the author dead, creative genius has been replaced by irony. Yet without the claim of genius, art cannot compete with the juggernaut that is popular culture. Besides, it is embarrassing to rally around irony for more than ten minutes.

To mix metaphors that are themselves encrusted with connotations, there is a brave new world along the digital frontier. Having conquered the alphanumeric realms of computation and data storage, the computer has moved into areas formerly outside the purview of the programmer and hardware manufacturer: graphic arts, performance,

The high-tech trade show is at the very center of commodity camaraderie and the TechnoVolksgeist. "Working the floor" at a show entails setting up a vast array of computer equipment, manning a booth in the huge, cavernous space of a convention center, and then enticing passers-by to participate in on-the-spot demonstrations.

The SIGGRAPH Trade Show. Courtesy of SIGGRAPH 98.

creative writing, music. Like all outposts, these technocultures configure their own social and cultural practices. The question becomes how to talk about them, how to move beyond reviewing contemporary technologies, as nothing dates faster than such journalistic enterprises—except, perhaps, predictions of future wonders. What I propose is a discussion of some technocultural communities and their artifacts. What follows is a future archaeology.

## Commodity Camaraderie

There are new artistic communities, emergent technocultures, being built around computer-driven media. These communities are in their formative stages. They are often tenuous, more dispersed geographically than their cultural antecedents, often uneasy in their alliances, but they are communities nonetheless. These communities have attracted attention not just as novelties, nor simply because they have become major economic players, but in large measure because of their high rates of cultural production, although within them, the usual boundaries of art, music, entertainment, and information tend to blur to the point of meaninglessness.

The personal computer first promised to make each man his own secretary (with word processing) and accountant (with spreadsheets and databases).[1] With the advent of graphical interfaces, WYSIWYG ("What You See Is What You Get") desktop publishing, and increased multimedia capabilities, the computer was marketed and taken up as a tool to transform every user into something more "elevated"—an artist.

Of course, this is not the 18th century, the era of Immanuel Kant, who in his *Critique of Aesthetic Judgment* confidently asserts that "fine arts must necessarily be considered works of *genius*."[2] In our age, though cultural producers continue to produce, the idea of a singular author has become suspect. This notion, often literalized as the "death" of the author, first surfaced in literary theory, gained credence in the art world, and seems to well describe a moment in which hyperlinks connect everyone's work to everyone else's.[3] This is all well and good, yet in the absence of such venerated concepts as genius and transcendence, digital artists find themselves stripped of the ethos around which most previous artistic communities were founded.[4] Beyond neophilia and millennarianism, around what centralizing concept can these artists build community? I would propose that the cohesive force binding them together is less a shared sense of destiny than the common use of similar *tools*—what I refer to as "commodity camaraderie."

Before going any further, I should clarify terms by engaging in a transtemporal dialectical exercise: citing Karl Marx to theorize cybernetica. In the *Capital*'s seminal essay on the fetishism of commodities, Marx discusses the distortion of social relations brought about by the tendency under capitalism to emphasize the "exchange value" of the commodity over its "use value." Commodity production impels the development of social relationships among producers. But for Marx, this relationship becomes obscured with the fetishism of commodities—wherein the relationship between producers is taken metonymically as the relationship between commodities. Producers see "a social relation, existing not between themselves, but between the products of their labor."[5] This misunderstanding of the relationship—taking it as one between things rather than human beings—is a prime, if primitive, condition for the production of ideology, or to put it in terms that Marx himself transcended, false consciousness.

The production of commodities intrudes upon the social order because the human producers come into contact with each other only when they "exchange their products, [and] the specific social character of each producers' labor does not show itself except in the act of exchange."[6] Marx wrote this in an era we now call early capitalist. Whether we are presently in capitalism's late period, as some claim, or merely in the middle of one of its succeeding stages of ascendancy is another issue. I want to analyze the radical changes in the nature of commodities generated by the advent of digital hardware and software.[7] First of all, among coders, software engineers, hardware manufacturers, and the end users of new media systems, "the social character of private labor"[8] is vastly more apparent than it was according to Marx's model. The commerce of goods from which Marx drew his theories of commodity has now been joined by, and sometimes supplanted by, the commerce of tools.

Technocultures are awash in tools. Generally considered the most important of the cybernetic tools, the computer is actually more of a workbench, or desktop, upon which one works with ones tools. The word processors, nonlinear digital video editing systems, database managers, Web server softwares, interactive multimedia programs, and even esoterica like virtual reality "world-building" kits are what constitute the tool commodities of the technoculture. These commodities are not simply consumed; instead, they produce new commodities and new work. It is, then, no longer a case of sellers and buyers, but of a relationship between hyphenates: between manufacturer-producers and consumer-producers.

This exchange relationship grows out of but remains distinct from the so-called "high-tech gift economy." This gift economy is an outgrowth of computer hackerdom, where individuals dedicate their time, energy, and talents to winning esteem—rather than direct financial reward—from their colleagues. This is an economic model that functions, obviously, within an environment of plenty rather than scarcity, but the hacker's emphasis on openness and prestige also owes an obvious debt to academic science, where research is publicly disseminated via journals to add to the field's growth as a whole and the reputation of the publishing authors. The prestige the hacker seeks is one confined to a small community of elites, though one that expanded enormously in its reach with the development of world-wide computer networks like the Internet.[9] When a broader base of users and consumers enters the equation, the gift economy shifts into the "commodity camaraderie" of the aforementioned manufacturer-producers and consumer-producers.

Let us return to the market, follow the development, launch, and perpetuation of a product in the technocultural system.[10] After the manufacturer-producer concludes the preliminary development process—the alpha stage—the software is sent out to a privileged group of consumer-producers for what is known as beta testing. Beta testers help work out the problems, the ubiquitous bugs, and file detailed reports, register complaints, and make suggestions, all while remaining in close contact with the original development team. The product is then released to the general population. The early consumer/producers are a brave group, because the first release of the commodity, even after extensive beta testing, is sure to be flawed. They accept this risk as a condition of getting the newest technology fastest, and the manufacturer-producers rely on this group for a post-beta analysis and a critique of their commodities. The manufacturer-producers facilitate the feedback process by including reply cards with the products, maintaining Web sites, and staffing telephone help lines to offer advice and accept criticism. This feedback loop remains intact as the commodities go through various modifications and releases over the course of time. It must be noted that this feedback loop tends to function better the more diverse the community of providers. As economies of scale grow and consolidation occurs, the communication loops so essential to commodity camaraderie can become blocked to the point of frustration. This has famously happened with Microsoft and its "Windows Everywhere" goal. With Windows users everywhere all trying to communicate with one company, distributed, nodal communication becomes dominated by a core/spokes model, leading to the classic user complaints about hugely powerful companies that do not listen to their customers (complaints as ubiquitous about Microsoft as they once were about IBM).

To return to the model of smaller-scale, nodal communication: throughout the cycle of production, distribution and updating of the commodity, the relationship between the manufacturer-producers and the consumer-producers is distinguished from Marx's model of the fetishism of commodities by the continued personal contact maintained among the parties. Although the commodity still retains its awesome power, the "made" character of the technocultural commodity is consistently foregrounded for the consumer-producer.

Commodity camaraderie, generated by this contact, creates a sense of neo-community that is palpable at a massive trade show like Macworld. This show, which concentrates on products and services for the users of machines manufactured by Apple Computer, Inc., was famously successful in creating a conspiratorial cohesiveness among its participant. The official corporate pronouncements of Apple, the editorial content of magazines like the now-defunct *MacUser*, and the buzz on the trade-show floor all combined to reassure Apple customers that they were creative, rebellious, and right on the edge. Consumer-producers referred to the "Mac Universe," and trade shows like MacWorld reified a metaphorical construct that semantically bonded a disparate user population.

Obviously, hobbyists of all sorts have their own special vocabularies and subcultures have their rituals of inclusion and exclusion, but the technoculture has achieved such a mass of specialized semantic and syntactic elements that one can truly speak of a language specific to it. Indeed, these technologies have become so pervasive that we are forced to assimilate their language into the culture as a whole.

## TechnoVolksgeist

Throughout the 1990s, new media artists were just one of the groups generating and using these new languages, joining reality hackers, phreakers, smart drug advocates, artificial intelligence proselytizers, and digital shamans in making up what was variously called the technoculture, the cyberculture, and even "the new edge."[11] As these groups extended their commodity camaraderie from software to platform to network, they transform the idea of a geographically specific Bohemia into a broader concept of the user group as proto-social formation—a "TechnoVolksgeist." In eighteenth-century Germany, Johann Gottfried Herder discussed the "Volksgeist," the communal sensibility that develops as individuals struggle to form groups with others with whom they share a deep culture. Political philosopher Sir Isaiah Berlin, this century's greatest exponent of Herder, framed the need the Volksgeist fills in this way: "Loneliness is not just the absence of others but far more living among people who do not understand what you are saying."[12]

Sidestepping the ease with which a debased Volksgeist can transmute into mere nationalism, or worse yet, virulent xenophobia, Berlin sees the concept as a localizing rather than universalizing influence, of use to a world searching for a respite from the failures of totalizing theories like fascism and Leninism.[13] Herder wanted individuals to come together because they shared a common culture, not because they pledged allegiance to a sovereign or state. It is the individual's conscious choice to socialize, as opposed to the demands of the power structure, that gives legitimacy to the Volksgeist. For Herder, the base of the Volksgeist is language—the repository and transmitter of culture. Herder was not championing a specific culture or language, however, as he saw diversity not univocalism as the wellspring of human growth. The "international transmission of social cultures" was for Herder "the highest form of cultural development which nature has elected."[14]

In positing a TechnoVolksgeist, I hope to foreground the most progressive aspects of Herder's thought, even at the cost of smoothing over both its nuances its contradictions. The TechnoVolksgeist can and often does degenerate into the pretensions to culture of a pampered network of elites. If the self-proclaimed digiterati refuse to promote access and include the dispossessed, their rhetoric of revolution through technology will seem nothing more than the callous justification for unregulated accumulation of personal wealth.[15]

The cohesiveness of the TechnoVolksgeist has yet to be proven, but on the other hand, the very diversity of its discourse indicates strength. Digital artists and their extended communities generate a staggering amount of material. They are quick to master the intricacies of new media and the creation and mining of information resources: from the first desktop published "zines" to disk-based hypertexts and multimedia CD-ROMs; from the dedicated bulletin boards systems (BBSs) to specialized listserves and the explosion of digital communities on the Web. These publications, hypermedia, and Web sites disseminate not merely ideas and techniques but style, that most precious of contemporary attributes. The TechnoVolksgeist is driven in large measure by info-addicts looking for a fix on the next data cloud.

When Paul Virilio wrote *Speed and Politics* in 1977, he warned of the deleterious effects of the "dromocracy": the society ruled by speed.[16] But along with their evident dangers, world-wide computer networks and instantaneous telecommunications have made possible the creation of a transnational TechnoVolksgeist. Commodity camaraderie encourages inclusion not by blood, but rather by chip.

## Post-'89: New Media and New Theory

For all of my hyperbolic dismissal of contemporary politics at the start of this chapter, it would be absurd not to situate commodity camaraderie in a political context. For a generation, historians and critics have been talking about art and theory in relation to the pivotal year of 1968, the assumption being that somehow the failed revolutions of that heady year so demoralized the avant-garde that all cultural production since then has been irrevocably altered. This kind of periodization is what cultural historians do, of course, and it has the same relationship to actual developments as the map does to the road—it is a useful guide, but only an approximation of the terrain. Yet other markers have sprung up since then, and in terms of technocultural production, it strikes me that 1989 has become the new dividing line.[17] That year saw the Czech Velvet Revolution, the fall of the Berlin Wall, the reunification of Germany, the eventual fissioning of the Soviet Union, the emergence of the Baltic states and the continued extension of market reforms in China (which coincided with the political repression of Tiananmen Square).[18] With the disintegration of state-sponsored socialism and communism throughout Eastern

Europe and the former Soviet Union, and the market-oriented reforms in the People's Republic of China, this may not have been "the
Final Victory of Capitalism," as Susan Sontag ambivalently characterized it a decade later.[19] Even so, it would be impossible to argue against
the notion that capitalism is in yet another of its periods of ascendancy.

With tribalism and fundamentalism appearing to be the only other
options on the political scene attracting adherents, postindustrial capitalism would seem at this point as inevitable and all-powerful to the
artists of the West as the Christian church must have been to artisans
of 11th century France. In other words, for those coming of age in a
post-'89 world, an alternative to capitalism is not simply unlikely but
almost completely unthinkable. Post-'89 theories of aesthetic production, then, begin with the centrality of the market and its forces. This
is as opposed to both pre- and post-'68 theories, which were originally
predicated on a direct opposition to the culture of the market (classic
Marxist/Leninist doctrine).

For artists and critics on the left before the events of '68, that is,
the emphasis was on making art and theory with a specific use value:
inciting rebellion. With the repression and/or exhaustion of revolution
in the streets, however, the focus shifted inward, from fomenting social
action to analyzing social imaginaries. Critics who had been pulling
up paving stones moved from the barricades to the text. They, and
even more generally their students and interpreters, spent the
thirty years after 1968 mining all forms of cultural production for
"sites of resistance" to capitalist alienation. By the time that the discipline of cultural studies was firmly established in the 1990s, Anglo-
American scholars were looking at consumers who watched *Dynasty*,
listened to Madonna, or read *Hustler* and writing as though any smid-
gen of cultural bricolage was a revolutionary act and every fan club a
conspirators' cell. Post-'68, what intellectuals had formerly regarded as
capitulating to the spectacle was coming to be seen as sly resistance.[20]

What formal analysis was done under this rubric was always predetermined in its purpose, to locate "cracks and fissures," i.e., those
moments in which the ideological mask slips and the repressiveness of
the dominant discourse is revealed. Post-'89 theory is more elastic. It is
rigorously historicized: it lives in its moment, eschews nostalgia, and

acknowledges that oftentimes, consumption is acknowledgment of rather than subterranean resistance to the global market. At the same time, it is vitally concerned with determining the formal characteristics of contemporary art and culture—especially in their digital and electronic flavors—as opposed to moving directly into a discussion of their "revolutionary" use value. This is not to say that a post-'89 theory worthy of its ambitions functions in tandem with the marketers of the digital "revolution," degrading the latter word more fully than even the most mediocre cultural studies analyses: post-'89 theory completely rejects the mercantilism of futurism. But, as has been noted, it eschews any spirit of renunciation. Art historian Marcelin Pleynet notes that the history of the last hundred years "may well go down as the history, above all, of conflicts and debates surrounding the intelligence and unintelligence of the attitudes, the ways of being, and the modes of thinking that have been conditioned by the irresistible evolution of technology."[21] Post-'89 theory lives in, with, and through these technologies in complex and entirely self-conscious ways, wherever it lead. It is enough to say right now that post-'89 theory is wary of using nineteenth-century analyses of industrial capitalism to engage with the post-industrial, interconnected world, with new social formations like commodity camaraderie and the TechnoVolksgeist.

A breach in the Berlin Wall in 1989. That year marked the end of the rigid dichotomies of East and West, and has replaced 1968 as the defining moment for contemporary theories of culture.

Photo: Frederick Ramm, 1989.

# CYBORG ECONOMICS:
# DEMO OR DIE

At the MIT Media Laboratory, . . . the academic slogan "publish or per-
ish" has been recodified as "demo or die". . . . When we started the Media
Lab, I kept telling people we must demo, demo, demo . . . . Forget technical papers and to a lesser extent theories. Let's prove by doing.
*Nicholas Negroponte*

Right now, somewhere in the wired world, there is a graphic designer
booting up her electronic portfolio trying to convince a client that she
can develop a complex corporate-identity system for the company.
Right now, somewhere in the wired world, there is an artist having
difficulty navigating through his complex interface for the benefit of a
curator he hopes will give him a show. Right now, somewhere in the
wired world, there is a team of digital post-production media specialists cursing silently as their presentation to the director crashes for the
third time. Right now, somewhere in the wired world, there is a poet
demoing her first hypertext, and marveling that it's actually working.[1]

## Defining the Demo

The demonstration, or "demo," has become the defining moment of
the digital artist's practice at the turn of the millennium. For artists
and designers who work with technology, no amount of talent, no
ground-breaking aesthetic, no astonishing insight makes up for an inability to demonstrate their work on a computer in real time in front of
an audience. The demo, as immortalized in the MIT Media Lab's
credo "Demo or Die," is now at the heart of the professional
imagemaker's life. Artists and their machines are on display. This does
not simply presage the artist as cyborg; it also augurs the transformation of digital presentation into live performance.

Digital presentation as command performance: F. Joseph Pompei, a graduate student at the MIT Media Lab, gives a demo to Britain's Prince Andrew.

The floppy disk, the portable hard drive, the CD-Rom, the DVD and the World Wide Web all serve up the artists' multimedia image/text/sound matrices. But this service is never trouble-free. The computer, no matter what the platform, software, or format, is a remarkably unstable mechanism with which to exhibit work, not least because the goal of so much new work is precisely to test and extend the technical capabilities of the system with which it was created. To examine the demo-or-die aesthetic is to address a series of related questions. What is it to put work out to the world using inherently unstable platforms? How do people enter into synergy with their machines? Are users fast on their way to becoming cyborgs, if only for the fleeting moments of the demo? How does the demo increase techno-anxiety, even among those who would seem to be Masters of the Electronic Universe? How is it that a technology that promised to replace face-to-face communication in fact demands it?

Artists and designers giving demos are quintessential post-'89 cultural producers, as defined in chapter 1, "Commodity Camaraderie." In this context, it is no wonder that the demo or die aesthetic is caught up in a presumption of artistic labor with definitive use value. In order not to die, the demo must perform: it must work within the constraints of the ideology generated in the wake of digital technologies. In other words, this aesthetic is one perfectly suited to contemporary capitalism.[2] Technologically intensive practices of any kind—military, scientific or artistic—require sources of capital support, and computer media have been no different. From the start of the modern computer age, first government and then corporate investment were an essential part of the production of electronic art and digital media.[3] From the $200,000 and up that corporate donors use to buy into the MIT Media Lab (the original audiences for demo or die) to the Deutsche Telecom galleries of technological art at the SoHo Guggenheim, digital art is the product of transnational corporate capitalism.[4]

### Speaking with Media

Much of the impetus for this chapter comes out of my own experiences giving and organizing demos. For a number of years I was well within the belly of the postindustrial capitalist beast, working in the computer graphics industry.[5] My responsibilities included working trade shows like the National Association of Broadcasters (NAB) and SIGGRAPH (the Association for Computing Machinery's Special Interest Group on Computer Graphics). "Working the floor" at a trade show means setting up a vast array of computer equipment, manning a booth in the huge, cavernous space of a convention center, and then trying to entice anyone passing by to listen to you talk about the firm's line: offering on-the-spot demonstrations of the products. I have never felt as in control of a digital system as I did while in the midst of what we referred to as "demo-mode." There were a set series of routines we would run through and—ideally—a certain sync between human and machine would settle in for the three or four days the show floor was open. In chapter 1, I discussed the intensity of the trade show floor's commodity camaraderie, but what bears mention here is how focused the experience of the demo is for the presenter, indeed, how much of a performance it is.

Since returning to academia to teach in a graduate program in communication and new media design, I have continued to note the importance of performance to the culture and pedagogy of digital art and design. Each term my seminar "Digital Dialogues" features a different guest each week. I also coordinate *mediawork:* The Southern California New Media Working Group, which meets regularly to look at demos and develop cross-disciplinary discourse about electronic culture. Thus, at least once a week I have the opportunity to watch the way artists, designers, scientists and architects struggle to describe—better, to show—the importance of their work. This goes beyond the technical questions of making the machines work; it concerns the way in which we develop a syntax to "speak" of—and with—these media. Yet being witness to it is not enough to understand the impact of the demo or die aesthetic. One must consider the history of the way that artists and designers have presented their work through the course of the twentieth century, when art and design exploded out of the atelier and into the mainstream of cultural production and commerce. One must also take into account how the computer industry developed, how it sells itself to the public (and just as importantly, to itself), and how its particular mix of marketing and evangelism has migrated into the realm of art and design.[6]

Artists and designers rarely send out original work to curators or cart it to meetings with commercial clients. Instead, they make reproductions, either in portfolios or as slides. The advantages of the portfolio are its success at reproducing print work, its impressive physicality, and its obvious stability. Slides solve size and reproducibility issues and, with their standardized format, they have achieved universal penetration into every gallery, advertising agency, museum, editorial office, artists' collective and classroom.[7]

The move towards the digital in contemporary art and design might seem to make the physical presence of the maker even less necessary than in the above scenario. Disc-based archives make it as cheap to send out color images as black and white ones, and the cost of distributing a thousand images on one disc is no greater than that of sending out a single image. The Internet can serve as a distribution medium for image files, with even fewer costs and farther and faster reach. Finally, with the World Wide Web, images can be accessed from anywhere in the wired world at any time, obviating the need for portfolios and slides entirely.

This, at least, is the theory. While it sounds wonderful and may yet be wonderful, as of the present moment there are innumerable problems to overcome before the dream becomes commonplace rather than merely plausible. For disc-based archives, these problems include incompatibilities between operating systems and imaging softwares, and nonstandardized storage media to transport and play back the work. For Internet and Web applications there is also the ever-present problem of insufficient bandwidth to transfer large files, and even less control over graphic design and typographic issues than in disc-based presentations. Finally, there is the universal problem for all monitor-based presentations: the size, color, luminosity and registration of the image are different for each and every display (even when the monitors are made by the same manufacturer).

On top of these inherent difficulties, there is the issue of interactivity to consider. Interactivity is one of the grails of the computer industry, and right now—for good or for ill—being able to demonstrate the capacity to create interactive media is the *sine qua non* of the demo. Yet all the interface instabilities noted earlier are only exacerbated by the complexities of interactivity. As hard as it is to move still images from one place to another and have them look something like they are supposed to, it is exponentially more difficult to ensure that interactive projects look, much less operate, as they were designed to. Thus it is that cutting edge interactive projects are so often demonstrated by the artists/designers themselves—in person. What was perhaps intended to replace or augment person-to-person communication becomes the occasion for just such interaction. And it is here that the demo demands that presentation become performance.

### Performing Technology

It may sound strange to discuss performance in relation to the computer, since that particular technology comes replete with stereotypes of the nerdy recluse, uncomfortable doing anything other than hacking code in the lab. But in fact the demo has been a space of performance within the technological arena for decades. In 1968, Stanford Research Institution computer scientist Douglas Engelbart gave perhaps the most important demo ever presented. Working at a custom workstation, Engelbart gave the first public showing of a mouse (a device he had invented) and used the mouse to control a graphical user interface complete with windows of hypertextual materials and video teleconferencing. It took years to get this vision of personalized, interactive multimedia computing out to the general public, but Engelbart's ability to demo a working prototype was an inspiration to the assorted hackers, engineers and entrepreneurs in his audience that day. This was more than a thought piece in a journal or chit-chat around the water cooler at Bell Labs; it was an "existence proof" of the kinds of ideas Engelbart had been proposing for almost a decade.[8] More than twenty years after the historic 1968 Fall Joint Computer Conference where Engelbart performed this *real-time proof of concept*, Howard Rheingold interviewed some of those who had been present. A startling percentage of those who witnessed Engelbart's demo were, like Alan Kay of Xerox PARC fame, to become key figures in the development the personal computer. As Rheingold characterized it, Engelbart's demo was "electrifying to everyone who attended. The assembled engineers, programmers, and computer scientists had never seen anything like it."[9]

In the decades that followed, certain figures emerged as masters of the demonstration (or "demo gods"), individuals capable of taking technical explanation and product marketing to a feverish pitch. To watch Apple cofounder Steve Jobs work arena-sized crowds was to witness a great evangelist at work. Both Jobs's colleagues and his competitors acknowledged the "reality-distortion effect" with which he could seduce audiences from one to ten thousand to follow his lead, imagining a world filled with "insanely great" technological wonders.[10] Andrew Hertzfeld, an Apple veteran who went on to cofound the General Magic software company, is famed for his real-time feats of programming during a demo. "'He seems to enjoy having his system crash in mid-demo," another programmer noted in *The New York Times*, "'He'll say something like, 'Oh, I know what that is,' and then quickly type a hex command in his debugger. You're never really sure if he has rehearsed it or he's just really good.'"[11] Two other figures to reckon with are Michael Backes and Scott Billups, who claim a measure of credit for nurturing links between Silicon Valley and Hollywood (a much hyped union occasionally derided as "Sillywood"). Backes, a screenwriter and cofounder of the computer games company Rocket Science, and Billups, a desktop digital media production guru, are legendary.[12] For a decade, they coordinated the American Film Institute's (AFI) Advanced Technologies Program's seminal Tuesday Night Salons, serving as hosts for the myriad demo gods who passed through the AFI's campus, just below the Hollywood sign. The two offered complementary public personae, Backes playing the polymath intellectual to Billup's brash, garage-band techno-junkie. Backes spoke in a language comprehensible to the "suits"—marketing executives from Northern California, movie producers from Southern California— while Billups's hands-on know-how appealed to the "gearheads"— hardware and software engineers from SGI, Apple, and Radius, and movie crafts people like cinematographers, film editors, and special effects artists from Warner, Disney and Universal.

So pervasive is the computer industry's demand for the demo that often people who have neither the technical facility to bear up under the pressure nor an appropriately performative personality are drafted into demoing products. Yet what concerns me here are not the marketing errors companies make in "casting" their demos, but rather the way in which *the demo has become an intrinsic part of artistic practice.* What we have seen is a movement of the demo or die aesthetic outward from the Media Lab's computer science milieu into the general realm of culture. From Stewart Brand's ground-breaking book *The Media Lab: Inventing the Future* in the late 1980s to the impact of *Mondo 2000* and *Wired* on the publishing community beginning in the early 1990s, to the ubiquitous coverage of all things digital in the general media at the moment, the demo has moved to center stage.[13] There is now an expectation that artists and designers will be able both to craft sophisticated media and demonstrate them live in front of clients and audiences with Jobs's missionary zeal, Hertzfeld's steely nerves, and Backes and Billups's glitzy showmanship.

## Crit Culture

The demo or die aesthetic would seem to challenge the facile stereotype of the artist who lets the work speak for itself. Yet for almost 20 years, the training of artists and designers has actually taken an

The demo or die aesthetic is related to the rarefied rhetoric of the art school critique, or "the crit," as it is here lampooned.

Daniel Clowes, "Art School Confidential," panel. From the collection *Orgy Bound* (Fantagraphics Books, 1996).
© Daniel Clowes.

increasingly discursive bent. In an unexpected way, the demo or die aesthetic is related to the rarefied rhetoric of the art school critique. The crit, as it is better known, is one of the central pedagogical tools of arts education.[14] The crit comes in many flavors, but customarily students present their work (often in their own studios) in front of each other and their instructors, with detailed (and often sharply pointed) discussion by those in attendance, followed by spirited defenses by the student showing the work. With the ascendancy of conceptual art practice in the 1960s and the infiltration of critical theory from the late 1970s on, the crit has tended to take an increasingly linguistic turn, especially in the elite schools of art and design, one in which discourse about art discourse is at least as important as discourse about art.

This elevation of the crit to its present preeminent position has been controversial, but there is no denying that it has created a generation of artists and designers extremely conversant about their own practice, and not at all shy about engaging in polemics. For many young artists and designers, demoing their digital work is simply an extension of their mastery of the studio crit, and the demo's demands for performative prowess is a natural corollary to their investment in the narcissism inherent in the artist's role. Yet the present moment does give off a slightly odd vibe: artists as trade show flacks, in strange symbiosis with their machines. Yet, as noted earlier, this symbiosis is never stable, the partners—human and machine—forever jockeying for dominance.

Consider the work of the Australian artist Stelarc who, in an exploration of the performative aspects of the demo, challenges our inherited understandings of the body's place in a technological culture. Stelarc gained a reputation as an artist willing to put his body on the line. Beginning in the mid-1970s and continuing for more than a decade, Stelarc engaged in a series of body suspension projects, involving flesh-piercing hooks, ritualized body modifications and pain-induced trance states. He has since been pushing the limits in the human/machine interface. In *Stomach Sculpture* (1993), he inserted into his body a self-illuminating, sound-emitting, extending and retracting capsule structure actuated by a servomotor and logic circuit, and recorded the sculpture with endoscopic medical imaging cameras. In other words, Stelarc pushed the demo or die aesthetic to the literal limit in *Stomach Sculpture*, which almost killed him.[15]

Stelarc moved into exploring the body and its relationship with technology as manifested on the Web, creating what can be taken as the ultimate meta-demo: *Ping Body: An Internet Actuated and Uploaded Performance* (1996). With *Ping Body*, he extends his investigations into the posthuman body by linking his neuromuscular system to the pulse of information on the net. Pings are like the sonar of the Internet, going out and then bouncing back to measure response time between

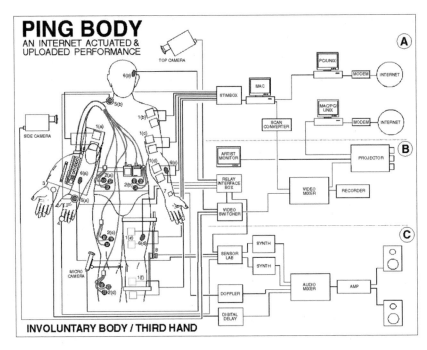

*Ping Body* links the posthuman body to the World Wide Web, creating a meta-demo in which the pulse of information on the net drives the artist's own neuro-muscular system.

Stelarc, *Ping Body: An Internet Actuated and Uploaded Performance* (1996), schematic.
© Stelarc/Merlin Integrated Media.

local and distant nodes on the net. Stelarc interfaces directly to the ebb and flow of data traffic by having the low level Internet ping protocol drive electric muscle simulators capable of delivering 60 volt jolts that he attaches to his body. The frequency and intensity of the pings drive Stelarc's "enhanced" body: his neuromusculature jerks and spasms beyond his conscious control. Stelarc often needs to be carried from the stage after the performance because the experience of being "driven" by the network so completely depletes him. *Ping Body* is obviously a limit text for the performative aspect of the demo, but the best quality of Stelarc's practice is the way it brings forward and makes manifest our subconscious anxieties about technology—in particular, our fears about its performance of us.

## Poetics of the Dynamic Nonconscious

How are we to discuss the techno-anxiety that "demo or die" generates? For Sigmund Freud, anxiety functions as one of the most common symptoms of neurosis (if not the most common). Anxiety is of particular interest because it is manifested physically as well as psychically. It is both a feeling of dread and a series of physiological changes: the breath shortens, heart quickens, muscles tense, and sweat pours. Yet Freud himself seems to have been anxious about his definition of anxiety, since he made a major correction to his early work on the topic when he published *The Problem of Anxiety* in 1926, towards the close of his career.[16] Whereas Freud first saw anxiety as a result, he later viewed it as a sign of things to come. That is to say, the early theories saw anxiety as a manifestation of repression—generally repression of the libido—whereas the later work concentrated on how anxiety functioned as a warning sign of the movement from the unconscious to the conscious of repressed impulses or feelings.

Techno-anxiety, as I choose to define it here, draws from both of Freud's definitions as well as from less analytical, more general understandings of anxiety. For one, the techno-anxiety engendered by the demo or die era is not a free-floating nervousness about technology. It is neither the result of the split between the two cultures of the sciences and the humanities, nor a general Luddite skepticism about the engineered world. This is not about fearing that the automatic teller machine will eat the bank card, or that the microwave will overcook the roast, or that the VCR is not programmed to record the show. Techno-anxiety is instead a sensation specific to those who know their machines and systems intimately. It is a nervousness that can in no way be termed neurotic. The artists and designers who have given form to our technocultures are nervous about system crashes when people come to visit their studios precisely because their systems crash regularly. When these creative people leave their own specially configured systems of hardware, software and displays, their fear of a lack of compatibility increases because they have encountered software clashes and missing functionalities dozens of times even in their own studios. The old adage, "Just because you're paranoid doesn't mean they aren't out to get you," plays itself out every day in every presentation (even if it seems to viewers that the experience was flawless).

Freud was dealing with anxiety in its relation to the dynamic unconscious—a struggle between parts of the human mind. Techno-anxiety extends this metaphor to deal with the dynamic *non*conscious. To emphasize: the demo (and to an extent all higher-order computer-mediated communication) further complicates the relationship between the human user's split psyche—conscious and unconscious—by adding to this already volatile mix the non- but pseudo-consciousness of the computer. The dynamic nonconscious, then, is the machine part of the human computer interface. Techno-anxiety can be seen as either the result or the harbinger of the repressed pressures of the cyborg artist. To invoke the cyborg artist as I have done throughout this chapter is, of course, to engage with the most quoted, misquoted, and over-quoted essay of the recent past, Donna Haraway's "A Cyborg Manifesto."[17] The cybernetic organism (or cyborg for short) contains elements both organic and technological, and its defining limits are always contested. Does the wearing of eyeglasses mark the start of the process? What are the effects on subjectivity of the sliding scale of meat and metal (to appropriate the language of cyberpunk science fiction)? Is there a human essence that is leached away through the process? Or, on the contrary, are the incorporations of technological systems into the body expressions of the very essence of *homo faber?*

Let us not forget that the melding of human and machine has had its poets as well. J.G. Ballard's 1973 novel, *Crash*, remains unmatched in its evocation of the *unheimlich* qualities of our own era. Ballard's eroticized evocation of the automobile wreck, the human morphologically merging with the machine, retains its power decades after it was penned:"

I lifted my nervous legs into the car and placed my feet on the rubber cleats of the pedals, which had been forced out of the engine compartment so that my knees were pressed against my chest. In front of me the instrument panel had been buckled inward, cracking the clock and speedometer dials. Sitting here in this deformed cabin, filled with dust and damp carpeting, I tried to visualize myself at the moment of collision, the failure of the technical relationship between my own body, the assumptions of the skin, and the engineering structure which supported it.[18]

Here, however, I am less interested in the debate over the posthuman qualities of the cyborg than I am in how the ideal of the cyborg affects the demo-or-die aesthetic. The goal of this aesthetic, as should already be clear, is the presentation with a seamless interface between the human and the machine. This attention to presentation as performance further extends the theatrical metaphors for digital cultural production so well stated by Brenda Laurel in her classic work, *Computers as Theatre*.[19] Laurel was concentrating on interface design in relation to the stage, whereas the demo or die aesthetic concentrates on the specific relationship among those human beings doing the demonstration, their machines and those human beings watching it. A technical paper entitled "Demo or Die: User Interface as Marketing Theatre," by two SunSoft engineers, is one of the purest expressions of the demo as performance. Annette Wagner and Maria Capucciati designed a system that was never a "real" product, but that was instead an impressive interface designed specifically for "marketing events, most notably the product announcement." The two "knew that reality would not be as important as perception in the presentation."[20]

## Sleight of Hand

One of the most fascinating aspects of the demo as performance is the way in which it mimics the particular rituals of the close-up magic show. The close-up magician, who specializes in sleight of hand and card tricks, must master the technique of misdirecting attention and forcing audience choices. Most good demos have a similar quality of prestidigitation. During the demo, users are subtly directed to pay attention to the interface's flourishes, maneuvered to those areas of the program that are hot (that is to say, programmed to offer active response to user input) and away from unfinished or buggy sections (those that are prone to failure). The magic show has to create the appearance of seamlessness: it is a mutually agreed-upon fiction that the coin comes straight from the ear, the cane emerges from the handkerchief, the dove from the hat. If there is a real magic in magic, it is of a psychological nature: a gifted magician is the master of others' perceptions.

A good demo retains something of the flavor of sleight of hand: there is the pleasure of being taken for a ride. So, what then can we say definitively of the demo-or-die aesthetic? Like so much else of interest, it contains a multitude of contradictions. It purports to be about technology, but demands the presence of the body. It speaks the language of progress but brings about an odd return of the cult value of the art object. It is both sales pitch and magic show. It is, in the words of advertising, the way we live now.[21]

# HYPERAESTHETICS:
# REAL-TIME THEORY

## Nostalgia for the Future

Infinitely tiny partitions of time contain the equivalent of what used to be
contained in the infinite greatness of historical time."
*Paul Virilio*[1]

I suffer from nostalgia for the future. I am one of those people who
works with computers, a ubiquitous trade within the information
economy. I find myself missing systems, softwares, tools, and products
before they are even gone. I miss them because I know that the ever-
redoubling speed of digital technologies will render them obsolete
memories in the blink of my too human eye. If I do not prepare myself
emotionally for their absence even before the moment of their release,
I will be less able to adjust to the immediate future that will regard
them either as detritus or charming anachronisms. Only nostalgia for
the future allows me the mental space to confront the convergence of
digital technologies and cultural production.

## The Future/Present

An enthusiastic respect for the word 'future,' and for all that it conceals is
to be ranked among the most ingenuous ideologies.
*Georges Duhamel*[2]

Remember future shock: the new boldly announces itself, cuts through
the quotidian fog, and forces you to confront tomorrow. It is already
tomorrow, however, and the future does not shock—it simply exists
alongside the present. Grammarians speak of the future perfect tense,
which indicates an action that begins in the past or the present and will
be completed later. Example: "The snow *will have melted* before you
arrive." Explanation: Melting of snow *has begun, is continuing,* and will

Must we adopt a science-fictionalized discourse to critique a science-fictionalized world? Or is the trick to oscillate between temporalities, never privileging the past, present, or future in theorizing digital media?

Ridley Scott, *Blade Runner* (1982), film still. © Warner Brothers and the Blade Runner Partnership.

soon be completed. There is need for a similar term to describe the contemporary moment—no longer simply the present but rather a future/present, a phenomenological equivalent to the future perfect tense. Example: "In the future/present, digital post-production techniques *will have become obsolete* by the time you learn them." Explanation: The technologies *have been developed*, *are being refined*, and *will soon outstrip* your expertise.

That the cycles of development, maturation, and decay of future/present environments are ever accelerating has been noted by others too numerous to mention. In fact, the blossoming of metacommentary—in books, journals, 'zines, newsgroups, listserves and Web sites—is itself an aspect of this speedup. This explosion of discourse indicates that if we are to wrest meaning from contemporary experience, we must deal with the future/present ubiquity of the computer.

The cybernetic realm metastasizes faster than cancer, and classical aesthetics is not the diagnostic tool it once was. Yet who said the culture is more pathological now than it has ever been? It is not. Etymologically speaking, to diagnose is to distinguish, and distinguishing one from the other—*a* from *b*, apples from oranges—is the basic function of cognition. Once we distinguish a technoculture and its future/present from that which preceded it, however, we need to move beyond the usual tools of contemporary critical theory. Methodologically sophisticated as this theory has become, it remains imbricated in analog systems. As constituted over the past three or four decades, "contemporary" critical theory has proven itself only partially competent to account for these new digital objects and electronic systems. A critical reading of the technoculture must involve more than the facile overlay of well-worn vocabularies and paradigms onto new objects of investigation. Three representative strategies for confronting the future/present have developed, each with its own temporal orientation. The first invokes the past to battle the present, reinvigorating the machine-breaking ideology of the Luddites. The second races frantically to keep pace with the present, manifesting itself in an almost hysterical neologizing. The third looks forward, deploying a discourse that mimes the structures and concerns of science fiction. I conclude the chapter with a fourth alternative, a hyperaesthetic that encourages a hybrid temporality, a real-time approach that cycles through the past, present, and future to think with and through the technocultures.

### Neo-Luddites

All technologies should be assumed guilty until proven innocent.
*Jerry Mander*[3]

There are those in our culture who do not suffer from what Allucquère Rosanne Stone refers to as *cyborg envy*: "the desire to cross the human/machine boundary" that computer technologies and their interfaces seem to promise.[4] Studies like *War in the Age of Intelligent Machines*, *Cyborg Worlds: The Military Information Society* and *The Closed World: Computers and the Politics of Discourse in Cold War America* offer compelling arguments that the new cybernetic technologies are still too dependent on their roots in the military's obsession with

C³I (Communications, Command, Control and Intelligence) to be seen as entirely beneficent.[5] Yet as cautionary as these critiques are, they do not go as far as others. In deference to the Luddites, those early nineteenth-century bands of English mechanics and their supporters who set themselves to devastate the manufacturing machinery in England's midlands and north, we can call the furthest wing of techno-critique neo-Luddite.[6] Neo-Luddite thought approaches the manifestations of digital culture as phenomena that must be examined with the focus firmly on the past—looking at historical and even prehistorical models of a more "humane" relationship between technology and the environment. The neo-Luddites do more than risk the approbation of technophiles; they court it. Author and provocateur Kirkpatrick Sale has gone as far as smashing computers with sledgehammers during public lectures.[7]

When impassioned ex-advertising executive turned ecological think-tank director Jerry Mander maintains "the importance of the negative view," he is expressing an exhaustion with the pro-social rhetoric of technology boosters. Philosopher Langdon Winner succinctly asks the question: "What kind of world are we building here?"[8] Though there is no neo-Luddite catechism, they would certainly agree that the ills of the future/present can be solved only by paying attention to the lessons of the past. There are groups not always willing to accept the label of neo-Luddite, much less one another's positions—ranging from Earth First! (the radical environmentalist group) to the *Processed World* collective (publishers of a magazine about the horrors and boredom of the electronic workplace)—that find themselves mutually in sympathy with this perspective on the past.[9]

Critical theorist Andrew Ross, by no means a Luddite, neo- or otherwise, posits that "the high-speed technological fascination that is characteristic of the postmodern condition can be read . . . as a celebratory capitulation to the new information technologies."[10] For those who adhere to this reading, the effect of the move to the digital merely atomizes, accelerates, and renders instantly accessible the violent, racist, sexist, consumerist, and anti-environmental excesses of postindustrial capitalism. If so, who needs it? What use theorizing that which deserves merely scathing condemnation?

The hard-line neo-Luddite stance offers a critique of an expansionist, consumption-oriented technology from a conservationist, pacifist point of view, often inspired by the philosophies of aboriginal peoples. Attempts to apply the neo-Luddite approach to the aesthetics of digital arts and media tend to situate computer-inflected arts as mere handmaidens to the ubiquitous entertainment industries of post-'89 global capitalism discussed in chapter 1. Poet and essayist William Irwin Thompson positions the citizenry of the technoculture as the "electropeasantry in the state of Entertainment."[11] In *Generation X*, a novel far more interesting than the marketing label it became, Douglas Coupland is less concerned with technopolitics, which he labels "bread and circuits," than in post-baby boomers and their numbed personae. The technocultures have ever-expanding borders, and their endless engorgement contributes to what he has termed "option paralysis: the tendency when given unlimited choices, to make none."[12]

Yet we must make choices, especially if we reject Mander's complete skepticism about new technologies. The question becomes, how do we reason or feel our way vis-à-vis the technoculture without relying too heavily on a perspective focused on the past? As noted in Chapter 1, digital cultures tend to have embryonic and oddly amalgamated politics. They profess on some levels to being inclusive and open to divergent voices—the digital democracy of the electronic meeting house so central to wired populism (Ross Perot's quixotic 1992 presidential campaign was the first major manifestation of this particular delusion in North American politics). Digitizing a culture is a cash-intensive proposition that dramatically demonstrates the split between rich and poor, North and South. Regardless of the growing presence of women and people of color online, there is still a poor enunciation of gender consciousness, and questions of race are often elided in the airy discourses of technopositivism. Whole swaths of these cultures still maintain their gnostic and nerdy insularity, with experts happily plying their trades for whoever buys them equipment and rents their time. As powerful as the neo-Luddites' position can be, their central arguments almost preclude their abilities to address the very audience that most needs to hear them: technophiles who could broaden their conception of who they are, what they do, and how they could strive for so much more.

## Lexicographers of the Future/Present

Rasterbator—A compulsive digital manipulator. A Photoshop abuser.
*Entry in* Wired's *"Jargon Watch"*[13]

To enter a community and practice its crafts, an individual must learn to speak a specific language. The editor of *The New Hacker's Dictionary* writes of the computer community's "almost unique combination of the . . . enjoyment of language-play with the discrimination of educated and powerful intelligence" to account for the prodigious rate at which it coins new words, acronyms, and slang to describe and comment on the systems it creates and utilizes.[14] Critical discourse's adoption of the hackers' penchant for neology is evident throughout the myriad academic journals and conferences that are springing up to confront the technoculture. The venerable *South Atlantic Quarterly*, founded in 1901, published an issue almost a century later titled "Flame Wars," with essays such as "Compu-sex: Erotica for Cybernauts."[15] In the acronymic triads of the humanities CAA, SPE, MLA, and SCS (the College Art Association, the Society for Photographic Education, the Modern Language Association, and the Society for Cinema Studies), panels and papers bulge with references not merely to cyberspace and cyberpunk (the direct descendants of Norbert Weiner's "cybernetics") but also their distaff cousins: cybersex, cyberfunk, cyberbunk, cypherpunk, cyburbia, *et cetera*, or perhaps *ad nauseam*. This *neologorrhea*—to coin a phrase—is a response to the foreshortening of the horizon of new technologies.[16]

Neologizing is neither new nor intrinsically bad, of course, and as Thomas Jefferson noted, "Necessity obliges us to neologize."[17] But as the future/present barrels along, the critical community can too quickly follow the lead of developers and hackers by continually refashioning the language to account for the novelties it confronts. This accounts for the neologizers' fascination with the immediate present. These scholars are in a breakneck race to enunciate the moment. Yet one of the features of the future/present is that novelties—and the vocabularies that grow with them—have ever-quickening half-lives before they turn into either constituents of the general culture or painfully anachronistic clichés. Less than a decade after the release of William Gibson's *Neuromancer*, the term "cyberpunk" was already beginning to feel creaky. When a movement makes the cover of *Time* magazine, it is usually over, and so here entered into evidence is the magazine's cover blurb for February 8th, 1993: "Cyberpunk: Virtual sex, smart drugs and synthetic rock'n'roll! A futuristic subculture erupts from the electronic underground." This typically exploitative feature—which could have borne the alternate title, "Are Cyberpunks a Danger to Your Kids?: A Time Warner Guide for Parents"—served to foreground the problems of chasing furiously after the present.

Each successive digital technology that catches the mass media's attention adheres to the same cycle of hype followed by a backlash of fear-mongering. From the movement of the computer onto the desktop, to the waxing and waning of interest in virtual reality discussed in chapter 7, "*Camera Rasa*," to the explosion of the Internet's World Wide Web, excitement quickly morphs into hysteria. The elevation of pedophilic Webmeisters to the level of agents of international communism in the 1950s and rogue terrorists in the 1970s is evidence less of the terrible perversion of the pedophile gone digital than of a national security apparatus in the West searching for reasons to exist in a post-'89 world.[18] This kind of excess is proof that hysterical neologizing is not enough. There must be more than mere naming: care must be taken to develop a process for contextualizing the new words and concepts generated in and by the future/present.

### Vapor Theorists vs. Digital Dialecticians

Media philosophy attempts to move beyond existing institutions to imagine and fashion possibilities that *might be*.
*Mark C. Taylor and Esa Saarinen*[19]

Driven by both the market and the laboratory, technomediated cultures are constantly mutating, leading critics such as R.L. Rutsky to observe that we do not read science fiction so much as live it. Rutsky maintains that it is a conceit to imagine that we are capable of stepping outside of the future/present to comment on it from a "stable" position. He follows the lead of Donna Haraway, who has suggested that we make the best of this and metaphorize our present condition as a kind of science fiction, imagining possible worlds.[20] All this talk of imagining announces that the temporal focus of the science-fictionalized discourse of the technoculture is the future. But is this the best strategy? Must we adopt a science-fictionalized discourse to critique a science-fictionalized world? The danger here is that the critic can be too easily drawn into a ever-escalating cycle of conjecture and unsubstantiated speculation, which generally sorts out into odd combinations of utopian longings, dystopian warnings, and technomysticism. Are scholars to critique the material conditions of the future/present or to weave the phantasmic?

The computer industry respects a hierarchy of realisms: there are the market-proven products on the shelves at your local electronics superstore, and there are new releases to be purchased only by the brave; there are beta packages out with testers and alpha versions that are not even allowed out of the developer's lab. Furthest out is vaporware, that most ineffable of all products, which is to be sold only to exceedingly gullible venture capitalists. Are critics to follow suit, offering a brand of dialectical immaterialism—a vapor theory of ruminations unsupported by material underpinnings?

This is certainly not to say that the science-fictionalized discourse should be banned, but rather that too many theorists are modeling their methods after works such as Haraway's brilliantly speculative "Cyborg Manifesto" without acknowledging that the insights contained within her work grow from a long-standing inquiry into the material history of science and its practices. In *Future Hype: The Tyranny of Prophecy*, Max Dublin refers to sociologist Daniel Bell's particularly insidious notion that just as historians create "retrospective history," futurologists are writing "prospective histories." Dublin creates a savage image of a "time-telescope" first focused on the past, then mechanically flipped around "one hundred and eighty degrees" to the future.[21] My complaint about the science-fictionalized discourse of contemporary theory is that serious investigations into the technocultures should be scrupulously differentiated from the wretched excesses of professional futurists. Those who contemplate the future/present should ground their insights in the constraints of practice, speculating *after* thorough investigations, not *before*.

Subsuming the neologizing and science-fictionalized discourse to the investigation of the production, consumption, and use of computer-inflected media technologies is a strategy I have already defined as the digital dialectic. Digital dialecticians will educate themselves in the ways of these new technologies, thinking not only of their theoretical potentials but also of their practical limitations. Here, for example, is critic and curator Timothy Druckrey, who in calling for a new approach to interactive art forms also insists upon a thorough investigation of the modes of production and dissemination of this work: "A model of interactivity will have to include an assessment of the fragmentation of knowledge, a reformulated concept of identity within discourse as well as the creation of media to manage information dispersal, and a refigured model for access and distribution."[22] Also in line with a digital dialectic is the work of N. Katherine Hayles, whose book *How We Became Posthuman* situates her theses about virtuality within a scrupulously researched account of information theory as it relates to cybernetic technologies.[23]

As will be demonstrated in chapter 7, "*Camera Rasa*," some areas of discourse, especially those around virtual reality, seem entirely removed from any conception, much less comprehension of computer graphics technologies. Why discuss economizing the use of graphics primitives or the intricacies of interface design when you can wax rhapsodic about the mechanisms of virtual sex? It was one thing when a figure like the founder of pioneering virtual technologies corporation VPL, Jaron Lanier, crafted a public persona both gnomic and visionary. After all, he had a start-up company he needed to hype. It is quite another when a theorist like Anne Friedberg discusses the complete dissolution of gender through the adoption of virtual identities, as though this were technically feasible or even likely to move beyond mere masquerade.[24]

Mark Pesce's occasional excesses on behalf of the utopian potential of Virtual Reality Modeling Language (VRML), which included launching it with a technopagan ceremony/rave he called the CyberSamhain, are understandable and even refreshing coming from the software's co-creator.[25] Yet too often, otherwise interesting thinkers let their discussions about the impact of the Internet and the World Wide Web spiral into airy theosophizing about Teilhardian noospheres and Gaian consciousness. For example, Pierre Lévy concludes his book *Collective Intelligence: Mankind's Emerging World in Cyberspace* by dismissing anyone who questions how realistic a prospect it is that a world brain machine will come into being. "The process has begun and we do not yet know, within the context of its overall movement what limits it will shift or how far it will shift them. Its ultimate finality will be to place the reins of the great ontological and noetic machine in the hands of the human species considered as hypercortex."[26] As Erik Davis ably counters in his book *Techgnosis*, "the notion that computer networks are booting up the mind of the planet is not a technoscientific scenario at all, however much the language of complex systems or artificial intelligence may help us get a handle on the Internet's explosive, out of control growth or its mindlike properties."[27]

The danger of vapor theorizing is not simply that it often mutates into technomysticism but, more important, that it can lead even exceptionally able thinkers into a hype-driven discourse that dates incredibly quickly. Williams College's Mark C. Taylor and the University of Helsinki's Esa Saarinen basked in the mediasphere's attentions for the requisite fifteen minutes when they conducted an educational experiment in 1992. They co-taught students in America and Finland, linking their classrooms together by computer networks, as well as phone, fax, and video transmission. Two years later they published their online discourses in a very highly designed volume entitled *Imagologies: Media Philosophy*. Taylor and Saarinen demand that we "move beyond existing institutions to imagine and fashion possibilities that might be," eliding rigorous investigations of what "was" and what "is." In the end, just about nobody but Marshall McLuhan regularly succeeded with this gambit, and, truth be told, McLuhan's observations, or "probes" as he called them, failed at least as often as they succeeded. No less than the neo-Luddites and the hysterical neologizers, those who practice a science-fictionalized discourse about the technocultures need to focus on more than one temporality at a time.

### Hyperaesthetics in Real-Time

When a poetic structure attains a certain degree of concentration or social recognition, the amount of commentary it will carry is infinite.
*Northrup Frye*[28]

Traditionally, the study of aesthetics is the study of stable forms. In literature the ancient genres of the epic, the lyric, and the dramatic still generate debate. The discourse around art has concentrated on the concrete object: painting, sculpture, and architecture. The advent of the computer, however, has destabilized these formations, blurring categories and boundaries. This engenders the categorical error that many make in their critiques of technocultural work: aesthetics particular to the static object are being applied to the dynamic arts. The neo-Luddites focus on the past, the neologizers on the present, the science-fictionalizers on the future. A dynamic system, however, requires constant recalibrations in focus, a shifting between three temporalities. Hyperaesthetics requires theorization in real-time.

In computer graphics, one of the goals is to create three-dimensional systems in which any changes to a model will be reflected immediately, without waiting for a new object or scene to be rendered. The more complex the three-dimensional structures, the more difficult it is to create and refine them in "real time." Real-time theory does not posit a prelapsarian past, as do the neo-Luddites; it eschews the hype-mongering of hysterical neologizing, and it condenses vapor theory into a discourse grounded in the constraints of production. Real-time theory strives for balance while maintaining passions both positive and negative. The question becomes, then, how is real-time theory to be encouraged, and where can it be found?

It is one of the glories of the Internet that for all its fabled, and often failed, hype, it can nurture new forms of discourse and production. The development of bulletin boards, chat rooms, and Web sites has added a dimension of instantaneity to the discussion and critique of digital culture that printed texts for the most part lack. In academic publishing, the twin requirements of peer review (books and articles go through lengthy vetting by anonymous reviewers) and disciplinarity (the idea that literary scholars should talk about literature to other literary scholars) tend to slow down and calcify the discussion of contemporary culture. In contrast, more immediate print media such as magazines and the even quicker, dirtier 'zines often do not profess a strong interest in developing much more than an instantly reactive model of consumption and response as opposed to the longer project of developing sustained critical and theoretical discussion.[29]

The obvious solution to the bottleneck of print would appear to be the Web, which so famously makes everyone with access their own publisher. In the abstract, it should be the new medium most open to the development of a hyperaesthetic. Yet while Web pages and electronic 'zines flourish, they are too often like flowers in the desert, popping up, lasting for a short time, and then dying or going dormant until the next rain. In other words, these sites are closely modeled on magazines and journals, a model that their publishers have difficulties maintaining after launch. Even should the site's content change on a regular basis, there is the problem of informing readers of these updates and getting them to return.

Usenet, a technology that predates the Web and continues to prosper on the Internet, would seem to offer the solution to the problems outlined above. On Usenet, people read and post to newsgroups, which are usually organized around themes or interests. As interesting as these newsgroups are, however, one still has to seek them out (using either a dedicated newsreader or a newsreading functionality built into a Web browser). To use an analogy from the world of print, reading a Web page or a posting to a newsgroup is like buying a single copy of a magazine. To enter into the community of readers of that particular publication, the reader has to make the conscious and regular choice to return to the newsstand.

What all magazine publishers are looking for, of course, is an escape from the "cover-driven" business of single-issue sales. Publishers want subscriptions to ensure a stable readership, and (in the ideal) readers subscribe because they do not want to miss the publication's ongoing conversation and they want to know that something they care enough to commit to will arrive regularly.

Listserves, humble as they may be, solve these problems and are the best hope for theory in real time. Listserves are electronic mailing lists to which users subscribe. Subscribers post written comments that are then automatically distributed to all the other subscribers. This structure can be totally open or the owners of the listserve can moderate the list, screening out unwanted mass commercial mailings (better known as "spam") and messages they deem inappropriate to their mission. Discussions build over time in a contained though often expanding community, as subscribers' mailboxes fill (sometimes hourly) with the latest posts. Readers turn into writers with the touch of a reply button: commenting, challenging, diverging, and sometimes combining all three in the same post.

Push media—which stream unchosen (and often unwanted) materials to an Internet user's desktop—were hyped as a revolutionary way to "move seamlessly between media you steer (interactive) and media that steer you (passive)," as a now infamous cover story in *Wired* put it. The problem with this process was that it felt more like TV than anything else, and the self-styled digiterati were quick to revile a return to "broadcast," regardless of *Wired*'s boosterism. Listserves, on the other hand, have proven to be push media that people actually want.[30]

There are listserves about everything from collecting Barbie dolls to making avant-garde films to community organizing. Howard Rheingold has defined these curious hybrids of community, publication, and dialogue as a sort of "invisible college."[31] Three lists that have contributed to the dissemination, reception and strengthening of real-time theory through the 1990s are The Thing, Rhizome and <nettime>.[32] From the start, these lists determined to be more than simply places to post notices and engage in electronic chat. These lists serve as collaborative text filters for the contributions of their regular posters, who compose a formidable international collection of theorists, artists, and intellectuals.

Jordan Crandall, an artist based in New York who has developed his own listserves, writes of how these lists resist "the market boosterism of the 'digital revolution,'" attempting "to forge a new kind of media criticism from informed positions deeply embedded within the networks" and fostering "groupware" collaborations among their dispersed communities.[33] These lists have featured long-running threads on the development of hybrid net-based forms of English, manifestos on the technopolitics of the Zapatista movement, disquisitions on the aesthetics of net.art, and a hodgepodge of whatever their subscribers find interesting. Subscribers regularly post work they have written for other venues, but it never feels like repurposed shovelware (that bane of the commercial software business in which preexisting "content" is shoveled into new media) or like résumé building (as with the republication of so many academic articles).

With listserves, there is also the pleasure/terror of not having full confidence that those who have signed their names to something are the people they claim to be, shifting theory into the raw material of detective fiction.[34] But the reality of identity is not always the most important issue, as when someone claiming to be the conceptual artist Jeff Koons posted the following to <nettime>. I include both "Koons"'s post and my response to give a flavor of how theory in real-time emerges.[35]

Dear List,
I've been following this list for a while now in complete and utter astonishment.

I'm sure all posts are incredibly interesting but is there actually anyone reading all this? Or are you just trying to build a Borgesian library?

Yours truly,

Jeff.

My response:

The recent spate of falsely attributed postings to this and other lists makes me gunshy about responding to this particular post, but I'm willing to adopt nomenclature from the music world—The Artist Formerly Known As Prince (TAFKAP)—and refer to the author (or authors) of this post as The Artist Assumed To Be Koons (TAATBeK). TAATBeK raises the point that <nettime> generates quite a bit of text, and wonders if I/we/you actually read any of these missives.

<nettime> is push media, and TAATBeK seems to feel that push media like listserves carry with them the impression that everything should (must?) be read. For TAATBeK, e-mail thus retains something of the urgency of a phone call (with all but the most egregious spams having at least a slight pull on one's time and attention).

Would TAATBeK ask this same question about a printed magazine or a journal? I think not . . . . The assumption I make with <nettime> is that some pieces are interesting enough to read carefully, some get a quick skim, and a large percentage get deleted after the first paragraph or even at the Subject line. This is exactly how I treat print (doesn't TAATBeK read *Artforum* the same way?). The major difference is that <nettime> posts do not come all at once (though many lists, including Rhizome, do digests that mimic their print forebears exactly).

All told, I prefer this kind of dedicated push media to webzines and e-journals, which I dutifully investigate, bookmark, and then ignore. In the end, <nettime> serves as a refuge for long arguments and sophisticated discourse, two forms that most other media have long since abandoned, and I like the list's mix of focus and breadth, constancy and surprise. But then again, I'm both an academic and a text addict, so my innocence is sullied (and anyway, I'd be first in line for a Borgesian Library Card).[36]

Listserves depend not only on the relentless energies of their moderators but also on the interest of their subscribers. Most of the best hyperaesthetic listserves maintain archives so that interested parties can thread through their postings, but the question of how the extraordinary explosion of thoughtful commentary on new media generated in these venues will survive is an open one. When these lists finally come to their entropic ends, will their archives simply atrophy, shedding bits until nothing is left of once vibrant debates and polemics? What happens to their particular real-time piquancy when they are archived, especially when bound into the no-time/all-time flavor of the book?[37] There are no answers to this, though it is probably a good thing that the bulk of any era's discussions disappear. The future deserves its opportunity to cycle through temporalities, fabricating its own theories in real-time about the past, our present.

# HYPERTEXT:
# THE ALPHANUMERIC PHOENIX

The sixteenth-century shift from manuscript to print was pushed in large measure by the populace's demand for copies of the living word of God. The 20th century's escape from the Gutenberg Galaxy into the realms of the nonlinear, the hypertextual, and the multimediated was driven by something far humbler—the memorandum. The generation of ever more paper in an information economy produced a demand for computer systems to create and store documents. These systems became smaller and less expensive with each passing business quarter until they reached a point when users moved the machines out of their offices, on the road, and into their homes.

The proliferation of word-processing systems and screen-based reading environments like the Internet has engendered a radical reorientation in the way that people write and read, and hence think. Rather than having to rewrite every text from start to finish, the contemporary writer/reader enters a text at any point and amends it, with all the other elements shuffling themselves into a new order—a fluidity the term nonlinear is meant to describe. This shift has taken place not just in the sheltered laboratories of academia and industry but as well to a majority of those people who write in the information economy.

No longer stationary on the page, the word once digitized is afloat in a universe of polyvalent databases. Reading becomes less a matter of following than a process of extracting. The user enters the database like a miner after precious metals. The search may take unexpected turns, but extraction is the paramount concern. The pressing need for a system of extraction encouraged the next shift away from the stable universe of the book, a shift that took full advantage of the computer's ability to link disparate bits of data instantaneously, regardless of their origin.

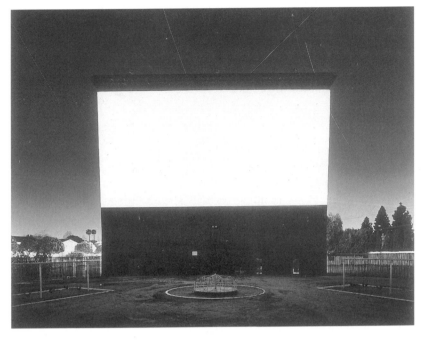

The very vastness of the cinematic screen challenges our preconceptions about how type and text should be displayed: a movie is a billboard, not a page.

Hiroshi Sugimoto, *Studio Drive-in, Culver City* (1993). Courtesy of Sonnabend Gallery, New York, and Angles Gallery, Santa Monica.

The word "hypertext" was coined in the 1960s by visionary systems designer Ted Nelson, who defines it as "non-sequential writing—text that branches and allows choices to the reader, best read at an interactive screen."[1] The interactivity of the most sophisticated hypertexts allows users to choose their own paths through materials contained in the computer or in any electronic database to which it is connected. As a technology, it is the most sophisticated manifestation of the computer's impact on writing and reading. At its best, then, the medium of hypertext opens up the static book to nonlinear exploration, exegesis, and, of course, extraction.

There has been an explosion of literary critical writing about hypertext.[2] Once exposed to electronic language's open-ended, multi-user, multi-creator documents, theorists (ever resourceful) have noted similarities to poststructuralist notions of the production of meaning. Clearly, digital environments complicate questions of authorship, as noted in chapter 3, "Real-Time Theory." They also seem to offer a privileged space to explore theorist Roland Barthes's valorization of "writerly" textuality, wherein the reader does not encounter a work whose meaning is fixed, but rather (re)writes the text through the process of reading. The "writerly" is opposed to the "readerly" qualities of classical fiction, wherein the art object is static and the hierarchy of creator and consumer is rigidly maintained.[3]

In the early 1990s, there was a surge of interest in the possibilities and accomplishments of hypertextual fictions in the popular media. On the same Sunday morning, the book sections of both the *Los Angeles Times* and the *New York Times* had front-page reviews of hyperfictions.[4] The *New York Times*'s was actually the second cover piece the newspaper ran by novelist Robert Coover on emerging hyperfictions. Coover included a long review of Stuart Moulthrop's *Victory Garden*,[5] short reviews of ten other hyperfictions (occasionally scathing, a refreshing change for a field where breathless praise for the new is the norm), a theoretical overview of hypertext, and a resource guide for ordering the works reviewed. In other words, *The New York Times Book Review*, the most powerful critical organ of the publishing establishment, took hypertext seriously.

One of the most evocative hypertexts published in the 1990s was *Agrippa: A Book of the Dead*. *Agrippa* was a collaborative project among book publisher Kevin Begos, artist Dennis Ashbaugh, and author William Gibson, best known as the author of the previously mentioned *Neuromancer*, the most influential cyberpunk science-fiction novel. *Agrippa*, however, is something quite distinct. Described as "a black box recovered from some unspecified disaster," *Agrippa* opens to reveal charred-edged pages, covered with repeated letter patterns: "AATAT / TACGA / GTTTG."[6] After a moment, the realization comes that these are not merely couplets of concrete poetry, that, in fact, they are the signifiers of the genetic code, sequences of deoxyribonucleic acids. The pages of DNA codes are intermingled with Ashbaugh's engravings of subjects ranging from guns to telephones. Embedded within *Agrippa*'s back cover is a computer disc that contains the text of Gibson's poem: "The sweet hot reek/ Of the electric saw/ Biting into de-

*Agrippa* plays with temporalities; the past, present, and future implode as an integral part of experiencing the work.

*Agrippa: A Book of the Dead* (1992). Text by William Gibson, etchings by Dennis Ashbaugh. Photo © by Ken Showell. © 1992 Kevin Begos Publishing.

cades" closes one stanza. What is unusual is not simply that the text is designed to be read only on the screen—many hypertexts are written to be read in this way—but rather that Gibson's work is meant to be read once and once only. The floppy disk is programmed to destroy the text as soon as it is read. The poem itself is about family and memory, which are usually considered to be elements of our lives that endure. *Agrippa* plays with temporalities; the past, present, and future implode as an integral part of experiencing the work. That the material is intended to be read once and only once, and then to deteriorate, is in itself the deftest of hyperaesthetic gestures—"biting into decades" indeed.

This kind of disk-based hyperfiction, no matter how packaged, did not emerge as a marketable commodity within the constraints of the publishing industry. Its spirit, however—and many of its forms—moved gleefully onto the World Wide Web. "Avant-pop" hyper-

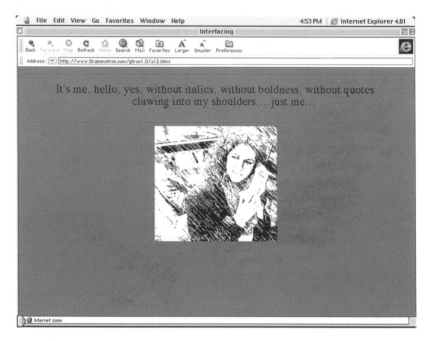

It's me, hello, yes, without italics, without boldness, without quotes clawing into my shoulders....just me...

*Grammatron* is a hypermedia narrative environment that expands into audio and animation, complete with "Grammatron magic cookies" connecting users to pages determined in part by which links they previously followed.

Mark Amerika, *Grammatron* (1999). Screengrab from *<www.Grammatron.com>*.

author Mark Amerika is perhaps the best known author of sustained hyperfictions on the net. Amerika describes *Grammatron* <www.Grammatron.com> as "a public-domain hypermedia narrative environment," a work that expands into audio and animation, one that comes complete with "Grammatron magic cookies" that connect users to pages determined in part by which links they previously followed.[7] That these magic cookies might indeed be reading the reader is a new twist on McLuhan's observation that "schizophrenia may be a necessary consequence of literacy."[8]

## The Rebirth of Text

The development of hypertext came at the close of a century that had been a great one for the printing business, but ironically, an awful one

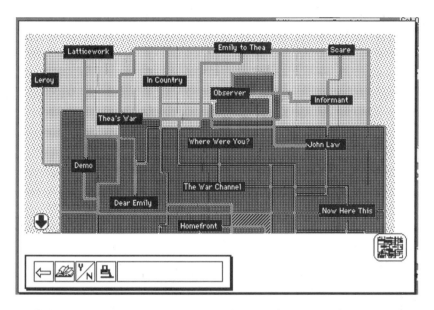

No longer stationary on the page, the word once digitized is afloat in a universe of polyvalent databases, like this hyperlinked map. Reading becomes less a matter of following than a process of extracting.

Stuart Moulthrop, *Victory Garden* (1993), screen grab from the hypertext.
© Stuart Moulthrop and Eastgate Systems.

for the culture of literacy. For one hundred years, commercial and governmental bureaucracies generated a terrifying tower of paper at the same time that print was losing its primacy as *the* source for information, for education, and for entertainment. Audiovisual mass media, especially cinema and television (those bastard children of the photograph and the radio), have poisoned the environment for text.[9] It is not simply that audiences are seduced away from typographic culture by the moving image, it is that it is almost impossible to read text within linear audiovisual media like film and TV. One of the defining qualities of printed text is that readers can skip around, return to previously read passages, linger or push on—in other words, set their own pace. Chapter 3, "Real-Time Theory," noted the ways in which the Web can push media on the Internet, but it is important to remember that film and television are the original push media: their forward movement is uncontrollable and it is impossible to refer back to that which has come before.[10]

It is this linear dynamic that accounts for the central importance of overdetermination in the dominant narrative forms of entertainment media. Plot points, character names, vital props, important locations, all must be constantly reiterated if they are to make their required impact on the spectator. Commercial film and television are thus quintessentially overdetermined media. Like everything else in film and television, text in linear dynamic media spews out at a predetermined and uncontrollable rate, and can neither be referred to nor reversed.[11]

As well, film and television subject text to specific technological abuse. Though the resolution of 35mm film is higher than electronic displays, the very vastness of the cinematic screen challenges our preconceptions about how type and text should be displayed: a movie is a billboard, not a page. If the overwhelming size of the screen is a problem in the cinema, television offers different limitations. NTSC video (the North American standard) is a terrible medium for all but the largest fonts.[12] As commercial videotext providers learned in the disastrous experiments of the 1970s, people do not like to read from their television screens. NTSC is an interlaced video system, meaning that only alternating lines are refreshed by the scanning gun, contributing to American TV's overall blurriness, which in turn leads to eyestrain and headaches whenever text is present.[13]

The computer, on the other hand, solves both of the major problems presented by cinematic and televisual technologies. The computer monitor's scale is obviously more intimate than the screen in a movie theater. Ergonomically, a computer workstation offers a more amenable distance for reading than the typical living-room layout of a couch placed far from the television.[14] In addition, computers use much higher resolution non-interlaced screens, which offer vastly better legibility. Beyond these technological differences, the higher-order possibilities of nonlinear access, hypertextual linking, and interactivity that distinguish digital media can combine to offer the kinds of temporal control we expect from print rather than audiovisual media. In other words, the user of an interactive entertainment has the opportunity to go back, to linger, or to speed ahead, just as with a printed magazine or novel. Dynamic, yet free to escape from the constraints of overdetermination, digital media are open to text and subtle typographic treatments. Alphanumeric text has risen from its own ashes, a digital phoenix taking flight on monitors, across networks, and in the realms of virtual space.

## The Technics of Text

It is not simply that computers are technically suited to revive typographic culture; users, for decades now, have been conditioned to view computers first and foremost as machines to create, store, manipulate and deliver alphanumeric text. From early word processing systems like those offered by the Wang Corporation to spreadsheet programs like Lotus 123 that made the PC ubiquitous within the business economy and the PostScript typographic printing technology that powered the desktop publishing explosion, users have come to expect text to be a major component of digital environments.[15] Even as processing speed improved enough to make computer-driven multimedia a marketable commodity, users continued to demand some sort of textual interface. When, for example, digital publishers repurpose film and television properties, the first thing they tend to do is add textual supplements. The Voyager Company did just this with its 1993 QuickTime version of the Beatles film *A Hard Day's Night* (Richard Lester, 1963). The disc hyperlinked the audiovisual materials with texts including the original script and an essay by the critic Bruce Eder on the band, their music and the movie.

Just because the technical capacity exists does not mean that text will reemerge in a form that transcends logos and info-bytes. Too easily glossed over in all the excitement are the questions that nonlinear authoring and use raise about the creation of textual and hypertextual meaning. Examine the temporality of text: the action of reading is always linear; meaning is formed by stringing words together one after another in sequence. Yet in the future/present, the computer allows nonlinearity in the way that authors present materials and users extract information. The constant play between interlinked nodes of information transforms our conceptions of rhetoric: we can no longer know where a proposition will come in relation to other propositions. Our situation is somewhat akin to that facing the originators of quantum physics. In 1913, Niels Bohr observed that the position of the electron within the atom had more in common with musical notes on a piano's keyboard, which make definite jumps from key to key, than with the notes of a stringed instrument that can flow smoothly from one to the other.[16] This brings to mind the contrast between the discrete steps of digital imaging systems and the continuity of change in analog photographic technologies. In 1928, expanding upon Bohr's work, Paul Dirac described the atomic structure as an "arbitrary electronic field of potentials."[17] The most we can know of a microparticle, then, is its partially defined state—its contribution to an irresolvable ensemble. This is quite different from the ability to pin down the exact location of a particle in the Cartesian grid at place $x$, $y$, and $z$ and at time $t$. In a like manner, we can no longer count on the physical unity of the book, and cannot precisely determine the position of the proposition within a hypertext system. We simply accept its position as a probability and make do with that level of uncertainty.

### Extracting the Nano-Thought

The author can assume no a priori knowledge on the reader's part because hypertext allows that reader to enter, exit, and augment the work at any point or time. One strategy that hyperauthors have developed is the repetition of key topics throughout the linked nodes.[18] To laud the use of these small textual units, or *lexia* as Barthes coined the term, as base reading units is to acknowledge a condition of nonlinear production and reception—the difficulty of pre-structuring complex arguments of extended length.

But are all ideas, metaphors, and images, then, to be processed down to their smallest units, the nano-thought, and repeated *ad nauseam* throughout digital databases? In this analogy, the nano-thought represents "information," the raw data of science or the undigested facts and factoids of the essay—or even fictional—form. This is not to say that intriguing ideas cannot be generated by sifting through nano-thoughts, just that a regime of nano-thinking to the exclusion of other conceptual practices is probably going to lead to an impoverished discourse. To evaluate hypertextual systems, then, we must ask how they aid the user towards "knowledge," much less the even more quicksilver "wisdom." If we accept that a hypertextualized, database-driven culture will perforce encourage the proliferation of nano-thoughts, the next issue becomes ensuring that this new form can be used with precision, and wit towards those ineffable goals lauded above. Rhetoric is the study of language as the art of persuasion, and its ancient lexicon can be mined for tools to address the nano-thought. Two terms in particular, *multum in parvo* and *mise-en-abyme*, offer insights into how to ensure that hypertextual systems do not completely atomize discourse.

Susan Stewart notes that a "reduction in dimensions does not produce a corresponding reduction in significance."[19] Collapsing the *Oxford English Dictionary* from twenty-four volumes to two, for example, and then to a single CD-ROM, does not affect the dictionary's content. Precisely how, though, does one collapse discourse without completely losing its meaning, much less its significance? The Latin phrase *multum in parvo*, "much in little," describes those turns of phrase that condense larger ideas and concepts into pithy aphorisms, epigrams, and fragments. Our culture is awash in the *multum in parvo* without ever calling it by name. Bumper stickers advising us to "Think Locally, Act Globally," T shirts that assure us their wearers are recovering "One Day at a Time," and even the little tags (annoying or edifying) that senders attach to their e-mail signatures all are signs that attempt to condense meaning rather than simply dice it into ever smaller shards. The aphorism was Marshall McLuhan's favorite form of the *multum in parvo*. He contrasted the unfinished quality of the short "probe" to the overly explicit (at least in his view) essayistic form he had been trained in by the dons at Cambridge. The essay tells; the aphorism teaches: "For instruction, you use incomplete knowledge so people can fill things in; they can round it out and fill it in with their own experience."[20] The *multum in parvo* takes a sure hand to keep from sliding into banality (and McLuhan stumbled there regularly), but a phrase like "the medium is the message" is truly "much in little," and those crafting their thought hypertextually have in McLuhan's work a model worth striving for.

The *mise-en-abyme* is less a feat of condensation, though it is that, than a sleight of structural hand. This term implies that a book, story, film, CD-ROM, Web site, or hypertext contains selected passages that play out within themselves, in miniature, the process of the work as a whole. At its limit, the *mise-en-abyme* is an almost infinitely regressing series of mirror reflections of a work's most significant concerns and structures. The *mise-en-abyme* is a mini narrative that encapsulates or somehow reflects the larger structures within which it is held: it is a mirroring of the text by the subtext. As Gregory Ulmer puts it, the *mise-en-abyme* "is a reflexive structuration, by means of which a text shows what it is telling, does what it says, displays its own making, reflects its own action."[21]

The relevance of this term to hypertextual environments is that the *mise-en-abyme* allows the unfolding of meaning; it makes feasible a Romantic conceit: click on the acorn, and the tree majestically unfolds. One of the central questions for the design of the Web is how to make information accessible, attractive and meaningful. By developing introductory or covering structures that contain within themselves in miniature the concerns of the work as a whole, and offering direct access to that whole or to those other relevant parts, the hypertextual, networked *mise-en-abyme* can help to stem the gush of unconnected nano-thoughts.

Michael Heim notes, "Thought must now learn to live in a new element if it is to live at all."[22] Hypertext systems must offer users the ability to craft or follow linkages among the nodes of information that build arguments, construct plots, even search for epiphanies. Only by planning for and incorporating ongoing synthetic processes can hypertextual systems overcome the tendency to let the screen's size determine the length of discourse. In a networked environment, the scope of the database is almost limitless, and this is one of the most exciting qualities of our era. But we must not forget that so much of that data must display itself in the concrete blocks of text determined by the limited real estate of the single screen. If we are justifiably wary of our culture's overflow of nano-thoughts, info-bits, unsustained characterization, plotless narratives, and sound bites, we need to determine how to use the short forms dictated by the medium to craft longer forms of argumentation and narrative.

# DIGITAL PHOTOGRAPHY:
# THE DUBITATIVE IMAGE

### The Alexandrine Dream

In the third century B.C.E., Ptolemy I of Egypt called on "all the sovereigns and governors on earth" to send him volumes of every kind, by "poets and soothsayers, historians, and all the others too."[1] Thus the Ptolemaic dynasty set itself the task of housing all "the books of all the people of the world" under one roof in the Library of Alexandria. The word, once written down, has always been subject to reproduction, and the fact that there could be more than one copy of a book has long encouraged such totalizing fantasies in the realm of language.[2] A few short centuries after Ptolemy I, the fabled Library of Alexandria burned to ashes. Yet the desire to spatialize and totalize knowledge within a repository has thrived through the millennia.

The technologies change but the dream remains. Michel Foucault mentions that in 1538, after the advent of printing, La Croix du Main proposed a space "that would be at once an Encyclopaedia and a Library, and which would permit the arrangement of written texts according to the forms of adjacency, kinship, analogy, and subordination prescribed by the world itself."[3] As the word has been digitized, the Alexandrine dreams have shifted from architectural space to hyperspace. For decades, Ted Nelson (who, as discussed in chapter 4, coined the word "hypertext" in the 1960s) has been pursuing Project Xanadu, a computer-based system to digitize and link the totality of text, making possible "a common publishing repository for the writings of humankind," a clarifying system of order.[4] The computer here serves to meld Hellenistic structure and Renaissance method.

What, then, of the image? Through most of human history, reproducing the image has been vastly more problematic than replicating the word. Not even the most megalomaniacal of tyrants ever proposed bringing all of humankind's art works together in one place—the

Compositing a photochemical shot of a live model, a digital photo of a 12" physical model of the monster, and electronic manipulation of chromatics, lighting and shadows, this piece is typical of the next generation of fine art digital photography, which takes as a given the dubitative qualities and potential of the medium.

Charlie White, *The Inland Empire* (1999), from the series *In a Matter of Days*. Courtesy of Muse X Editions, Los Angeles, and Andrea Rosen Gallery, New York.

prospect of uniting so many unique objects has always been too daunting. The advent of photography held out the possibility that what the tyrant could not assemble as booty, the scholar could gather as representation. In 1859, Oliver Wendell Holmes prophesied:

The time will come when any man who wishes to view any object, natural or artificial, will go to the Imperial, National, or City Stereographic Library and call for its skin or form, as he would for a book at any common library. We do now distinctly propose the creation of a comprehensive and systematic stereographic library, where all men can find the special forms they particularly desire to see as artists, or as scholars, or as mechanics, or in any other capacity.[5]

### Photography, Art History, Semiotics

Analyzing the methods and assumptions of art history in the modern era, Donald Preziosi notes that in addition to making comprehensiveness possible in the realm of the image, photography—specifically the projected transparency so important to nineteenth-century archival practices—reduced "all analysands to a common scale and frame for comparison and contrast."[6] It is thus no exaggeration to say that the invention of photography made the discipline of academic art history possible. The slide format homogenizes size, style and era, naturalizing art history's teleologies: allowing seamless transitions from massive, ancient Parthenon to miniature, medieval icon in Art History 101; letting scholars segue without breaking stride from Pablo Picasso's *Les Demoiselles d'Avignon* (1907), Cubism's signature canvas, to Robert Smithson's *Spiral Jetty* (1969–1970), the pivotal earthwork constructed on the bed of Utah's Great Salt Lake. Moreover, photography's mechanistic regime of representation is a linchpin of the development of a semiotic of the image. Photography is both the apotheosis and challenge to painterly notions of realism. The very idea of a science of signs, of semiotic discourse, relies on the "photography effect."

Yet today, photography as both medium and object of discourse is undergoing a most radical confrontation with electronic imaging technologies. The computer's capacity to electronically represent any image as simply another graphic is a serious challenge to photography's previously secure position within the archive as the *primus inter pares* of representational media. That is, the photograph was formerly the representational medium under which all others could be subsumed, distributed, and analyzed. Today, that role must be allotted to the computer graphic. Under its domain, the photograph is transformed into simply one among many representational forms. A critique of digital photography, therefore, must take into account this subsumption of the "photo" to the computer "graphic."[7] With this subsumption comes a shift in the very way we conceptualize the photographic image: both in terms of the way we read it as a sign, that is to say its position within a semiotic, and the way that we consider it within contexts, that is to say in terms of its place within art history.[8]

The development of electronic imaging technologies, of which digital photography is but one part, has posed a challenge to both the conception of semiotics and the discipline of art history. We are only just now getting around to understanding the impact the computer has had on the discourses developed around the photographic object, discourses not just technological but epistemological.[9] Writing in 1961, at the height of his structuralist phase and under the influence of the science of signs, or semiology, developed by Ferdinand de Saussure,[10]

Roland Barthes observed that "the photograph is not simply a product or a channel but also an object endowed with a structural autonomy."[11] Moving on from there, he identified the crucial specificity of the medium: while there may be a reduction of visual information from the object to its image (proportion, perspective, color), there is no "*transformation* (in the mathematical sense of the word) . . . the image is not the reality but at least it is its perfect *analogon* and it is exactly this analogical perfection which, to common sense, defines the photograph."[12] But as film scholar Rick Altman notes, "conventional wisdom is always about yesterday's technology; that's how it became commonplace."[13]

### Digital Photography?

We know there has been a rupture between photochemical photography and electronic imaging technologies. In *The Reconfigured Eye: Visual Truth in the Post-Photographic Era*, William J. Mitchell offers a clear delineation between these two technologies of image production. "A photograph is an analog representation of the differentiation of space in a scene: it varies continuously, both spatially and tonally."[14] This differs from any computer image, whether originally photographic or not.

Images encoded digitally by uniformly subdividing the picture plane into a finite Cartesian grid of cells (known as *pixels*) and specifying the intensity or color of each cell by means of an integer drawn from some limited range. The resulting two-dimensional array of integers (the *raster* grid) can be stored in computer memory, transmitted electronically, and interpreted by various devices to produce displays and printed images."[15]

Digital imaging can take input from a vast variety of sources, among them analog cameras, digital still cameras, video, scanners, and camcorders, and can be displayed on monitors or in hardcopy outputs including thermal wax, dye transfer, inkjet, laser printing, filmcameras, imagesetters, and—for large-scale applications—computer-to-press and computer-to-plate systems. But those who, like Mitchell, insist that there has been a revolutionary, systemic shift between chemical and digital imagery on a formal level are overstating their case. As digital imaging improves, the human eye finds it harder and harder to distinguish between the fine details and flowing curves we associate with chemical processes and the pixellated images of electronic systems.

Even the much touted differences between the composition of each type of image can be overemphasized. Following Barthes and a host of others, the "revolutionary camp" concentrates on the analog nature of conventional photography—positing a one-to-one relationship between object and photograph. This concentration leads them to key in on the physical differences between the mechanical photograph and the electronic image. But while they note that with every copy of an analog picture, detail is lost (a process best thought of as a re-presentation) while presumably nothing is lost with digital transfers (a re-production), the realities of digital practice prove otherwise. For example, in most commercial systems, image compression is a vital component of digital imaging, in order to keep file sizes, transfer rates, and archiving manageable. With each compression and expansion, the digital image suffers at least its own mutation and degradation, just as does its analog predecessor. Uncompressing digital images does not reproduce them, it rewrites them. Networked environments promise to worsen, not lessen, this situation, due to the need to compress images before sending them out, only to unstuff—and thereby rewrite—them at the other end.

Thus the truly radical transformation is not from chemical to digital systems of production—as Mitchell and the others would have it—but rather in the composition of the output, which has shifted from the discrete photograph to the essentially unbounded graphic. It is here that the "revolutionary" shift can be located. The "unique" photograph is now forced to merge, even submerge, into the overall graphic environment. There formerly discrete photographic elements blend even further into the computer's digital soup of letters, numbers, motion graphics and sound files: what is crucial is that all of these and more are simply *different manifestations of the data maintained in binary form.*

Whereas this quality of digital imaging seems to be an extension of the mechanical reproduction of photography, the nature of computer imaging—of which digital photography is only a subset—engenders a radical shift. Because the digital image is composed of discrete pixels that have mathematical values assigned to them, the whole of the digital image can be shifted by modifying the definitions given to those pixels. The computer allows the artist to morph, clone, composite, filter, blur, sharpen, flip, invert, rotate, scale, squash, stretch, colorize, posterize, even swirl an image around a single point, making the photographic look like it is being sucked into a black hole.

While photography has always had an inherent mutability, the digital photograph is so inextricably linked to the other elements of computer graphics that the formerly unique qualities of photography as photography disintegrate. Within the realm of the digital, all images are subject to the visual alchemy of the paint program, which offers the user a set of tools to modify every quality of the pixel. This linkage of electronic imagery and digital paint programs is at the heart of the subsumption of the "photo" to the "graphic." When all images are created or modified by the computer, the photographic is no longer a privileged realm of visual communication, segregated by its machined qualities.

### The Semiotics of Dubitative Images

The inherent mutability of the digital image poses a challenge to those who have striven to create a semiotic of the photographic. Having already mentioned Saussure's model, we can also look to the influence of his American contemporary, Charles Sanders Peirce. Film theorist Peter Wollen maintains that Peirce offers an even more precise semiotic for the analysis of the visual image than Saussure.[16] Peirce created three classifications of signs: icon, symbol, and index. The icon is a "sign determined by its dynamic object by virtue of its own internal nature." This is akin to the painted or sculpted image, a relationship of likeness. A symbol is a linkage based on convention, as in language, an arbitrary relationship between a dog and the word "dog." A third type is the index, "a sign determined by its Dynamic object by virtue of being in a real relation to it." With the index, there is a causal link between the object and the sign, like wisps of smoke curling in the distance that indicate the presence of fire. In regards to photography, Peirce was quite explicit: "Photographs, especially instantaneous photographs, are very instructive, because we know that in certain respects they are exactly like the objects that they represent. But this resemblance is due to the photographs having been produced under such circumstances that they were physically forced to correspond point by point with nature. In that respect then, they belong to the . . . class of signs" known as the index.[17]

It is hard to imagine a science of signs, especially Peircian semiotics, developing in a pre-photographic age. The classical aesthetic dichotomy divides poetry and painting. A science of signs develops only after technology adds a new dimension to the signscape of the symbolic representations of literature and the iconic representations of painting. Peirce was born in 1839, the same year in which photography was invented. Both he and Saussure developed their ideas contemporaneously with the development of the cinema.[18] Only after the mechanical photographic apparatus ruptures the dichotomy developed between writing and painting—between the symbolic and the iconic—is semiotics developed. The mechanical apparatus of photography vastly expands the realm and power of the indexical sign. What has happened to this class of signs, and to the semiotics of the image in general, with the advent of *digital* photography?

With electronic imaging, the digital photographic apparatus approaches what avant-garde filmmaker and photograoher Hollis Frampton refers to as painting's "dubitative" processes: like the painter, the digital photographer "fiddles around with the picture till it looks right."[19] The dubitative—defined as "inclined or given to doubt"—has long been present in photography, but now it is located at center stage. While critics and theorists have long rejected the idea that the photograph is somehow "true," the very fury of the debate over digital imaging proves that the public sphere still holds the evidentiary nature of photography in high regard. Yet, as Mitchell and others point out, in the era of the dubitative digital photograph, the public is forced to trust in the source of the image, or in the veracity of the image's context.

In this, the digital photograph must now be treated as having the same truth value (or lack thereof) as a written text. We have thus returned, in some sense, to the aesthetic of the pre-photographic era, to a signscape that is once again reduced to the dichotomy between the word and the image, though now both are merely different outputs from the same binary code. This insistence on context and interpretation is, of course, not unique to electronic imaging, but the digitizing of the photographic has made it ubiquitous.

Gisèle Freund recounts a story about photographer Robert Doisneau that illustrates the importance of context. Doisneau was famous for his shots of Parisians in cafés and on the street.

One day, in a small café on the rue de la Seine where he was accustomed to meeting his friends, he noticed a delightful young woman at the bar drinking a glass of wine. She was seated next to a man who was looking at her with a smile that was both amused and greedy. Doisneau asked and received permission to photograph them. The photographs appeared in the magazine *Le Point*, in an issue devoted to cafés illustrated with Doisneau's photographs. He handed this photograph, among others, to his agency.[20]

All this was well and good, of course, until his agency started to sell the picture without Doisneau's involvement. The man in the picture objected strenuously when the photograph was used by an obscure regional magazine to illustrate a piece on drunkenness and temperance. Doisneau offered his profuse apologies, and the man, a drawing instructor, though incensed that he should "be taken for a boozer," accepted them. The agency then turned around and sold the photo to one of France's leading scandal rags. As is the wont of a scandal rag, it did a story about vice and captioned the picture: "Prostitution in the Champs-Elysées." At this point, all bets were off, the drawing teacher sued the magazine, the agency, and Doisneau. The court fined the magazine and the agency but found the photographer an "innocent artist."[21]

As already noted, the ways in which digital technologies break down whatever remains of our inherited faith in the indexical relationship between the photograph and its object are of obvious importance to the epistemology and politics of an image-saturated culture. This overwhelming attention to the dubitative, to questions of fraud and forgery, though, tends to obscure the developments in another area of discourse around photography. The breakdown of the indexical relationship between the photograph and its referent, and the concurrent obliteration of photography's assumed truth value, have had the same impact as the destruction of the aura occasioned by the advent of photography itself.

### Electronic Auras and the Aesthetics of Mutable Form

Walter Benjamin's essay "The Work of Art in the Age of Mechanical Reproduction" has become a central text for those trying to understand image environments in an age of mass media. Benjamin observed the transformation of culture under the pressure of mechanical technologies of reproduction, examining the impact of reproductive techniques like printing, woodcuts, lithography, and especially the mechanical arts of photography and film on the reception and appreciation of art. Prior to the advent of these technologies, there was a singular importance to an artwork's "presence in time and space, its unique existence at the place where it happened to be." This anchoring in place and in moment is a prerequisite of the art work's "authenticity," which in turn adds to its "aura"—its specialness, its roots in myth and ritual, its fetish characteristic. "That which withers in the age of mechanical reproduction is the aura of the work of art."[22]

In "The Photographic Activity of Postmodernism," Douglas Crimp takes a fresh look at what had happened to the concept of the aura by the 1980s, the decade that not coincidentally saw the wide deployment of electronic imaging technologies. In the photographic work of postmodern appropriationists Cindy Sherman, Sherrie Levine, and Richard Prince, Crimp finds an acquired aura lifted from the "original" work from which the artists appropriate. Cindy Sherman is best known for her "Untitled Film Stills" (1977–1980) in which she photographed herself adopting the poses, attitudes, and styles of anonymous B-movie denizens. In one image she is the librarian, in another the gun moll, and in a third the office girl in the big city. Sherman's film stills are reverberations rather than instances of origin and narrative. Sherrie Levine came to fame when she rephotographed famous images from the canon of photography, exhibiting them as her work, albeit with new titles. Her "After Walker Evans" (1981) challenges both the idea of authorship and the sexual politics of the art world in which men are masters and women are models. When Richard Prince worked as a layout artist in the New York magazine world in the late

Richard Prince's appropriation of the imagery, but not the trademark and pitch text, from Marlboro cigarette ads lends his photograph an acquired aura. Although not produced electronically, the photograph presages the ways in which digital images can seem utterly familiar, yet remain ultimately estranged.

Richard Prince, *Untitled (cowboys)* (1987). Courtesy of Barbara Gladstone Gallery, New York.

1970s on early digital imaging systems, he looked at advertising, pondering the relationship between the images and their identificatory texts. His appropriation of the imagery, but not the trademark and pitch text, from Marlboro cigarette ads left him with images that seemed utterly familiar, but ultimately estranged.

Crimp sees Sherman, Levine, and Prince as developing work in which the acquired aura is now a "function not of presence but of absence, severed from an originator, from authenticity. In our time the aura has become only a presence, which is to say a ghost."[23] The aura as ghost is a stimulating idea. This emphasis on absence and severing from the origin points to a way to characterize the rupture between the photographic and the post-photographic eras.

There has long been a bifurcation in photography—between the photograph as documentary evidence and the photograph as "art" object. This opposition between realistic/documentary/journalistic photography and art photography is one that has generated some of the most impassioned critical writings on the medium. As we enter the digital era, the age of the dubitative, this bifurcation will no longer function, for all digital photographs—no matter what their makers' intents—are analogous to the art photograph.

As noted above, the reigning fiction about photographic practice is that it relies upon mechanical and chemical means, relatively unaided by human intervention, to re-present the outside world. It is thus taken to be an ideally suitable medium for an "objective" presentation of that exterior world. But what of those who would employ photography to render inner states? These are the artists who have chosen to use the camera to concentrate on those qualities that Abigail Solomon-Godeau describes as "the issues and intentions . . . associated with the aestheticizing use of forms of the medium: the primacy of formal organization of and values, the autonomy of the photographic image, [and] the subjectivization of vision."[24] "Fine art photography" has always been less reliant on truth value than have documentary and news photography. Much of art photography has been happy to mime the developments of other art forms, looking to painting as an exemplar of the "serious" art—from Edward Steichen's "Self-Portrait with Brush and Palette" (1902) to Joel Peter Witkin's monstrous *memento mori* of cadavers, sexual freaks, and the deformed from the 1990s. The *tableaux vivants* and still lifes, the concentration on formal questions of light and shadow, the quest for the limits of photographic practice—all these are the hallmarks of the modern work, no matter what the medium.

In another essay, Solomon-Godeau points out that regarding art photography as "the expression of the photographer's interior, rather than or in addition to the world's exterior, has been almost from the medium's inception *the* doxa of art photography and a staple of photographic criticism since the mid-nineteenth century."[25] This is the obverse of the truth-value question; it is the question of the aesthetics of form. Yet, as we move into the digital, the aesthetics of form become more and more involved in the aesthetics of mutable form.

# Techniques of Observation

The man beholdeth himself in the glass and goeth his way, and straight-way both the mirror and the mirrored forget what manner of man he was.

*Oliver Wendell Holmes*[26]

A mutable hyperaesthetic acknowledges that as imaging technologies change, so must analyses of the art object evolve. As we enter an era of digital photography on demand, image re-production via electronic spigot, we are challenged to create a context that does not completely devalue other forms of production and presentation. In essence, it forces us to re-invent art history, which was born with the advent of photography. Of what will the new art history, perhaps better formu-lated as a hybrid approach to both new and old media, consist?

Additionally, we must question how great a revolution these new media will bring on. As Jonathan Crary points out in *Techniques of the Observer*,

Photographs may have some apparent similarities with older types of images, such as perspective painting or drawings made with the aid of the camera obscura; but the vast systemic rupture of which photography is a part renders such similarities insignificant. Photography is an element of a new and homogeneous terrain of consumption and circulation in which an observer becomes lodged. To under-stand the 'photography effect' in the nineteenth century, one must see it as a cru-cial component of the a new cultural economy of value and exchange, not as part of a continuous history of visual representations."[27]

We know we are involved in a similar era of change with regard to our techniques of image production; we must now determine whether we are in the formative stages of a similar transformation of our tech-niques of observation.[28]

One reason that Ridley Scott's 1982 film, *Blade Runner*, retains its hold on the contemporary imagination is that it offers a compelling in-terrogation of the relationship among photography, memory, and truth. *Blade Runner* continues to offer insight into our emerging and imagined techniques of observation.[29] This science-fiction film con-cerns Rick Deckard (Harrison Ford), a bounty hunter, known here as a blade runner, who tracks down androids who have escaped from slavery in off-world colonies. These androids, called replicants and sold with the tag line "more human than human," are extremely difficult to detect, and the possibility of "retiring" a human by mistake makes Deckard's job even more distasteful. As the narrative develops, Deckard encounters Rachel (Sean Young), a replicant who has been so fully implanted with false memories that she thinks she is human. When he confronts her with this news, she insists that this could not possibly be true, because not only does she remember growing up, she has photographs to prove it. She tries to show him a print of herself as a child in her mother's arms. Deckard refuses to even look at it, and badgers her into accepting her status as a replicant by forcing her to acknowledge that he knows things about her innermost and unvoiced thoughts—things about her past that he could know only if he had been provided access to the memory files with which she was programmed. She then drops the photograph and flees the apartment. Deckard picks up the photograph, and the image fills the entire frame—the photo becomes the totality of the film image. At this point the extraordinary occurs: the "still" image of the photograph begins to move—a ray of light wavers, as if obscured by a cloud, and the girl and her mother seem to shift just slightly.[30] This short flickering can be taken as a sign of a new era of the image—the mutable aesthetic of the electronic era made visible.

In *Slippery Traces* (1995), artist George Legrady has reified this mutable aesthetic, drawing from *Blade Runner* while making his own comment on the informatics of the electronic image. As with so much contemporary computer-inflected work, *Slippery Traces* blurs genres and technologies. Legrady creates an arranged universe of three hundred postcards that have been scanned and "linked according to literal and metaphoric properties."[31] These photo-graphic images are projected on a screen, with a cordless infrared mouse resting on a podium in front of the image on screen. The user/spectator uses the mouse to search out up to five hot spots on the images which then lead to one of the other cards, which in turn has its own hotspots. *Slippery Traces*'s interface replicates the look and sound of a memorable piece of imaginary technology from *Blade Runner*. In the film, Deckard inserts a photograph of a replicant's apartment into a machine that allows him

All THE HOT SPOTS FOR THIS IMAGE

9 Aden Camels

FROM  White smoke in the sky        AT  Camel carrying tree branches

George Legrady makes visible the mutable aesthetic and informatics of digital images, linking a series of appropriated postcards according to their literal and metaphoric properties. The interface draws inspiration from the Esper, *Blade Runner*'s fictional photo-analyzer.

George Legrady, *Slippery Traces* (1995). © George Legrady/ZKM, Karlsruhe.

to search, scan, enlarge and navigate through the represented space of the image. He calls out instructions to the machine: "Move in, stop . . . pull out, track right . . . pull back, stop . . . track 45 right, stop . . . center and stop . . . enhance 34 to 36 . . . " and eventually, when he has found the precise detail he was looking for, "Give me a hard copy right there." The photo-analyzer, known as the Esper, responds on cue, clicking distinctively with a mechanical precision, creating a fantasy of photographic omniscience, if not omnipotence. The Esper's user can extract an almost limitless amount of information from a single still.[32]

*Slippery Traces* appropriates the Esper's sound and interface to play off the link between the realm of high art, emergent digital practice, and the mental geographies colonized by the forces of popular culture. Like replicants, we have a vestigial memory of a photo analyzer that never existed, except as a flickering few moments in a movie now de-cades old. As a culture, we are starting to understand that the truth value of the photo-graphic is gone. What is still up for grabs is the ef-fect this will have on the narratives we tell with these dubitative im-ages—our electronic arts, enhanced televisions, and digital cinemas—and the analyses we craft about the new techniques of observation that will emerge from them—the emergent semiotics of the mutable imagescape.

# THE WORLD WIDE WEB:
# IN SEARCH OF THE TELEPHONE OPERA

### Euretic Pleasures

Listen to me now or listen to me later. . . . Gonna get it together, watch it. Gonna get together, Ma Bell. Like Ma Bell, I got the ill communication!
*Beastie Boys*[1]

It is in the process of the use of equipment that we must actually encounter the character of the equipment.
*Martin Heidegger*[2]

When logging on to local Internet service providers via a dial-up service, the first sound heard is a familiar one: the reassuring seven tones of a local telephone call. While not quite as homey as the clicks of a rotary dial (which are now to the ear as the lithograph is to the eye), these dial tones anchor most explorations of the World Wide Web.[3]

Links between the telephone and new media forms are not as circumstantial as they might first appear. One might begin with the oft-repeated maxim, "cyberspace is where you are when you're on the phone." It is hard to overestimate the impact of Bell Labs on the history of computing. The net's nodal construction is based on the Cold War model of the interstate telephone system, which could switch routing almost instantly to ensure continuous communications even in the event of nuclear destruction of major urban centers. For the past decade, major telecommunication companies have been exerting growing pressures to determine how online environments will be billed—which is one of if not *the* defining issue affecting the next growth phase of the Web. And since the advent of cellular systems, telephones are suddenly sexy again.

These collaborative images are generated by a game—one artist creates a drawing and describes it over the phone to his partner, who then makes a new drawing based on the verbal description of the first. This process reflects the conceptual turn taken by most telephone art.

Michael Coughlan and Jory Felice. *Telephone ("It Doesn't Taste Like Chicken")* (1998). Courtesy of works on paper, Los Angeles.

The present relevance of "telephony" prompts a reconsideration of the history of art as communication in the twentieth century, and the related question of how technologies carry the weight of art. With the instantaneity of electronic mail bringing about a resurgence of epistolary culture, the Internet is—like telephony—a communicative medium par excellence. The Web has excited cultural producers as no technological development has since the arrival of video. From the start, people have been drawn to its communicative properties, its ability to create a dialogue between producer and audience, the first step towards the hazily grasped goal of fully interactive aesthetic practice. With the Web, the computer becomes an instrument unique in the history of audiovisual media—for the first time the same machine serves as the site of production, distribution and reception.

Rather than artists' homepages, arts information resources, interactive tool chests, and those Web galleries that repackage existing work, I choose here to concentrate on Web-based art that specifically explores point-to-point communication—a technologically mediated reciprocity between producers and their audiences. I begin by examining the specific communities that came together to create the Web. Next, I offer a history of the use of the telephone within art practice, creating a context for the hyperaesthetic experiments now being conducted on the Web. This is followed by an analysis of the strengths and weaknesses of the two strategies that are as the Web's default settings for such a practice—what I refer to as the Electronic Corpse and the Digital Questionnaire. I conclude with a series of provocations about the relationship between conceptualism and communication art in an era of ever-expanding networks.

How, though, to frame the discussion? With a medium that is still emerging, the scholar's usual hermeneutic approach is not always appropriate. Hermeneutics is the science of interpretation, a tradition based on Biblical exegesis. The Web, however, has no Pentateuch, and exploded too quickly to have generated a canon. Gregory Ulmer has proposed, rather than hermeneutics, a "euretic" criticism, one based on the Archimedean "eureka!"[4] A euretic methodology explores the joys and stutters of discovery. My observations about the Web are, in this sense, essentially euretic: a series of inquiries into my own astonishment at what I have seen, and a subsequent questioning of whether this astonishment leads to the kinds of pleasures I expect from other arts and media.

## Communities and Communication

Understanding the history of the Web is important, not so much to grasp its technological development (well covered elsewhere), but rather to get a sense for the communities that came together to create a visually based, point-to-point communications medium.[5] Consider two distinct user groups: those who communicated with digital graphics and media, and those who used text-based networking to bring about interaction. This is not to say that graphics programmers did not have electronic mail accounts or that Internet Relay Chat and newsgroup users did not download image files. Though substantial numbers were card-carrying members of both groups, there were many who belonged to one or the other, each with its own history, emphasis, and argot. I write now in the past tense, because with the advent of the World Wide Web, these two groups effectively merged. Artists now create images that compress effectively for transmission, and dungeon masters incorporate graphics into on-line MOOs.

Yet we must question whether the specificities of each of the communities—what it was that drew people to them in the first place—have not been lost in the merger. What happens to the ever more highly nuanced digital image as it is subjected to the compression algorithms required to pipe it around the globe? Just as important, what becomes of the egalitarian community of text, which seemed to defy the usual social hierarchies by making the same channel open to anyone, credentialed or not?[6] And how does this egalitarianism affect the question of what constitutes art in this technologized and mediated era?[7]

### Telephone Art

Those looking for sophisticated strategies to transform the Web into a medium capable of bearing the weight of the aesthetic object would do well to examine earlier communications media. Will the movement from communications medium to art form be more successfully negotiated on the Web than it was over the telephone? One way a hyper-aesthetic critique can generate new questions, if not answers, is to investigate how artists have utilized the open and responsive channels of other, earlier media to effect aesthetic interventions.

Has there ever been any important art created specifically *for* the telephone? And is this different from the issue of whether there has ever been any art *on* the telephone? A distinction is needed because in its first decades, telephonic communications also functioned as proto-mass-medium distribution systems, along the lines of contemporary cable television. Starting as early as 1881, there were experiments in Europe and the United States using telephone lines to pipe news, sermons and entertainments from one place to another. Royalty had live lines installed from the opera houses, heads of state from parliament, and "nickel-in-the-slot" public telephone stations piped in the latest from the popular theater. To comment on just one renowned user, in 1911 Marcel Proust subscribed to Paris's Théâtrophone; thus the neurasthenic novelist could remain at home, listening to the operas of Wagner and Debussy from his beloved bed.[8]

The most sustained point-to-point telephonic distribution system lasted over three decades in Hungary, where Telefon Hirmondó was a fixture from 1892 to 1925. Targeted at the Magyar-speaking, nationalistic upper classes, Telefon Hirmondó offered a schedule of market reports, news of politics and foreign affairs, sports, and nightly performances from the likes of the Royal Hungarian Opera House and the Folk Theater.[9]

The first proposal for a specifically telephonic art was an unrealized provocation offered by the Dadaists in 1920. The *Dada Almanac* proposed that an artist could call in an order for a picture by telephone, and have it made by an artisan.[10] In 1922, Lázló Moholy-Nagy claims to have indeed ordered five paintings in porcelain enamel by telephone from a sign factory. According to Moholy-Nagy, these *Telephonbilder*, as he called them, were created when he sketched out his paintings on graph paper with the color chart from the factory in front of him, and relayed his instruction via the telephone to the supervisor of the factory at the other end of the line. Moholy-Nagy wrote years later of the process: the supervisor "took down the dictated shapes in the correct position. (It was like playing chess by correspondence.)"[11]

It makes sense that in the heyday of conceptualism, the telephone made its way back into artistic practice. In 1969, Chicago's Museum of Contemporary Art (MCA) opened a show titled "Art by Telephone." The MCA asked over thirty artists, including noted conceptualists like Joseph Kosuth, to telephone in to the Museum, or to answer the Museum's call, and then to instruct museum staff about what their contribution to the show would be. The Museum then produced the pieces and displayed them. A "record-catalogue" was produced, replete with recordings of the telephone engagements between artists and Museum.[12] My favorite proposal for this show was English Fluxus artist George Brecht's poll of public opinion on his plans to move the land mass of the British Isles into the Mediterranean Sea.[13]

In 1980, Allen S. Bridge founded the Apology Line in New York City. In a project that tested the boundaries between art and the mass media's evolving culture of confession, Bridge posted flyers around the city offering a telephone number that people could call anonymously to apologize for sins, real or imagined. These confessions were then re-purposed as installations, audio tapes, and, after transcription, published in *Apology Magazine*.[14]

In the past decade, artists have explored the aesthetic possibilities of our most stable communication technology.[15] In Santa Monica, CA, Martin Kersels wired his dealer's telephone and fax to trigger a cacophony of taped sounds so that anytime a ringer went off the whole assemblage would erupt in a frenzy, bringing any kind of discussion in the gallery to a grinding halt.[16] Ian Pollock and Janet Silk organized *Local 411* (1997), a telephone project about the uncompensated displacement of 4000 people to clear the way for San Francisco's Museum of Modern Art and the Moscone Convention Center. *Local 411* featured sound installations and live performances centered around an interactive voicemail system that played narratives about the area for anyone who called in. As the artists wryly noted, while admissions to *Local 411* were the price of "regular telephone calls," any "long distance toll charges apply."[17] In "Telephone" (1998), Michael Coughlan and Jory Felice create a game to generate work:

> Player A creates a drawing.
> Player A telephones Player B.
> Player A describes the drawing to Player B. (If Player B is not home, Player A may leave a message.)
> Player B attempts to recreate Player A's drawing based on this description.
> Player A and Player B's drawings are placed side by side.[18]

Coughlan and Felice's telephone drawings slyly point out that language's encapsulation of the visual is a hit-or-miss proposition. "Try, try again" offers two remarkably similar boxed cacti with human hands emerging, while "Footloose"—two drawings of a severed limb emerging from a Christmas stocking—could not be more dissimilar.

Though this survey of art for the telephone is incomplete, its abbreviated nature is indicative of the telephone's limited influence on the course of twentieth-century art, avant-gardist or popular. This is obviously in stark contrast to the impact of film, radio, and television.[19] Telephone art—from Moholy-Nagy to Coughlan and Felice—has not developed forms or strategies specific to the medium itself. Telephony can not lay claim to a unique aesthetic practice, as sound recording can to the three-minute pop single, or television (and radio before it) to the half-hour situation comedy, or the cinema to the ninety-minute feature-length narrative. Indeed, this chapter's title invokes something that is not; there has been no telephone opera, no Wagnerian total work of art, or *gesamtkunstwerk*, for this communication medium.[20] This is not to imply that telephony is not important (the telephone has molded modernity at least as much as broadcast media), just that it is not a system that has generated a sufficient number of discrete cultural objects to slot into the discourses of criticism and art history.

### The Electronic Corpse and the Digital Questionnaire

So what do ruminations about telephone operas as yet unborn offer to a euretic investigation of the Web? Start with two default uses of the Web as communication art: the Electronic Corpse and the Digital Questionnaire. The Electronic Corpse is the digital era's take on the Exquisite Corpse, the Surrealists' parlor game in which paper was folded over and phrases or images were inscribed on the quadrants, each person unaware of the contributions of the others. The paper was then unfolded and the sentence or drawing seen in its splintered totality. The game takes its name from the first sentence produced using its method: "The exquisite corpse shall drink the young wine." Though created to take advantage of an unmediated communication between individuals in proximity, the Exquisite Corpse has been the inspiration for generations of experimentation and its extension into communication media has been inexorable.[21]

There are innumerable projects on the Web which ship bits and bytes of art from one point of transformation to another, and artists continue to explore the potential of the Electronic Corpse as a discontinuous continuum. The best of the Electronic Corpse pieces, Douglas Davis's 1995 Web-based text project *The Sentence: Breaking Out (of the Virtual Closet)*,[22] is a hypertrophied provocation—the combinatory sentence has simply grown too long to read. Davis's piece is less about juxtaposition than the sheer additive mass of almost countless contributions from browsers of the site. While this strategy can be productive when text-based, things become muddier—literally—when visual images become involved.

In 1964, two years before his death, André Breton maintained that one of the intents of Surrealism was to "attain the point at which . . . painting 'must be made by all, not by one.'"[23] The Web is circling around that point insofar as images can be shipped remarkably easily from one person to another. Bonnie Mitchell's group at Syracuse University has been pursuing online versions of the Exquisite Corpse for some years now with projects like *ChainArt* (1993), *Digital Journey* (1994), and *Diversive Paths* (1995). Mitchell describes *Chainreaction* (1995) as "a worldwide collaborative art project that involves digital image manipulation and networked integration of visual communication and the visual environment . . . [artists] collaborate to build a structure of images that reflects the multiplicity of the experience."[24]

Mitchell is not alone in her desire to use the communicative potential of the Web to ship images around the globe, but the question of whether this effort is justified goes unasked.[25] The problem with the Electronic Corpse is that the additive processes and multiple manipulations do not necessarily reflect a "multiplicity of experience," and in fact too often end up in a dismal sameness of murky rasterbations. Artists (and site developers) tend to create Electronic Corpses simply to show that they are capable of networked collaboration, not because the collaborative effort will result in something richer or more complex than work done individually. Telematic artists too often forget that collaborations between people seated side by side are not made more interesting on any level beyond the technical if some of the artists are in Addis Ababa and the others are in Jakarta. Electronic Corpses tend to be demonstrations of creative potential rather than systems worthy of critical engagement.

If the central concern of the Electronic Corpse is shipping data from point to point, then that of the Digital Questionnaire is responding to data. The best known of the Digital Questionnaires is Komar and Melamid's *Most Wanted Paintings* (1994). Their project uses the ubiquitous point-and-click forms of commercial Web sites, that is to say, a series of questions and answers spread over several pages. These questions are about personal aesthetics, with queries about favorite colors and sizes, preferences for "traditional or modern style," and the wonderfully loopy "Would you say that you prefer seeing paintings of wild animals, like lions, giraffes or deer, or that you prefer seeing

When Komar and Melamid moved their brilliant observations on polling and market research to the Web, they created the ultimate Digital Questionnaire, simultaneously exploiting and critiquing the utopian promise of direct response.

Komar and Melamid, *Most Wanted Paintings* (1994), screen grab of *America's Most Wanted* from *<www.diacenter.org>*.

paintings of domestic animals, like dogs, cats or other pets?," limiting the answers to the three equally nonsensical choices of "wild animals," "domestic animals," and "both."[26]

Responses are organized by the respondents' nationalities, and Komar and Melamid then paint two canvases based on this empirical material, yielding what this method determines to be each country's most and least wanted paintings. The next step is posting thumbnails and larger images of the paintings themselves which (as Internet propagandists trumpet) are then available twenty-four hours a day, from anywhere, by anyone with a modem. The United States' *Most Wanted* painting is a large-scale landscape with deer standing in a lake under a blue sky with George Washington looking on. The Least Wanted (modernism be damned) is a small, reddish abstraction of triangular forms.[27]

Ever since emigrating to the United States from the Soviet Union during the Brezhnev era, Komar and Melamid have been honing their Russian irony to investigate populism in art, in both the East and the West.[28] From their detournements of Socialist Realism in the 1970s, to their proposals to recycle Communist monuments after the dissolution of the Soviet Union, to the *Most Wanted Paintings*'s brilliant observations on the West's obsession with polling and market research, Komar and Melamid explore and critique the utopian promise of the artist's direct response to the desires of the audience, without ever succumbing to that promise. The Digital Questionnaire is so obviously resonant with the communicative capabilities of the Web that artists have created dozens of variations, from the Techno-Ethno-Graphic Profile at Guillermo Gómez-Peña, Roberto Sifuentes, and James Luna's *Cybervato* site to Victoria Vesna's *Bodies© INCorporated.*[29] What artists want with all this information is not a question to deal with here—it is more important to address what they do with that data. Specifically, if artists request data from their users and in turn pledge to respond to that data, are they obligated to follow through on their promises?

The correspondence logs of *Bodies© INCorporated* raise precisely this issue, which is perforce an ethical one. The site invites participants (Vesna prefers this term to user) to construct a virtual body from predefined body parts, texture maps, and sounds. The participant's virtual body then joins the site's larger body-owner community. The possibility of creating a representation of the self (however modified or fanciful) has its appeal, and many people responded to Vesna's questionnaire in hopes of seeing their individualized bodies rendered at the site. *Bodies© INCorporated* promised a payoff for participating, but did it deliver? In the summer of 1996, one Borsi Tebroc posted the following messages to the site's communal bulletin board:

ATTENTION BODY OWNERS!!!! HAVE YOU WAITED OVER 3 MONTHS, SIX MONTHS, A YEAR!!! Do you sit expectantly at your monitor waiting for a response of some kind from the academics and tech heads that enticed you into this web site bodyshop?? Join the growing hundreds of body owners who wonder where their bodies are!! Horrors!!!. . . . Send us your testimonial,

Send us your grief, tell us your tales of woe!!!! WRITE THE BODY CON-STRUCTION GRIPE LINE . . .

It would seem, when first stepping into your website, that participation would render benefits to both parties. Yet, after several months of waiting and hearing from others having waited OVER A YEAR that concrete body is a one way street!! You have our data now what about your end of the bargain!!![30]

An integral part of communication is establishing a framework of reciprocity: if a work on the Web requests input from users in the promise of some form of response, there would seem to be an imperative to respond. Yet like any generalization in art, this one is meant to be transgressed, especially if the piece is conceptualized—specifically—to frustrate users seeking this kind of reciprocity, if its very function as communication art is to demonstrate the difficulty of communication.

## The Killer App?

Confounding this medium's ability to communicate is to challenge the very status of the World Wide Web as the Killer App of the Internet. The Killer App (short for "application") is yet another grail of the computer industry: the hardware/software combination that creates an entire market segment for itself. For the first generation of IBM personal computers in the early 1980s, the Killer App was the financial spreadsheet (specifically Lotus 123) that convinced millions of small businesses that they had to computerize to compete. For the Apple Macintosh in the late 1980s, it was desktop publishing (made possible by the development of PostScript and WYSIWYG—"What You See Is What You Get"—packages). For Silicon Graphics in the 1990s, the Killer App was three-dimensional animation (accomplished via programs like Alias, Wavefront, and Softimage). The Web itself has been hailed as the Internet's Killer App precisely because it added a crucial visual interface to a previously text-based medium.

Is conceptualism the Killer App of Web-based communication art? The answer to this is contradictory. First, claiming conceptual art as a Killer App violates the very premise of conceptual art, at least as Sol LeWitt defined it in 1969: "The conventions of art are altered by works of art. . . . Successful art changes our understanding of the conventions by altering our perceptions.[31] Therefore, if conceptual art were to function as a Killer App, it could do so for no more than an instant, because its very presence would alter the conditions of its production and consumption. On the other hand, Killer App or not, a rigorous conceptual phase could rescue the Web as communication art from the worst failings of both the Electronic Corpse and the Digital Questionnaire. There is a link here to the telephone art works covered earlier: those few projects had a conceptual edge because they did not simply involve communication; they interrogated the very idea of communication.

Too many artists have posted home pages without interrogating what the proliferation of individual representations implies for representation itself. If we can read Douglas Huebler's project of the 1970s, "To Photographically Document the Existence of Everyone Alive" as a conceptual lampoon of August Sander's plan early in the twentieth century to record visually every category of German citizenry, what are we to make of the Web? If everyone with a computer is well on the way to his or her own home page, then the Web is advancing towards Jorge Luis Borges' map as big as the world.[32] With the Web, Sander's catalog and Huebler's conceit—like Davis's *Sentence*—abandon the realm of metaphor and become literalized.

If we can indeed speak of schools in a medium just a few years old, then the "net.art" movement has indeed led the way towards a conceptually provocative practice for work on the World Wide Web. Net.art emerged as a subgenre of art on the net, and was composed of artists as diverse as England's Heath Bunting, Americans Cohen/Frank/Ippolito, the Berlin-based Slovenian-born Vuk Cosic, Russians Olia Lialina and Alexei Shulgin, and the Belgian/Dutch team of Joan Heemskerk and Dirk Paesman who live in Barcelona and go by the name JODI. Artists rarely like to be lumped together under rubrics like "net.art" (and Bunting claims that the term itself "for many of the practitioners is a joke and a fake"[33]), but there is no denying that these net.artists and a group of others shared certain approaches, emerged at the same time in the medium and communicated regularly with each other. As compelling as their investigations into the conceptual and material conditions of the Web are, net.art is also interesting because it is the first international art movement since the Second World War in which artists from Central and Eastern Europe and the former Soviet Union have been able to have completely unfettered communication with their colleagues in the rest of the industrialized world.[34] No other art movement has ever been so instantly accessible from so many different locales, and so fully primed for instantaneous critical discourse. Because the work is archived and searchable, there has never been an art movement whose history has been as easy to track as it evolved. If net.artists tended to make better communities than art works, creating a transnational TechnoVolksgeist around the aesthetics of the Web was no small achievement.

For a good period of time, the only non-gallery, stand-alone arts Web site to which I returned for pleasure—rather than out of a sense of information-age duty—was *jodi.org* <jodi.org>. Like so much of electronic media, Web sites should be critiqued along the lines of live performances (which are time based and not necessarily accessible to the reader) rather than as discrete objects (which can be cataloged, re-corded, and presumably visited in the same state in which they have been described). The discussions offered here on this paradigmatic net.art site have more in common with the way theater writers critique actors for their particular interpretation of a role like King Lear than they do with either the hermeneutics of textual criticism inherited from literary studies or the veneration of the unique object that still drives so much of art history and criticism. That noted, these are some impressions of *jodi.org* at a single moment in time.[35]

The first screen is simple: lines of green characters on a black screen, with a green highlighting function cycling down. Long-term computer users will find their experience tinged by nostalgia: for me, the font, colors, and black background were reminiscent of the first portable computer I ever used, a little Kaypro with a tiny monochrome screen. There are no identifiers, no marks of authorship or ownership, no indication that clicking on this essentially meaningless screen will lead into the rest of the site. The next screen to appear creates a vaguely three dimensional, gridded space with variously colored directional arrows. Clicking on any element of this page simply reshuffles the arrangement and direction of the arrows. This section is indeed interactive, but to absolutely no purpose. There are other nodes of the site: they are independent, but somehow connected in their interroga-

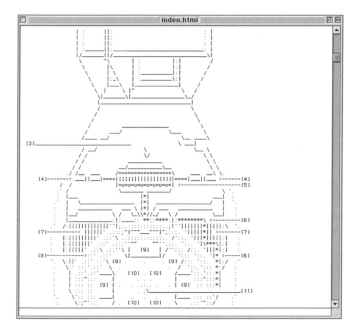

*jodi.org*'s pulsing green and black blankness is not so blank as it seems;
one just needs to know where to look.

JODI (Joan Heemskerk and Dirk Paesman), <*jodi.org*> (1997), screengrab.

tions of the schematic, from the 2.5-dimensional mapping of the first
grid, to machine age blueprints, to information era interfaces that
mock the icon-happy user friendliness of so much of the rest of the
Web. As the critic Susan Kandel notes, "www.jodi.org is ludic, entranced with the computer's potential for aesthetic play, but not at all
unserious."[36]

As enigmatically satisfying as the site is, *jodi.org*'s home page is
truly the center of the project, for there is a secret there. The gnosis
that opens up to the initiated confronts a central facet of aesthetic production on the Internet: the World Wide Web is a medium in which
the creative coding—hypertext markup language (HTML), virtual reality markup language (VRML), and whatever comes next—is visible
at the same moment as the audiovisual object.[37]

*jodi.org*'s pulsing green and black blankness is not so blank as it
seems, that is; one just needs to know where to look. In the browser's

tool bar menu, there is a command to view "Document Source." The source code comes up as a text document, and what is revealed is that there is a whole layer of pictorial, ASCII text art "below" the surface of *jodi.org*. This too is reminiscent of the early days of computer art in the 1970s, when Snoopys and Christmas trees composed of alphanumeric characters were spat out by teletypes in computer labs around the country. In referencing the Volksgraphics of the emerging digital class and in embedding this richly associative material in the site's HTML, *jodi.org* conceptualizes code as essential to the structure of the Web as communication art. So, is *jodi.org* the telephone opera, the Web's Killer App? Of course not, but what euretic pleasure!

# VIRTUAL REALITY:
## *CAMERA RASA*

### VR as an Object to Think With

Hollis Frampton once pondered an "imaginary relic," an image archive left by a mythical Atlantean society whose defining work was a series of miniature cityscapes designed to be photographed and then obliterated.

> And finally, as a crowning touch, the Atlantic masters fabricated a critical tradition to accompany the images: a puzzling collection of writings that is gathered into the so-called Atlantic Codex. It is precisely the opposite of its subject: the photographs are everywhere copious, exact, assured; the Codex is unrelievedly sparse, vague, and defensive.[1]

Frampton conceived of this fiction of a civilization that existed only to be rendered as image more than two decades before digital, three dimensional, immersive visualization technologies were obsessively feted in the early 1990s. Looking back, the imaginary relic of '90s digital culture was virtual reality. That decade's great technological imaginary exactly reversed the terms of Frampton's imaginary codex: virtual environments have tended to be sparse and vague, while the discourses of virtuality are copious and assured, if only rarely exact.

Sherry Turkle, psychologist and author of *The Second Self* and *Life on the Screen*, discusses how a theory like psychoanalysis has a certain "appropriability," a quality that allows people to use it as "an object to think with" and through the issues of a culture. In the process of disseminating these ideas, the professionals of a movement lose control over the theory and it becomes a culture. Although this diffusion is often described in negative terms, such pessimism implies that professionals always understand the "proper" use of a theory better than nonprofessionals. Yet, as cyberpunk author William Gibson so

3D images of lovers morphing into each other in virtual reality make for delirious Hollywood kitsch and demonstrate how the nontechnical public filled the *camera rasa* of VR with technophilic fantasies.

Brett Leonard, *Lawnmower Man* (1992). © New Line Cinema.

famously observed, the street finds its use for technology, and Turkle does not think that this "sociology of superficial knowledge," as she puts it, is a bad thing.[2] So, the point here is not so much the technological history of success and failure that VR carries with it, but rather the appropriability of virtual reality as an "object to think with."[3]

VR systems can be broken down into three major applications: desktop systems like architectural walkthroughs; hybrid hardscape/imagescapes that wed architectural spaces with imaging technologies to effect partially immersive environments; and fully immersive systems. Brenda Laurel, mentioned in chapter 2 as one of the leading theoretician/practitioners of new media, observed that this third type of system creates a "tight linkage between visual, kinesthetic, and auditory modalities" that fosters a "sense of immersion" for the user.[4] These linkages are created by a variety of human-computer interfaces, but the classic configuration included head-mounted displays (HMDs are helmet-like contraptions containing two monitors arranged like goggles, and are also known as "eyephones"), articulated datagloves containing sensors to detect and digitize movement, and sometimes even body suits to capture fuller ranges of movement.[5]

In these goggles and gloves systems, monitor input fills the users' full fields of vision, immersing them in a virtual reality. Users learn to navigate this space/non-space by controlling the graphical representations of their hands and bodies; they effect virtual actions, picking up objects, moving them, modifying spaces, even creating new objects. Immersing oneself in a well-made virtual world is indeed a revelatory experience, but it was nonetheless surprising how for a certain moment whole swaths of the media and academia promoted VR as a technology that would alter our positions as spectators, our perception of phenomena, even the solidity of our socio-sexual identities by opening up new, virtual spaces for human cultural interaction.

In the late 1980s and early 1990s, the so-called cybernauts of VR—complete with "face-sucking" HMDs, skintight black suits trailing sensors, and datagloved hands tracing mystic runes in front of them—caught the mass media's attention like nothing since the space race. Front-page newspaper stories trumpeted VR's promise. A dataglove flashed the victory sign on an *Artscribe* cover, and within there was much discussion of Jean Baudrillard and simulation. *M*, a men's lifestyle magazine, reported on virtual racquetball and other macho cybersports of the future.[6] Scanning the popular coverage afforded VR, what people seemed to be excited about was a fully immersive mimetic narrative medium that would somehow expand the cinematic experience into three dimensions and include not just mimetic representations but mimetic interactions. Such were the dreams of VR's promoters, cultists, and hangers-on. Inevitably, scholars as well were drawn into this, and they then began to hunt for poststructuralist game in cyberspace.

The only brake to all this excitement was that there were never ever any working, fully immersive VR environments that could live up to the phantom virtuality that so intoxicated journalists, visionaries, and theorists. Before proceeding, it is important to unravel "virtuality" from "virtual reality." Although there are undeniable differences between cinematic/televisual engagement and the "active" participation in virtual environments, the rhetoric predicting spectatorial revolution was overstated. The fabled interactivity of VR occurs in a virtual space just as constructed as the two dimensional space of film/video's linear progression, and therefore subjects its participants to analogous spectatorial and ideological positionings. Put more simply, the interactivity of VR is not as polyvalent as the promoters of virtuality would have it, because users immersing themselves in virtual worlds are more like visitors to a theme park—choosing between a limited number of prefabricated rides—than urbanites wandering the streets of the city.

What was said about the technology was dwarfed by what it implied about the general culture's desires.[7] Immersive environments offered the perfect opportunity to engage in the vapor theory of dialectical immaterialism discussed in chapter 3. In the discourses of virtuality, the imagination confronted a *camera rasa*—a blank room, the erased slate of the *tabula rasa* extruded into three dimensions—and rendered into it all manners of wonders. In proposing the concept of the *tabula rasa*, seventeenth-century philosopher John Locke presented "the mind to be, as we say, white paper, void of all characters, without any ideas." He went on to ask, "How comes it to be furnished?"[8] In a like manner, our technocultures, having built virtual rooms, sought to fill them.

### Teledildonics: Wetware, Wankware, and Vaporware

The human imagination has an unlimited capacity to fill emptiness, whether temporal or spatial, with sexual fantasies, and so it should come as no surprise that the *camera rasa* of virtuality quickly became furnished with all manner of digital fetishes. The desire to extend our libidos beyond the physical into virtual sexual interaction was irresistible and, needless to say, far outstripped the technology. Hollywood was quick to catch this trend, and so *Lawnmower Man* (Brett Leonard, 1992), the first major release incorporating the HMD/dataglove/bodysuit flavor of VR, created an instant cliché of virtual cybersex, one that the mainstream cinema has yet to escape. Jude, a learning-disabled gardener's assistant (the lawnmower man of the title), has been turned into a preternaturally powerful and intelligent Frankenstein's monster through the application of VR technologies. In a scene as creepy as it is unintentionally comic, Jude invites a woman back to the VR lab, where they both don body suits and HMDs and strap themselves into human-scale gyroscopes. The film than varies between computer-generated 3D images of the two "lovers" morphing into new permutations of coupling and shots of the two bodies writhing around in the gyroscopes, grimacing in that way bad actors do when called upon to simulate passion. This virtual sex is portrayed as so powerful that its pleasures and terrors leave Jude's partner blank-eyed and catatonic.

This is just the sort of delirious kitsch we expect from the movies. Asking a film industry that posits alien armadas defeated by a notebook computer (*Independence Day*, Roland Emmerich, 1996) to get VR "right" is completely to miss the point of virtuality as "an object to think with." And why would the hype machine not ponder virtual sex? The development of photorealistic image technologies, first chemical and then electronic, has gone hand in hand with the impulse to create and consume the graphic, the erotic, the pornographic, in short the media that contribute to what writer Chris Miller refers to as the "dynamics of solitude enhancement."[9] In 1870 visitors to Paris craved photographic "French postcards"; in 1887 Edweard Muybridge made his "scientific" motion studies of naked women; in 1927 for every Elks Club smoker there was a stag film; in 1972 that kind of "hard-core" moved into movie theaters with *Deep Throat*; by 1977 cable television was offering "explicit" materials both by subscription and as pay-per-view; in 1979, XXX videos ignited the VCR explosion; by 1986, people were downloading scanned, compressed images from "adult" bulletin boards, willing to put up with incredibly slow modem speeds to get the images they wanted.[10]

As noted in chapter 3, there is an inevitable hype cycle involved: after every great wave of public attention to a new technology there comes an inevitable crash. Artificial intelligence (AI), robotics, smart drugs, nano-technologies, even cold fusion, all of these and more follow a predictable pattern. Scientists and engineers toil in relative obscurity, making reputations among fellow professionals and rarely venturing out into the glare of the mediasphere. Then, somehow, a breakthrough either real (as with the increasing sophistication of AI systems through the 1960s and '70s) or imagined (the infamous cold-fusion scam) catapults the researchers, their popularizers, and other general hangers-on into the media's hype machine. Eventually, the claims made for the technologies—robot butlers! super-memory pills! virtual sex!—are either insupportable or so far in the distant future that the media blames the scientists and engineers for not delivering what they never in fact promised, and the long, dark winter of media avoidance sets in. Yet some of these fantasies are so powerful that they become perennials, sprouting up every year no matter what the climate in the media. Years into VR's now dark winter, AI researcher and scientific popularizer Raymond Kurzweil was still churning out prurient futurology like the following: "virtual sex will provide sensations that are more intense and pleasurable than conventional sex."[11]

Given teledildonics' hardiness, it should come as no surprise that when someone finally manufactured a full-fledged virtual sex system, the world and its media took notice. The short-lived but controversial magazine *Future Sex* finally gave shape to all these fantasies. There it was on the cover of the second issue: the CSEX 2 System, featuring "3D Stereo H.U.D., TDV Tactile Playback System, Simskin Components, [and a] context-sensitive interface," and promising that both the male version (featuring gloves, goggles and an enveloping crotch prosthesis) and the female version (with the same gloves and goggles, but with a piston-action prosthesis and the "Magic Hands™ CSex 2 Bra complete with articulated fingers") were "fully washable" and sensitive enough to allow the user "to experience sensations ranging from the tiniest brush of fingertips to the sting of a leather whip!"[12] Here, rendered in lurid purple and black, was the fulfillment of yet another term coined *avant la lettre* by Ted Nelson: "teledildonics," a system allowing for telematic, immersive mutual masturbation. No wonder people telephoned Lisa Palac, *Future Sex*'s much photographed young editor, from as far away as Germany, frantic to contact Reactor, the manufacturers of the CSEX 2 System.

Perhaps it would be better to refer to Reactor as the "manufacturer" of CSEX 2, because as anyone who looked twice at the cover or the interior feature would have seen, the entirety of these teledildonic wonders were computer-graphic renderings composited with photographs of live models. Reactor was a company formed by famed maverick comic book artist and games designer Mike Saenz. This was the same Mike Saenz who created the MacPlaymate and DonnaMatrix computer games, the same Mike Saenz profiled by the editor in that very issue of *Future Sex*, the same Mike Saenz who with Palac had whipped up the CSEX 2 as a quick joke.[13] Philip K. Dick observed that the "hallmark of the fraudulent is that it becomes what you would like it to be,"[14] and in this case, even a teledildonic joke became a telling comment on the discourses of virtuality.[15]

## The Edenic Fallacy

Journalists furnished the *camera rasa* of virtuality with teledildonics on demand, but of course, they never built any virtual worlds. Digital artists, on the other hand, did indeed construct working immersive environments, but interestingly enough, they regularly filled their virtual rooms with displaced guilt over spending so much money on hardware and software. As the debate raged as to whether or not the computer augured the twentieth century's last avant-garde, too many of those who employed its technologies offered a never-ending idyllicization of nature in the service of a feel-good eco-aesthetic. The call for a return to nature was a puzzling embarrassment: Why use million-dollar systems dependent on the latest hardware and software to create simplistic critiques of machine culture?

Canadian artist Char Davies's *Osmose* (1996) and *Éphémère* (1998), among the most impressive virtual reality art installations yet mounted, seem at first glance to fall straight into this trough. Davies' supporting texts are full of green thoughts; the interface is built around skin diving metaphors; and their environments are modeled on the organic eco-systems of the "natural" world: forest, stream, leaf, and earth. Yet Davies transcends her own rhetorical setup with an installation that's too clean to be green. For one, the physical environment she creates is highly aestheticized rather than simply thrown together as a mess of monitors, hardware, and wires with black cloth draped around the whole system (the usual affair in techno-art, unfortunately).

Based on the way that divers navigate underwater, *Osmose* and *Éphémère* use a unique interface mechanism: a vest with sensors to detect the motion of the chest. The user breathes in to rise, and exhales to descend. This apparatus offers a delightful spin on virtuality's standard repertoire of corporeal/aesthetic pleasures, so often limited to the head and hands. In terms of pleasure, these VR installations anticipate the needs of two entirely different audiences. Only the smallest

# CSEX!

## INTRODUCING THE CSEX 2 SYSTEM FROM REACTOR!

## FEATURES:

- *3D STEREO H.U.D.*
- *TDV TACTILE DATA PLAYBACK SYSTEM*
- *SIMSKIN COMPONENTS*
- *3D AUDIO*
- *CONTEXT-SENSITIVE INTERFACE*
- *FULLY WASHABLE*
- *TEMPEST SHIELDED*

**CSEX HELM 2**

At the core of the Cybersex Duo system is the CSEX HELM 2—an ultralight control helmet featuring fully adjustable stereoscopic displays and earphones. Full 360-degree freedom of movement, ribbed ventilation, feather-weight construction and wireless connection to the central unit make the CSEX HELM 2 the leader in comfort. You'll forget you're wearing it! (Chinstrap not shown.)

**CSEX GLOVES**

These gloves feature extremely accurate and durable touch sensors. The TDV™ Tactile Data Playback System allows you to experience

The teledildonic imaginary gives birth to the CSEX 2 System and its promise of techno-sublime rapture.

Mike Saenz and Reactor, *The CSEX 2 System* (1992).

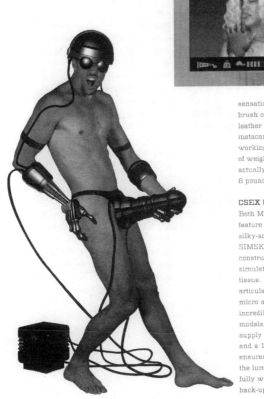

sensations ranging from the tiniest brush of fingertips to the sting of a leather whip! The patented metacarpal sleeve constricts gently, working to heighten the sensation of weight in your hands. You can actually feel the heft of objects up to 8 pounds!

### CSEX G-UNITS

Both Male and Female G-Units feature rugged construction and silky-soft SIMSKIN™ with TDV™! SIMSKIN's nitinol mesh construction and celastic casing simulates "Real Feel" erectile tissue. A complex array of smart, articulated servos coupled with micro air bladders gives TDV it's incredible performance. For both models, an independent power supply drives the playback system and a 10 megabyte data buffer ensures that you'll never be "left in the lurch." Shock-resistant and fully washable. (Multi-harness and back-up power supply not shown.)

**CREDITS:**

Concept/Article: Mike Saenz
Graphic Design: Ken Holewczynski
3-D Modeling and Graphics:
Mike Saenz and Norm Dwyer

Photos: Bill Weiss
Human Models:
Hans and Madison

**REACTOR**

This real-time frame capture from Char Davies's virtual reality installation showcases one of her highly aestheticized environments: though based on organic forms, they do not strive toward digital realism—the chimera of VR.

Char Davies, *Osmose (The Pond Red)* (1996). © 1995–1998 Char Davies/Immersence, Inc. and Softimage, Inc.

percentage of the museum's patrons actually get strapped into the vest and head mounted display so as to immerse themselves fully in the virtual environment; the rest participate less actively. Anticipating this, Davies creates a dialogue between the piece's "user" and the "viewers" (who wear polarized glasses and watch a large-screen stereoscopic projection of what the user sees). Blocked off from the viewers by a full-length pane of opaque glass, the user's back-lit silhouette twists and turns as she learns new ways of negotiating new spaces.

These virtual spaces are both lovely and strange. Perhaps their strangeness grows from the fact that these are so clearly acculturated bits of nature: though based on organic forms, their colors and textures do not strive toward the chimera of VR—digital realism. For users of *Osmose*, movement from cloud to tree trunk, from glen to riverbed, may be fluid and dimensional; for viewers, the images may have the quality of a languid series of long takes with the occasional fade. In *Éphémère* the feeling is more akin to a flowing between veils, as both transparency and seamlessness are prized. While the body, its organs, and its fluids form another level of visual metaphor within *Éphémère*, in *Osmose*, below the rocks and the riverbed is an environment composed of alphanumeric characters arranged in intersecting planes. This spatialized conceit about computer code and the way it undergirds techno-art is quite sophisticated visually. More important, though, its self-reflexivity denaturalizes the imagery, revealing the entire experience as a well-articulated series of electronic maneuvers.

When she made *Osmose*, Davies was the Director of Visual Research at Softimage, a high-end computer graphics software group eventually acquired by Microsoft. In other words, Davies is as imbricated in the brave new technological world as an artist can be. Davies's VR installations are at their best when they elide Edenic fallacies about the oneness of nature and concentrate on the shifting terrains of millennial technology.

### The Poetics of Virtual Space

Virtuality implies more than the shifting terrains we expect from movement through real space. VR environments also destabilize our sense of scale, and thereby of time and space. In *The Poetics of Space*, Gaston Bachelard contemplates the miniature and the immense.

The cleverer I am at miniaturizing the world, the better I possess it. But in doing this, it must be understood that values become condensed and enriched in miniature. Platonic dialectics of large and small do not suffice for us to become cognizant of the dynamic virtues of miniature thinking. One must go beyond logic in order to experience what is large in something small."

Further, he adds that "Miniature is an exercise that has metaphysical freshness: it allows us to be world conscious with slight risk." Immensity, on the other hand "is the movement of motionless man. It is one of the dynamic characteristics of quiet daydreams." All this talk of scale has profound implications beyond the realm of geography. "Philosophers, when confronted with outside and inside, think in terms of being and non-being."[16] The miniature and the immense transmuted into the virtual datascapes of the computer have immense effects on our epistemology, our ontology and our phenomenology.

A group at the School of Architecture at the University of Tennessee did a study that measured perceived passage of time in relation to changes in scale. Researchers had subjects investigate 1/6-, 1/12-, and 1/24-scale models complete with representations of furniture and inhabitants. They were asked to move scale figures through the environment, and to picture both these miniaturized representations and mental images of themselves doing things appropriate to do within that space. They were asked to indicate when they had been in this scaled down "lounge" for a half an hour. The researchers found that "the experience of temporal duration is compressed relative to the clock in the same proportion as scale-model environments being observed are compressed relative to the full-sized environments . . . [suggesting] that spatial scale may be a principal mediator in the experience of time." A 1/12 scale of 30 minutes is therefore 5 minutes, 1/24 is 2-1/2 minutes, and so forth.[17]

This speaks to both the opportunities and challenges in creating electronic spaces without a referent. There is a great deal of spatial confusion within the *camera rasa* and getting "lost" is far too easy: users can find themselves "above" or "below" the model, moving within a wall rather than through a room, facing away from the built structures out into the vast emptiness of the rest of the virtual world. The geographic and phenomenological discontinuities of VR both support and invert the "space-time compression" that characterizes the rest of our mediated experiences.[18]

Transarchitect Marcos Novak tells of an interesting inversion of the University of Tennessee study. At the Banff Center for the Arts, Novak had created a virtual environment of vast complexity, with innumerable virtual spaces, rooms, and structures. During VR exhibitions, users are usually restricted to very short immersion times, because of the public's demand to experience the environment. But one night, after hours, Novak invited the "metaphysician" of virtual reality, philosopher Mike Heim, to spend as much time as he wanted immersed in the transarchitectural liquid environment of *Dancing with the Virtual Dervish: Worlds in Progress* (1994).[19] When Heim unstrapped the HMD, Novak asked him how long he long he felt he had been immersed in the installation. Heim responded that he assumed about fifteen minutes, while in fact Novak knew he had been exploring the world for over two hours. Though this is, of course, anecdotal evidence, the almost exact inversion of the Tennessee results indicate that questions of scale—either of the miniature or of the immense—affect the time sense profoundly.

In this context, the miniature's condensation needs to be considered along with the oneiric qualities of the immense as they relate to electronic environments—those spaces built without concrete referents. Playing with scale brings both confusion and promise to the electronic arts. The hyperaesthetic, proprioceptive and spatiotemporal manipulations of artists like Novak and Davies make the flux and transformations of digital environments both visible and inhabitable. The *camera rasa* of VR will be far better filled with their discrete interventions than with journalistic hype or the fantasies of amateur futurists.

# HYBRID ARCHITECTURE:
# HARDSCAPES AND IMAGESCAPES

### Disney's Radiant City

In 1986, at the second Technology Entertainment Design conference (TED 2), the Walt Disney Company invited a select group of industry professionals, designers, scientists, and journalists into a spare and cavernous space. Once inside, the Disney Imagineers closed the doors and turned off the lights. They then hit a switch and the invited guests looked around and saw that they were no longer in an empty space—they were in a castle, complete with parapets, flying buttresses, and stone pediments.[1] The mere fact that there was no stone, nor any building materials of any kind, is immaterial—for that is exactly the kind of transformation of space that had occurred: an immaterial one. Using a sophisticated array of slide projections, the Imagineers had thrown up an environment that challenged the very concept of architecture. They had created a imagescape—a visual matrix for the space surrounding the users.[2]

How are we to characterize this phenomenon of castles at the flick of a switch? Where in this visual trickery is architecture's romance of brute labor—the Biblical saga of the Jews toiling on the pyramids, the centuries of labor on China's Great Wall, even the poignancy of Fitzcarraldo's carting a river boat over a mountain to build an opera house in the Amazon?[3] As the Imagineers' slides are outpaced by a battery of video walls, LCD panels, video projections, and large-scale computer graphic displays, we enter a new era of architecture, one in which the design of our lived spaces reflects and incorporates the electronic information and imaging technologies that are ever more central to our lives.

Michael Jantzen's computer-generated model of a beach home faced on the street with flat panel displays transmitting video signals from cameras mounted on the ocean side is a design for living that reflects and incorporates electronic information and imaging technologies.

Michael Jantzen, *Malibu Video House* (1998). Courtesy of the artist.

## After the Things of Nature

Consider D.E. Shaw & Co's twenty-four-hour digital office (1991). Architect Steven Holl approached this project as an opportunity to represent the ultra-modern spaces of information flows, "the invisible technology of electricity," commissioned by a company that uses sophisticated computer modeling to project future financial activities in the world's major markets. To create an environment for these postindustrial, information-dependent activities in "a way that is both visual and spatial,"[4] Holl simulates reflections of actual objects by cutting out slots in false walls to allow hidden, reflected colors to illuminate the room. The most emblematic of these phantom images is the blue phosphorescence emanating from behind one of the walls, the ghost of a phantom monitor. In the architect's words, "the invisible, untouchable, projected color is the manifestation of the electronic flow of the exchange."[5]

Rem Koolhaas's *Maison à Bordeaux* (1998) is another structure that relates built space to information space. Koolhaas had done a provocative design for the Center for Art and Media Technology (better known as the ZKM, or *Zentrum für Kunst und Medientechnologie*) in Karlsruhe, Germany in 1989. The ZKM plan features a "robot" on the south side, "an interpretation of the traditional scenery cage . . . [housing] various technical equipment and movable elements permitting the construction of an 'electronic décor' for each space."[6] Though his vision for the ZKM was never realized, the process of thinking through how to site, contain, display and contribute to emerging artistic practices had an impact on the *Maison à Bordeaux* in 1998, almost a decade later. Much of the house offers the Dutch architect's take on the fascination modernism has displayed for industry, constructing the environment out of huge, commercial-style plate glass windows, aluminum and poured resin floors, and concrete ceilings. But it is the central feature of the house that so completely identifies it as a product not of the industrial age but rather of the era of information technolology (IT) and its electronic décor. Pistons drive an 11′ by 10′ platform supporting a desk and a chair that functions as the "study" through the core of the house, allowing "smooth and open interface" to the entirety of a three story wall of glass and polyester bookshelves that house books, art and, in the cellar, wine.[7] Koolhaas's client was disabled just before the design work began, so there is a material justification for this structural mobility, but it is impossible not to read the platform as literalization of the search engine. The *Maison à Bordeaux* makes the display of and access to information (here primarily in the form of the book) both an architectural and cultural fetish.

Just as Holl stops short of incorporating actual computer modeling and display technologies into Shaw's office, choosing instead to represent these as visual simulations, Koolhaas is too savvy, and too witty, to fall prey to designing something for the moment only—like the industrial designers who put out a "Web surfing" ergonomic armchair which looked and even sounded obsolete the moment you took

Pistons drive a platform through the core of this house, allowing smooth and open interface to a three-story wall of bookshelves. The platform literalizes the search engine, making the display of and access to information both an architectural and cultural fetish.

Rem Koolhaas, *Maison à Bordeaux* (1998). Photo: © Todd Eberle, 1999.

in the idea. The *Maison à Bordeaux* draws from proven industrial meta-phors and the enduring information technology of print to comment on everything from the growth of the home office to the virtualization of contemporary architecture.[8]

Unlike Holl and Koolhaas, younger architects like Stephen Per-rella and Tony Wong early on in the 1990s proposed an "enculturated architecture:" a "design philosophy responsive to the digital informa-tion that surrounds us," replete with "'imaging wallpaper.'"[9] Note the title that Perrella and Wong gave their partnership: Studio AEM, which stood for "Architecture at the End of Metaphysics." A philolog-ical digression: *meta ta physika*, the Greek root, translates literally as "after the things of nature." In the modern era we generally under-stand metaphysics to concern the kinds of things there are and their modes of being. Digital enthusiasts follow the general postmodern tendency towards what Yve-Alain Bois calls the "millennarianist feel-ing of closure."[10] Thus, previously robust cultural forms are pro-claimed as dead and banished to the ashcan of history. The electronic novelties are then left to circulate in a vacuum of critical intelligence, afloat in the global market.

### Hardscapes at the End of Architecture?

Theoretician and digital artist Lev Manovich offers another endgame formulation. He suggests that rather than Architecture at the End of Metaphysics, what we have now is Architecture at the End of Archi-tecture. Manovich sees in the last two decades an unprecedented con-vergence of the death of architecture and the rise of computer graphics. As he sees it, "Architecture is becoming simply a support for computer-generated images. . . . The virtual space created by these im-ages replaces the physical space of architecture . . . the image termi-nates the space. Architecture is reduced to a shelter for the image, not unlike a TV set, a billboard, a movie theater, turned inside out."[11]

While agreeing with Manovich about the rise of computer graph-ics, I feel he dismisses architecture too quickly.[12] Architects must come to terms with a bifurcation within their field, a split that demands the development of a hybrid architecture: an approach that negotiates the relationship between the hardscape, a term I appropriate from the dis-course of landscape architecture, and what I have already referred to as the imagescape.[13] The hardscape is the physical space of buildings and sites; the imagescape is comprised of the electronic facades, linings, and elements on, in and throughout this hardscape.

That architecture will change, must change, under pressure from technology is borne out by even the most cursory examination of the last hundred years of building: indoor plumbing makes the bathroom an integral part of the home, first gas and then electricity transform the function of the home after darkness sets in outside; the telephone and the automobile combine to make even those living on the outskirts feel connected and mobile, encouraging the growth of suburbs; first radio and then television become the electronic hearths around which the rest of the home circulates. Most recently, the growth of telematic technologies has made possible, at least for some, the rebirth of the home as a site of production. The home was integrated with the farm for millennia, and was thus both shelter and the workplace. In the industrial era, the home was at first either refuge from or flop to recover in after the toil of the day. Later, after the introduction of broadcast media, the home became more and more a center of entertainment and consumption, along the lines of the suburbia so artfully mocked by fiction writers from John Cheever to Richard Ford.[14] Interestingly, for the telecommuting classes and home office workers, domestic architecture returns to its agrarian past: contemporary living spaces are being designed as both work and living spaces.

Today, sophisticated imaging systems and ever larger-scale projection surfaces will dictate the development of hybrid architecture. The high modern movement in architecture was, of course, enamored of technology, but tended to deploy it in line with a certain austere aesthetic, stripping down the machine to its most important parts, as it were. Yet the disillusion with such strict formalism and the more recent resurgence of ornamentation lead me to think that these architectural trends will intersect with growing acculturation to rapid stylistic change and user configurability engendered by advanced consumer markets and digital environments. One way to reconfigure architecture and maintain cost-efficiency is to hybridize it, to surround and infiltrate the hardscape with endlessly mutable imagescapes.[15]

The mutable imagescape, especially on the exterior, brings to mind the mirrored building—one of the hallmarks of modernism's use of new technologies. The reflective facade is obviously mimetic, masking the architectural into the sky and the land. The cinematic facade of the imagescape, on the other hand, need not be so directly reflective, and can be open to a wider range of notions. The visionary Californian architect Michael Jantzen has proposed an interesting way station between the mirror and the mutable imagescape with his unbuilt plans for the "Malibu Video House." This beach-front, two-level private home is faced on the street side with flat-panel displays transmitting video signals from cameras mounted on the ocean side.[16] The house thus effectively effaces itself in the manner of a mirrored structure, but at the same time offers up the tantalizing prospect of changing the channels.

### Throw a Bungalow at a Detached Garage and End Up with the Chrysler Building

Midway through the 1990s, the Fermi National Accelerator Laboratory announced the discovery of the top quark, the last undiscovered quark of the six predicted by current scientific theory. What makes this relevant to a discussion of hybrid architecture is that the top quark is more than 100 times heavier than the proton. This is a paradox: How can a component of the proton weigh more than the proton itself? A recent article on the relation between science and metaphor put it this way:

> Until recently, the reigning metaphor had it that quarks lay inside the proton just as protons lay inside the nucleus of atoms—like a box inside another box. But the . . . top quark is enormously more massive than a proton—which came as a complete surprise. Instead of opening one box and finding a smaller one, they looked inside the proton and found something more massive than the proton itself.[17]

To locate the top quark, physicists used the Tevatron supercollider to aim a proton at an anti-proton. The proton strikes the antiproton head on, they both smash to bits, and pieces fly off in every direction. Some of the bits that fly off are heavier than the proton and antiproton combined, including the top quark. The paradox of the parts being heavier than the whole can be solved more simply than it might seem, and involves the relationship between matter and energy.

Einstein's often invoked, if less often fully understood, equation $E = mc^2$ offers the explanation. $E$ stands for energy, $m$ stands for mass, and $c$ is the speed of light. The two quantities are tied to each other. Accelerating the proton and the antiproton to almost the speed of light gives them an enormous amount of energy. When they collide, most of that energy can turn into a corresponding amount of mass in the form of the particles that fly out of the collision.[18]

### The Paradox of Unfolding

The subatomic physics of the top quark resonates in an interesting way with the paradox of unfolding one finds in the aesthetics of hybrid architectures. When the transformations inherent in virtual space are situated within the stable structures of the hardscape, there is a confrontation between the illogics of the electronic image and the physics of building. Remember Zeno's paradox: Achilles can never beat the tortoise to the finish line because there is always half the remaining distance to complete, and the completion of an infinite sequence of acts in a finite time interval is logically impossible.[19] Yet there is a physical refutation of the paradox: after a finite number of decreasing intervals, the space of final intervals would be physically indistinguishable from the terminal point. Put more simply, Achilles is eventually bound to beat the tortoise by at least a nose, because his nose has an appreciable volume. Yet cyberspace offers us some intriguing ways to tweak Zeno, as density and volume are as mutable in virtual space as color or texture.

On the simplest level, take commercially available architectural walkthrough softwares. Walkthroughs are real-time 3D design packages that both spatial design professionals and amateurs use to conceptualize and communicate their ideas. The program integrates real-time perspective 3D rendering with object-model design, enabling users to move freely through the environment they create as if they were actually there. The program offers multiple views, 2D scenes and 3D objects. In some, changes made within the 2D model—or blueprint—can appear instantly in the 3D rendering. The physical properties of space, mass, and volume are constantly challenged by the visual conceit of approaching a wall and then passing through it to reach the interior spaces. Anyone who has lost their way in cyberspace—realizing they have just phased into what they had previously categorized as "solid" matter—will understand this example.

But what of those proposals for a virtual architecture in which the user approaches an object in cyberspace, moving towards it only to have it transform into a new object? In *Neuromancer*, William Gibson imagined these objects as data constructions—spheroids, pyramids, and clusters—that open up into more complex organizations of information as the user contacts them: "He punched himself through and found an infinite blue space ranged with color-coded spheres strung on a tight grid of pale blue neon. In the nonspace of the matrix, the interior of a given data construct possessed unlimited subjective dimension."[20] Here is a reorganization of the presuppositions of Zeno's paradox: the user dives headlong towards the virtual object in cyberspace only to have it transform into yet another space upon the moment of "contact."

Architect Michael Benedikt comments that if we want to use

the object in its largest context—that is in (cyber)space, along with other objects—and if, therefore, it is important that the object not be so large as to obscure others, we need to adopt [a method] for 'releasing' intrinsic dimensions, namely *unfolding*. . . . When an object unfolds, its intrinsic dimensions open up, flower, to form a new coordinate system, a new space, from (a selection of) its (previously intrinsic) dimensions. Data objects and data points in this new, unfolded, opened-up space thus have, as extrinsic dimensions, two or three of the ones intrinsic to the first, 'mother,' object. These objects may in turn have intrinsic dimensions, which can unfold . . . and so on, in principle, nested ad infinitum or until, at last, one has objects that have only one or two intrinsic dimensions and their self-identity left.[21]

In physical space there is only so much room between two objects. Yet cyberspace is a mathematical construct that can imitate the infinite regression of real numbers. Infinite regression means that between any two real numbers a third can be inserted.[22] Zeno's paradox, then, spatializes infinite regression. Interestingly enough, since the 19th century, there has been a fully implemented system inspired by infinite regression: the Dewey decimal system, still the most common worldwide. Following Melvil Dewey, librarians classify books by the broadest criteria with three digits, and then insert new subject numbers as they emerge, extending beyond the decimal point for subclasses.

The designers Charles and Ray Eames made a classic instructional film for IBM in 1968 called *Powers of Ten*, "a film dealing with the relative size of things in the universe and the effect of adding another zero."[23] The film begins with a couple having a picnic in a park in Chicago. As befits a project from the height of the space race, the perspective moves outward first, away from the couple, moving within a minute to a vision of the earth as a globe and within three minutes to a view of the Milky Way. This kind of movement, while brilliantly presented by the Eames, reflected the perceptual shift occasioned by photography from space in which the Earth figured as a "Big Blue Marble." But it is the movement from the large to the small that concerns us here.

The camera descends into the man's very flesh: moving from skin, to blood, to cell, to DNA, and ending at $10^{-15}$ meters with a visualization of subatomic structure. This kind of physical movement is perforce impossible; yet cyberspace, with its constantly enfolding and unfolding structures, offers us a way to imagine a permeable environment wherein we enter spaces forever smaller or larger.[24] The hybridization of hardscape and imagescape takes this previously disembodied experience and reintegrates it into the human spatial environment.

## SI + VR = UV (Unitary Virtuality)

Artificial reality pioneer Myron Krueger plans for the day when "the design of future buildings and the appearance of existing ones could be affected dramatically by responsive technologies . . . patterns could change in response to the people who moved through" them.[25] Krueger presents his plans as technological solutions to sterility and boredom, and his discourse, for the most part, is removed from the tradition of avant-garde critical architectural practice and discourse.[26] Yet the hybrid space of the hardscape and the non-space of the imagescape instantiate aspects of the radical and utopian discourse about architecture generated by the radical European movement, the Situationist International.[27]

In the aftermath of the Second World War, in western European countries emerging from chaos and destruction into a period of unprecedented prosperity, consumption, and consumer affluence (with the attendant increase in leisure time), a group of politically committed artists and intellectuals banded together to confront what they saw as advanced capitalism's extension of alienation beyond the Marxist models discussed in chapter 1. The SI posited an alienation not merely from the process of labor but from lived experience itself, a process that Guy Debord, the SI's chief ideologue, described as a "social relationship among people, mediated by images." This was, as Debord titled the SI's best known work, *The Society of the Spectacle*.

In French, the word *spectacle* means "show"; movies and theater are advertised under signs saying "*spectacle*." The Situationists used the term to mean the sum total of all looking, a single show that becomes the object of all of the apparently purposeless surplus production in our society: "*capital* accumulated to the point where it becomes image."[28] The spectacle is the sum total of all the movies, buildings, advertisements, propaganda, football games, boutiques, newspapers, televised wars, art museums, traffic jams, pornography, and anything else we watch—on screen, at home, or in the street. It is not the images themselves, however, that form the spectacle. It is the state of things in which communication flows only in one direction, from the powerful to the powerless. By the SI's account, in the society of the spectacle, we can't talk back, and, worse, we don't want to. In *Lipstick Traces: A Secret History of the Twentieth Century*, Greil Marcus links the SI back to the Dadaists and forward to the era of punk music:"

In the spectacle, passivity was simultaneously the means and the end of a great hidden project, a project of social control. On the terms of its particular form of hegemony the spectacle naturally produced not actors but spectators: modern men and women, the citizens of the most advanced societies on earth, who were thrilled to watch whatever it was they were given to watch.[29]

Situationism was devoted to jarring this social relationship, to creating situations that *involve* the individual—so that they are doing rather than watching.[30]

What makes all of this interesting for hybrid architecture is the SI's intimate concern with the place of the individual not only within ideology but, equally importantly, within space. As Thomas

McDonough observes, in their psychogeographic mappings and *dérives*, the SI attempted "to construct a more concrete collective space, a space whose potentialities remained open-ended for all participants in the 'ludic-constructive' narrative of a new urban terrain."[31] A rallying point for the SI was the concept of "unitary urbanism." This term they defined as "the theory of the combined use of arts and techniques for the integral construction of a milieu in dynamic relation with experiments in behavior."[32] Debord offered these comments in 1957:

Unitary urbanism is defined first of all by the use of an ensemble of arts and technics as means contributing to an integral composition of the milieu. This ensemble must be envisaged as infinitely more far-reaching than the old domination of architecture over the traditional arts, or than the present sporadic application to the anarchic urbanism of specialized technology or of scientific investigations such as ecology. . . . It must include the creation of new forms of architecture, urbanism, poetry, and cinema.[33]

The synesthetic fantasy of complete mutability that Debord offered in the 1950s and '60s has been recapitulated almost verbatim by the proponents of virtual systems. These theorists and programmers are not looking to remake urban spaces, but instead, to craft cyberarchitectures. The quest to create fully immersive virtual reality systems has been driven by the dream of a completely mutable, controllable environment. In 1993 Brenda Laurel noted that fully immersive virtual technology "represents both the grail at the end of the history of cinema and the beacon that draws creative energies towards the culmination of computing."[34] Yet even VR die-hards acknowledge that the "goggles and gloves" systems—those ubiquitous signifiers of VR discussed in chapter 7 that combine head-mounted displays and prosthetic input devices—lost ground in both the laboratory and the marketplace to hardscape/imagescape hybrids.[35]

What, then, does this hybridized space/non-space offer the architectural imagination? Remember that the Situationists were not simply looking to expand the spectacle, for the notion of urban space as a unified visual matrix for the display of commodified imagery would have filled them with loathing. The goal of unitary urbanism was to offer "a living critique, fueled by all the tensions of daily life, of this manipulation of cities and their inhabitants. Living critiques means the setting up of bases . . . on terrains equipped for their own ends."[36] The hybridized hardscapes and imagescapes I have been discussing are rarely as politically radical as the SI's proposals for unitary urbanism, but there are other forms of critique contained within them.

## A Magic Mirror

The desire to hybridize imaging technologies and architecture is as old as cave painting and only very rarely outdoes the frescoes of Renaissance Florence.[37] If we are to build hybrids of hardscapes and imagescapes, we must constantly return to the question of the body—as it exists in both real and virtual spaces. This notion of the body in space is central to the SI's concept of unitary urbanism, of course, and though the recent *Interaktive Architektur* of Frankfurt-based Christian Möller is much less overtly political than what the SI would have called for, Möller's work is as evocative as any hybrid architecture yet produced. Using highly sensitive condenser microphones, Möller has amplified the sound of grass growing, creating a space to contemplate the natural as it is transformed by the technological. He proposes to unroll a huge zootrope across the tunnel walls of the Frankfurt subway, emulating our ancestors' visual pleasures in simple animations while harnessing the speed of our high-tech vehicles to create the zootrope's illusion of motion. The facade of that city's Zeilgalerie is transformed into a skin that responds visually to environmental conditions—blue and yellow lights play across the glass panels, controlled by a workstation taking in information from a weather station on the roof about wind speed, temperature and light conditions. When it rains, flooded patches of yellow stream towards the ground.[38]

As much as all of these projects confront the relationship between the body and the new hybridized architecture, none go as far as Möller's *Electronic Mirror* (1993).[39] Hanging on a wall is a three-quarter-length mirror, unremarkable save for the discreetly glowing sensor located in the middle of the bottom framing element. From a distance, you see yourself reflected in space, as with any other silvered glass. It is only as you approach within a meter of the mirror and then

As one approaches the mirror, it begins to cloud. By the time one reaches the proper viewing distance to examine oneself, the mirror has become an opaque surface.

Christian Möller, *Electronic Mirror* (1993). Courtesy of the architect.

move closer, a distance better suited for the narcissism lurking within us all, that you notice the mirror beginning to cloud. By the time you have reached the proper viewing distance to examine the minutiae of your face, the mirror has become an opaque surface. As you retreat, your likeness comes back into view, tantalizing you with the inability to master even your own image.

Those who look at themselves in the "Electronic Mirror" become like Achilles under Zeno's tyranny of logic: their understandings of the physical constraints of space are challenged. Like the best magics, Möller's "Electronic Mirror" loses nothing of its power when its secrets are revealed: a Siemens Sonar ultrasonic sensor informs a 286 clone about the user's distance, the computer then sends commands to control the transparency of a variable control Priva-Lite large-size

LCD. None of this technical information changes the resonances: Narcissus and Zeno, *vanitas*, the curse of the Vampire to go without his reflection, the mirror pool in Jean Cocteau's *Orpheus*, Jacques Lacan and the mirror stage, the list goes on. Architecture is a form of communication, and the hybridized hard- and image- scapes of Christian Möller serve as models for the syntax we will need to keep this conversation alive in an era of electronic ubiquity.

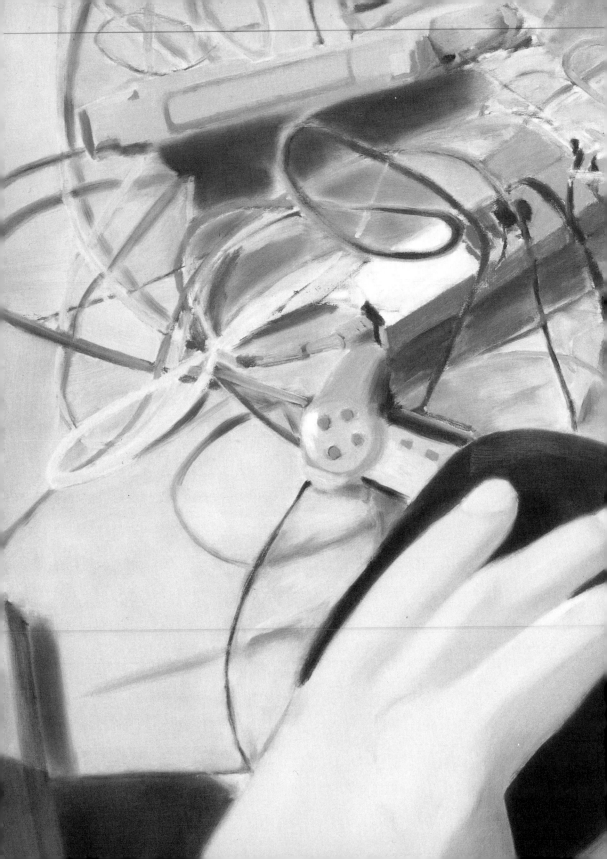

# Part III

# Makers

# HOLLIS FRAMPTON:
# THE PERFECT MACHINE

### Venues and Audiences

In a sense, the pixel is (or would like to be) capable of doing *everything*.
But the extent of this everything suffocates it, and leaves the computer
image with doubts about itself, in the grips of its own myth. . . .
*Raymond Bellour*[1]

The Shrine Auditorium in downtown Los Angeles is packed, with not
an open seat in the house. A Moorish palace of a theater, the Shrine
boasts the largest proscenium stage in the world. Host to innumerable
Academy Award ceremonies, tonight it throbs with excitement. A
twenty-minute countdown (displayed to hundredths of a second)
flashes on the screen. Inexplicably, dozens of people have laser point-
ers with them and they start to invent games, their laser lights tripping
across the stage. Little red dots race about, chasing each other, forming tight concentric loops, skittering around the ceiling, and criss-
crossing furiously. Anticipation cresting, the crowd of 6300 counts
down the final ten seconds. As the lights go down, the audience begins
to cheer. This is the Electronic Theater, the most important showcase
for contemporary computer graphics in the world, held annually as a
part of the trade show and conference known as SIGGRAPH (the Association for Computing Machinery's Special Interest Group on Computer Graphics).

The audience in the Shrine is there not simply to be entertained
but to see the new ways to see, to witness the imaging technologies and
strategies that have emerged the previous year. We (for I have long
been an enthusiastic member of the SIGGRAPH crowd) are there
both for pleasure and research. We cheer that which others would find
absurd. This year, a candle's realistic on-screen smoke elicits one of
the biggest responses. I remember, a few years back, the crowd bellow-

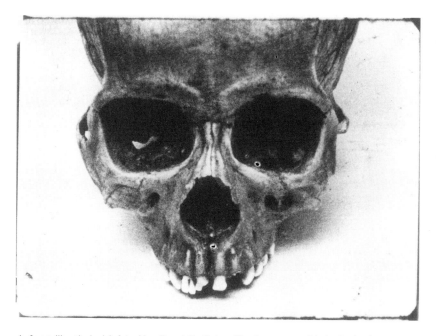

In forestalling the body's fate, *Magellan at the Gates of Death* resonates with the fascination contemporary digital culture displays for the posthuman technologies of life extension, death avoidance, and bodily transformation.

Hollis Frampton, *Magellan at the Gates of Death* (1976), film still. Courtesy of the Museum of Modern Art, New York.

ing with delight during Alain Guiot's *Rien Qu'un Souffle/A Slight Breeze*—this, at the sight of an animated three dimensional curtain blowing gently in an electronic wind. Over the course of three hours, we sit through 45 short films of scientific visualizations, artists' animations, student projects, and Hollywood special effects. We surge into the hot night air, enthralled, envious, exhilarated, desperate to talk about what we have just seen.

That same sweltering summer, I also attend a series of screenings of the *Magellan Cycle*, the last major work of structuralist filmmaker Hollis Frampton. Presented at Los Angeles Contemporary Exhibitions, a non-profit arts space in Hollywood that has seen better days, the screenings are organized by Filmforum, which once had a paid staff but has since reverted to an all-volunteer status. The parking lot is always empty. I pull up and park right in front of the door, which, though usually a sign of privilege in LA, feels melancholy in this case. I blink my way off the blistering tarmac and into the bleak, darkened screening space. Others straggle in after me. We sit apart from one another, sometimes as few as ten, never more than 25. We wait quietly for the projectionist to load the film and begin the program. This is what is left of the audience for the experimental cinema, at least in Hollywood, but, I suspect, around the rest of the world as well.

The lights go down, the projector whirs to life and I am transported, with my tiny band of cohorts, into the mystery of Frampton's last great cycle of films. One afternoon, I watch *Straits of Magellan: Drafts and Fragments [Panopticons]*, a 51-minute collection of 51, one-minute films. One segment offers an investigation of scratch animation, a virtual textbook on the cinematic apparatus. The next is a *realité* of a family eating breakfast together—"life as it happens," as the Lumières' reviewers used to say. There are pieces that offer such a multiplicity of exposures, such depth of optical printing that they approach the density of abstract painting. Another minute offers an extended take of traffic whizzing by, shot through a hole in a block of concrete—a distillation of the frame within the frame. Later, 60 seconds of playful savagery: a kitten bats around a still-living bird, the animal's blithe amorality both repulsive and entrancing. Still another moment of aestheticized violence: a butcher severs a cow's head from its body with a cleaver, the blood flowing everywhere, puddling on the ground, its rich sheen offering a purely formal pleasure, divorced from its charnel-house setting.

Midway through this compilation, I begin to take in *Drafts and Fragments* as a discontinuous whole, a blurry montage of disparate pieces that somehow cohere. This may be because many of the 51 films have in common the quality of the photographic gone dynamic. These are compact meditations that explode into movement, stills leaping into life.[2] In the course of viewing, the connections between the disconnected become naturalized, intellectual montage doing its work even on a field this fragmented. Chapter 4, "The Alphanumeric Phoenix" explored the *mise-en-abyme* in which the part plays out in miniature the work as a whole. In a quiet way, *Drafts and Fragments* functions as a *mise-en-abyme* of the entire cycle, enfolding *Magellan*'s tone and purpose.

The short films that comprise *Drafts and Fragments* are compact meditations that explode into movement, stills leaping into life.

Hollis Frampton, *Straits of Magellan: Drafts and Fragments [Panopticons]* (1974), film still. Courtesy of the Museum of Modern Art, New York.

As I watch these 51 minutes, I am struck ever more forcefully by the linkages both explicit and subterranean between this work and SIGGRAPH's Electronic Theater. I think back to *Rien Qu'un Souffle*, the simply presented animation of drapery swaying gently in the air that received such applause in 1992. Just as each Renaissance master's atelier had artisans who specialized in the detail work of painting clothing molded to flesh aping the "wet-drapery" look of Greek statuary, so too does the computer graphics field have a subset of specialists who work on mimicking textiles in motion. Yet beyond its insatiable appetite for photo-realism, the SIGGRAPH crowd was also reacting to the animator's reserve: *Rien Qu'un Souffle* creates a serene country window to frame the subtle motion of the curtains. This minimalist aesthetic is so unlike the rest of the program's techno-bombast—the expected dinosaurs, special effects reels, and morphing Mandelbrot chaos diagrams—that it becomes an affirmation that just looking can sometimes be as (or more) satisfying than the overamped distraction that dominates computer graphics.[3] As I was watching the *Magellan Cycle*, I came to wonder how the SIGGRAPH audience would have reacted to a similarly restrained minute of *Drafts and Fragments*, where Frampton shoots an uncut take of a silk-screened red cloth hanging in a window. For 60 seconds, we watch the fabric move slightly, shifting the shadows on the window frame, awed by the beauty of what in another context would be nothing to speak of, much less be transfixed by.

Can the gap between *Rien Qu'un Souffle* and this quiet minute of *Drafts and Fragments* be bridged? Is there a way to bring them together through their common concerns with seeing how to see? Even to attempt an answer to these questions is to confront the relationship between different eras of image technologies, between the lone artists who drove the American experimental cinema, the vast corporate entities who control both Hollywood and Silicon Valley, and those few artists trying to make work that matters using digital technologies. To do this via a reconsideration of the *Magellan Cycle* is also to dredge up a ghost that haunts the contemporary mediasphere. In other words, the ascendancy of the digital image has rendered experimental film ripe for a renaissance.

### Experimental Cinema as *Gesamtkunstmedium*

Artists have long invested certain technologies and art forms with the hopes of inducing radical synesthesia. By the nineteenth century, operas were lauded as *gesamtkunstwerke*, "total works of art" combining story and music, singing and acting, fantastic sets and heightened emotions. The cultural history of the past hundred years, contains a record not simply of the search for the *gesamtkunstwerk* but also for the *gesamtkunstmedium*. From the '50s to '70s, the experimental cinema achieved the status of *gesamtkunstmedium*.[4] Here was a conceptual space for collaboration between disciplines, a modern mode of production and distribution open to both representational and non-representational strategies, and a medium that excited artists and audiences alike. And then one day, it was all over.[5] I invoke this movement not to chronicle its decline and fall, but rather to note that in the '90s, the experimental cinema can serve as a model for computer-inflected art. I believe, in fact, that the most interesting new media works aspire to the condition of the experimental cinema without quite realizing it.[6]

Engaging with the work of a filmmaker like Hollis Frampton today engenders an interesting series of problems. While the structuralist cinema was never exactly a large draw, there was a period when those interested in the aesthetics of film felt a responsibility to at least acknowledge this brand of practice. At this moment, however, Frampton's legacy is much stronger in the art world than in contemporary film or new media circles. New York-based Robert Longo, who rose to fame in the 1980s, exhibited a massive series of drawings titled *Magellan* (1996–1997) in direct homage to the cycle. California projection artists like Diana Thater and Jennifer Steinkamp, whose work is discussed in the next two chapters, acknowledge the influence that the structuralist cinema has had on their work. These exceptions aside, however, I would hazard that structuralist film's period of influence is long since past, and that outside of an ever-shrinking coterie of longtime admirers and academic specialists, artists like Frampton are honored in the breach these days, if they are honored at all. But it is not simply the structuralist cinema that suffers from this fate, it is the vast majority of non-mainstream film.

To begin, there is the nagging question of what to call these films. Terms like "midnight movies" and "underground film" have clearly outlived their usefulness, while others, like the "critical cinema" or "alternative films," have never generated much support. The "independent" cinema, a phrase that once signified a narrative alternative to Hollywood production, has degenerated into a collection of calling-card films that young aspirants (often with freshly minted film school degrees) direct in the hopes of having the dominant Industry's producers, agents and distributors notice them.

This leaves the most widely used but also the most clearly problematic label of them all: "the avant-garde cinema." The value of this term is that it is fairly clear to readers and viewers who are already familiar with this body of films and discourses exactly what is being discussed. On the other hand, there is a certain embarrassment about using the term "avant-garde" these days. When MTV, video games, and the amassed technologies on high-tech trade show floors seem to push the formal envelope of the visual image as much or more than any self-proclaimed avant-garde, how can we continue to use this label at all? Thus it is that I have chosen to use the term "experimental" cinema, not necessarily because it is better (certainly it has its own categorical and descriptive flaws), but because it defamiliarizes these films from a category of reception and discussion while linking them to a broader concept of expanded media (to appropriate Gene Youngblood's concept of "expanded cinema").[7]

Further, it sometimes seems that the very theoretical and conceptual sophistication of the American experimental cinema militates against new readings and interpretations of its achievements. This movement generated a brilliant body of intensely engaged and partisan writings, with the artists themselves promoting specific aesthetics, ideologies, makers, and even the occasional expulsions.[8] Many of the major players in this debate are still alive, some are still making important work, and all maintain an active interest in directing the discourses about their own work.[9] As J. Hoberman notes, "the film avant-garde of the 1970s was as concerned with the production of theory as the production of films."[10] The desire of the artists and their partisan critics to remain vocal is admirable, but it does create a situation in which those outside the aegis of the original combatants join the fray at their own peril. To craft a new interpretative framework for the Pre-Raphaelites in the second half of the twentieth century would be easy enough, since everyone from Dante Gabriel Rossetti to John Ruskin is long dead. But those in the 1950s who wanted to discuss the formal rather than the political aspects of Surrealism found themselves under attack by the still strenuous polemics of André Breton. Likewise, in the 1970s and '80s, many an activist and critic was labeled "anti-Situ" by Guy Debord when they went through the materials generated by the Situationist International, drawing their own conclusions and lessons from the SI's legacy. So it has been for anyone interested in the experimental cinema today—they can find themselves wading into a Donnybrook that has been raging for decades.

Be that as it may, deference paid to the originators of the debate has in fact strangled off the possibilities for new readings of the films. Certain discourses about the experimental cinema became first canonized and then calcified, with the result that the films themselves have had their resonance with contemporary media makers severely muted. I am fully aware of the varied reasons for the precipitous drop-off of the audience for the avant-garde movement, and lament the loss of energy and purpose of this golden era of the cinema. On the other hand, I do not think that it will be possible to restore what once was to its original power and position. The question is not how to return to what was, but rather to determine how these films can find new audiences and with them, new meanings.

It is not necessary to invoke Harold Bloom's theory of creative misreading to acknowledge that this is simply the way that artworks and media stay alive.[11] Misreadings and misappropriations are essential, if contrary in spirit to academia's rote worship of artists and their objects. It is not that the artists and their coteries are necessarily wrong, just that in exerting too much control over the shape of the discourse, they may so inhibit new contributions to the conversation that the whole apparatus grinds to a halt. Yet the obverse is also true.

In the late 1970s, the reputation of William Burroughs was as low as it had been since he first came on the literary scene more than twenty-five years before.[12] Thought of as the junkie novelist who had done Norman Mailer one *worse* (not simply wounding his wife with a knife, but shooting her through the head), his later work was interpreted, if it was read at all, as the escalating masturbatory fantasies of an erotomaniac interested mostly in young boys and scatological violence. In 1978, Sylvère Lotringer, professor of French at Columbia University and *Semiotext(e)* publisher, organized a conference in the subterranean depths of New York's downtown called the Nova Convention (after the title of Burroughs's 1964 novel, *Nova Express*). Lotringer wanted to move the discussion of Burroughs's work away from the literary and critical milieu and into the street, as it were. Burroughs was present, and the event marked a radical shift: this was at the very start of the punk movement, and the energy that the young painters, musicians and writers drew from Burrough's work and the resuscitation that Burroughs experienced at their hands are a remarkable testament to the importance of letting a new audience encounter art in its own way, for its own purposes.[13] So, what hybrids, mutants and trans-genred (occasionally even trans-gendered) offspring result from cross-pollinating the experimental cinema with the emergent digital *gesamtkunstmedia?*

## Exploring *Magellan*

In *The History of Forgetting*, Norman Klein comments that most writing about memory, forgetting, and anesthesia perforce takes a turn toward fiction.[14] With that caveat in hand, pick through what follows as some fictions about the affinities between the now-forgotten histories of experimental film and the often ephemeral production of digital media. Fictions suit Hollis Frampton. A lionized figure of the glory years of the structuralist cinema, he was a visionary artist, a rigorous polemicist and a supple theorist.

In the early 1970s, Frampton conceived of a vast series of interconnected films, of varying length, to be shown daily over the course of a year and two days. Inspired by sixteenth-century explorer Ferdinand Magellan, the first person to circumnavigate the world, Frampton intended his epic to follow a similar movement, beginning and ending at the same point. Frampton mapped out a screening schedule that lasted 358 days, with some days having as few as two minutes' worth of screenings. That such a cycle would have massive difficulties finding a venue, much less an audience dedicated enough to make such a pilgrimage, was not paramount in Frampton's thoughts, for *Magellan* is as much a conceptual system as it is a series of films to be viewed.

The *Magellan Cycle* was so vastly ambitious and demanding that it seems almost to have been designed to be unfinished.[15] Frampton began it while he was in his early thirties; he was in his forties when he died, and had mapped out enough films for the cycle to keep him at work through his seventies, had he lived that long. I have written elsewhere that a defining quality of digital media is its "aesthetic of unfinish."[16] The endless malleability of digital media, the release of work in installments and upgrades, and the emergence of net.art—those telematic works discussed in chapter 6, "In Search of the Telephone Opera" that can change daily, even hourly—have further problematized the idea of a "finished" work of art. The *Magellan Cycle* certainly anticipates an aesthetic of unfinish, if only because its own scope was broad enough to prompt its maker to comment that although he hoped he could complete the cycle, "historically in the twentieth century your chances of finishing a very, very large work, if you undertake it, are certainly no better than fifty-fifty, and they're probably not fifty-fifty."[17] The importance of unfinish cannot be overstated: digital environments encourage an unending series of updates, upgrades, retoolings and revampings. The temptation to fiddle is virtually irresistible in situations where the costs of change are either nonexistent or minimal. Though Frampton was working in film, an expensive medium to change after the fact, the constitution of the *Magellan Cycle* itself was constantly being revised, with titles changed, orders reshuffled, and schedules for screenings under constant scrutiny.

The fluidity with which Frampton treated *Magellan* certainly anticipates the addiction to shuffling that nonlinear digital creation and presentation programs foster in contemporary artists. When Bill Barminski, Webster Lewin, and Jerry Hesketh put out an artist's CD-ROM like *The Encyclopedia of Clamps* (1997), they go through numerous versions, even after the disk's first pressing and distribution. Should another run be required, it would be expected that the disk would be changed from earlier versions, not only to catch and correct bugs, but also because the process itself precludes stability. Even the medium itself is unstable. Anyone making CD-ROMs today who expects their work to be legible in a decade is delusional, for the technology will have shifted so drastically (following the business cycle as well as Moore's Law[18]) that a disk released today will simply be inaccessible to anyone but the collector of arcane and obsolete equipment. When *Clamps*'s creators work on their Web site <www.deluxoland.com>, the issues of unfinish are even more pronounced.

Frampton may well have been making work for a less mercurial platform (though now 16mm film is itself in danger of obsolescence)—on celluloid with a longer life than the silver oxide of CD-ROMs—but his very fatalism about the prospects of completing the cycle, as well as his willingness to reshape it, continuously certainly point to an understanding of the media environment to come. *Magellan* and digital media both resist being read as permanent systems. As it was never finished, we must imagine the history of the cycle as it should have been, while accepting the fact that we can only engage with the films as they are. In this, then, I am not discussing *Magellan* as an eternally sacrosanct object so much as I am reporting on a discrete performance (much as I did in discussing *<jodi.org>* in chapter 6).

As noted throughout this book, reporting on an event in time is, in fact, the most appropriate way to approach digital media in general. It is not simply that these electronic objects and systems are inherently unstable: their very defining quality of unfinish means that different users will encounter very different instantiations of distinct things that go under the same names. This is a situation we associate with live-time performances—plays, music, dance—rather than what we feel about printed texts, recorded music, paintings, sculpture or films in general release.[19] What follows, then is not a complete accounting of *Magellan*, but instead a series of explorations designed to mine the cycle for congruencies between Frampton's work and the developing hyperaesthetics of digital media.[20]

## Mortality and Meat

If *Drafts and Fragments* is a *mise en abyme* of the cycle, the two part *Magellan at the Gates of Death* is the *abyme* itself: an abyss, a yawning chasm of mortality. Composed of shots of cadavers from an anatomy laboratory—both sexes, varying ages and races—*The Red Gate* and *The Green Gate* are among the most visceral works that this ascetic structuralist ever made: "encounters with death," as Frampton put it. Like *Palindrome [Second Dream]* (1969), *The Red Gate* initiates a sequence of images that will be replayed, but backwards and with a different tint, in *The Green Gate*. Palindromes, which yoke written language to mathematical notation, were important rhetorical devices for Frampton, who had a life-long fascination with science and mathematics and their influence on the arts. Palindromes read the same whichever way they are scanned (as with the most familiar one in English: "Madam, I'm Adam"), and have been a favorite challenge from antiquity (declined languages like Greek and Latin are well suited for such word play) to OuLiPo, the *Ouvroir de Littérature Potentielle* or "Workshop for Potential Literature" that has been active in Paris since the early 1960s.[21]

Yet beyond its quasi-scientific playfulness, the palindrome is important because it embodies radical non-linearity and offers a challenge to the temporal shackles on language, both textual and filmic. Linear narratives mimic the human condition: they begin and then wind to an end. As Frampton noted, like death itself, narrative "appears to be axiomatically inevitable."[22] The linear narrative, no matter how hard it struggles, is always subtended by mortality. In *Magellan at the Gates of Death*, Frampton trains his camera on lifeless bodies, using the cinematic apparatus to dynamize them. With this reanimation as his subject matter, Frampton redoubles the palindrome's innate recuperative powers. *Magellan at the Gates of Death* is as much about breathing life into cadavers as it is about mortality. The montage of legs, heads, arms, and torsos spirals out Red and returns Green: certain faces of the dead become as familiar and oddly vibrant as characters in a silent feature. *Magellan at the Gates of Death* acknowledges death while fighting on valiantly.[23]

In forestalling the body's fate, *Magellan* resonates with the fascination contemporary digital culture displays for the posthuman technologies of life extension, death avoidance, and bodily transformation. In chapter 2, "Demo or Die," I discussed Australian performance artist Stelarc and his devotion over two decades to augmenting and transcending his physicality through technology. In the United Kingdom, telematic pioneer Roy Ascott has been pushing artificial life art based on self-replicating and evolving software algorithms. In Los Angeles, Max More and his band of Extropians plot out digitally driven life extension techniques in their battles against entropy. In San Francisco, Mark Pauline and the Survival Research Laboratory (SRL) have developed their own form of *Grand Guignol* for golems, staging battles between lumbering, fire-belching robots that stand in for the bodies of human warriors. The aesthetic of the digital age is mesmerized by the machine's potential to escape meat.

One digital project that resonates with Frampton's less techno-utopian approach to the mortal body is *A Rehearsal of Memory*, a CD-ROM and installation by English artist Graham Harwood.[24] Harwood went to Ashworth Mental Hospital in Liverpool, where he recorded the thoughts and memories of the inmates. These include various serial killers, attempted suicides, and rapists: a panoply that the artist ironically refers to as "the psycho, the nutter, the mad dog." Harwood scanned the inmates' bodies, stored them in memory (note that *Rehearsal of Memory* abbreviates as ROM), radically modified the raw images, and created a series of composite naked figures to form the ground for his interactive art work. Using a mouse, users scroll across Harwood's patchwork prisoners.[25] As they pass over this fleshy sea of scars and tattoos, users trigger memories: with sounds from the hospital resonating in the background, the patients offer anecdotes about their crimes and sufferings. The artist writes that the CD-ROM "challenges our assumptions of normality and at the same time confronts us with a clean comfortable machine filled with filth, the forbidden and the demented."[26]

*A Rehearsal of Memory* is an interesting project, though it suffers from a romanticism about the violent and the mad more appropriate to the beginning of the twentieth century than its exhausted end (a sentimentalism blessedly absent from Frampton's more rigorous work). The connections Harwood builds between body and memory are elegant, though, especially the way he links the inscriptions of the body to multimedia writing. The tattoos and scars are inextricably bound to the sounds, texts and statements from which the work is built. These bodily marks become a mechanism of indexing, even an alternative orthography. In this, *A Rehearsal of Memory* participates in one of the defining qualities of digital aesthetics: the development and extension of textuality within dynamic media.

As noted in chapter 4, the computer, unlike the Hollywood movie theater or the television set, is a space where text and written language can and do thrive, and a number of new media artists have exploited this potential. In *Untitled, Game* (1998), Sara Roberts mimics the look and feel of a racing simulator at an arcade, with a full console, built-in gear shifter, and gas and brake pedals. But what distinguishes her game is that it is one concerned entirely with narrative textuality. Words appear one at a time on the screen, but the timing of their appearance is controlled by the user. These texts offer interior monologues about the quotidian, and thus how they are expressed has a direct impact on their import as "information." Stepping on the accelerator quickens the pace, shifting up makes the narratives less specific, less memory laden. Roberts's *Untitled, Game* cannot fail to bring to mind one of the most important artworks generated with digital tools, Jeffrey Shaw's groundbreaking interactive installation *Legible City* (1990).[27] This virtual environment takes its cues from the user who rides on an actual

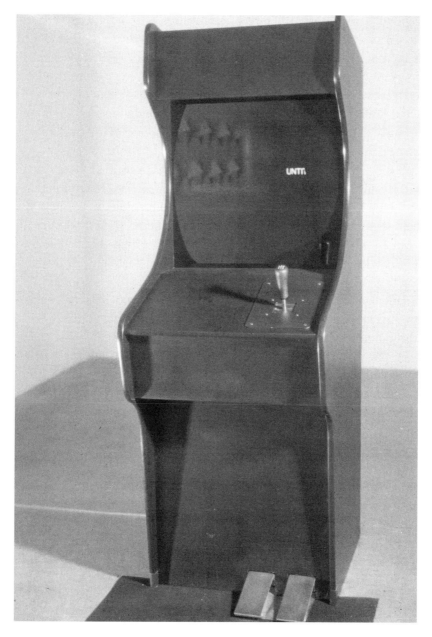

Mimicking the look and feel of a racing simulator at an arcade, this game is distinguished by its concern with narrative textuality.

Sara Roberts, *Untitled, Game* (1998). Courtesy of the artist.

bicycle. This is a city of literary architecture, of buildings-as-text, and as the user pedals and steers, she navigates through streets that in turn read as sentences. Work like *Untitled*, *Game* and *Legible City* point to ways in which digital media may revive typographic culture from the coma in which it has lapsed since the ascendance of televisuality.

Once again, Frampton is an exemplar for digital media: in his own words, "the place and use of the written and spoken word in film" was central to his entire career.[28] From the "Word Pictures" series of photographs in the early 1960s, to the on-screen script of *Poetic Justice* (1972), to the inter-titles of *Magellan*'s *Gloria!* (1979), Frampton practiced a sly displacement of signification systems. His work tracks the shifting terrains of meaning that text, voice, and music add to (and subtract from) film's visual field. *Zorns Lemma*, perhaps his best known film, makes manifest his approach to text and textuality in dynamic media.[29] The film is divided into three parts. The first section is a five minute soundtrack over black leader in which a woman's voice recites twenty-four rhymes from *The Bay State Primer*, a late eighteenth- to early nineteenth-century schoolbook for teaching children the alphabet. The second and longest section offers a succession of rapidly alternating shots of words and letters taken from the environment (from posters, architectural detail, store signs and the like). These letters are then organized in a recognizable alphabetic order, only to be replaced (least common letters first) by a series of recurring images: "B" by a frying egg, "W" by a tracking shot of a city's night skyline, and so forth. The third section is a long take (apparently seamless) that follows two people and a dog as they fade into a snowy field, juxtaposed with a series of female voices reading an obscure mystic text on the nature of light. Spoken language, textuality, and the cinematic vocabulary of light: these are the three interlacing subjects of *Zorns Lemma* and, in combination, they form the most nearly realized example of what Frampton referred to as the "perfect machine."

## The Perfect Machine

In his essay, "Film in the House of the Word," Frampton posits that Sergei Eisenstein—a figure to whom he constantly returned in his films and writings—may have been striving towards something beyond

An inter-title in white, jagged type on a luminescent green background and recognizable as being shot directly off now-antique computer monitors, from Hollis Frampton's first film to incorporate digital imagery.

Hollis Frampton, *Gloria!* (1979), film still. Courtesy of the Museum of Modern Art, New York.

intellectual montage: "the construction of a machine, very much like film, more efficient than language, that might, entering into direct competition with language, transcend its speed, abstraction, compactness, democracy, ambiguity, power. . . ."[30] A clue as to what this impossible, perfect machine might be is found in *Gloria!*, a film from *Magellan*'s final day. *Gloria!* is composed of a number of simple elements: found footage from the cinema's primitive era; textual "propositions" that serve as witty inter-titles; scratchy audio from an early recording of an Irish jig. These seemingly simple parts combine to form an exuberant meditation on memory and death. The early comedy is a version of the Irish legend of Finnegan, the hod carrier who comes back from the dead at his own wake when a few drops of whiskey fall on his lifeless lips. This folk tale is, of course, the kernel of

James Joyce's *Finnegans Wake*, and Frampton's sly reference here is important, for Joyce is another of the artists to and through whom Frampton spoke. Magellan is the modern world's Odysseus, for both were navigators striving to return home, and the voyages of Odysseus are, of course, at the heart of Joyce's other great novel, *Ulysses*. In the 1960s, Marshall McLuhan wrote of Joyce's importance to the "non-lineal logics" of the electronic age, and more recently, Donald Theall has discussed Joyce in terms of a techno-poetics.[31] Like the cadavers in *Magellan at the Gates of Death*, Finnegan is reanimated, and like the palindromic structures of the Frampton's films, Joyce's towering novels reinvent narrative, at least in part to cheat death.

It is the inter-titles, though, that give the perfect machine away: not their content, but their origin. They are alternately commonplace and amusing comments by and about Frampton's grandmother—"That she was obese. . . . That she kept pigs in the house, but never more than one at a time. . . . That her connoisseurship of the erotic in the vegetable kingdom was unerring"—in white, jagged type on a luminescent green background. To anyone whose digital experience goes back more than a decade, these texts are instantly recognizable as being shot directly off now-antique computer monitors. *Gloria!* is, in fact, Frampton's first film to incorporate digital imagery.

After taking a faculty position at the State University of New York at Buffalo, Frampton founded one of the first digital arts media labs, and he fully intended the *Magellan Cycle* to engage with electronic imaging and the emergent prospects of digital aesthetics.[32] A colleague from Buffalo's Center for Media Study, Brian Henderson, concludes his elegiac essay on the *Magellan Cycle* with the following paragraph:

Perhaps Frampton's Bayreuth was in effect, the computer. (He was still preparing it when he died.) That is where the last stages of the film were to be generated, and the film as a whole ordered and assembled. Perhaps even from that utopic site portions of the film, or copies of the whole, were to be dispatched to farflung sites of local exhibition. Quite probably the computer functioned in senses we do not yet know, in part because Frampton knew, better than we do, both the computer and the requirements of *Magellan*'s completion. He knew that the various technologies of realization, developed annually, might alter the execution—or even the structure of the whole. It was there, within and through the computer, that the work was ultimately to achieve its ideal realization.[33]

Frampton was working with digital media in the late 1970s and early 1980s, in other words, before graphical user interfaces became commonplace, before Hypercard, before interactive authoring programs like Director, before Photoshop, before commercial e-mail service, before the World Wide Web turned any computer with a modem into a combination of magazine kiosk, printing press, and broadcast studio.

Lev Manovich maintains that the loop and the database are defining tropes for contemporary digital media, and once again Frampton and the *Magellan Cycle* offer a remarkable meditation on these forms.[34] As Henderson notes, "*Magellan* is the largest loop film ever made, the longest film ever looped."[35] The loop is a way to escape the constraints of limited storage—a problem common to both the Kinetescope and the QuickTime movie—and can be seen as yet another mechanism to forestall entropy and death. In the early 1970s, Frampton posited "the infinite film": a forever unfinished cinematic system incorporating all modes of filmmaking, all examples of those modes, and one that could grow and change as its medium matured.[36] Frampton's "infinite film" is a Platonic database for our spectacular culture. It is the Alexandrine dream discussed in chapter 5, "Dubitative Images," distilled from the librarians who were promised by the Ptolemaic kings of Egypt that they would have the opportunity to catalogue every book of their era. As Bruce Jenkins writes, in Frampton's "attempts to wed the capabilities of the computer with the rich surfaces of celluloid, perhaps he was imagining the 'history of film as it should have been.'"[37] Or, alternatively, Frampton was seeking for the *neuen gesamtkunstmedium* that digital artists are in the process of inventing.

## Coda

An epigraph to *Gloria!* provides a dedication for the *Magellan Cycle*. It is a shot of some clumsily justified text taken directly from a computer monitor:

This work, in its entirety, is given in loving memory of Fanny Elizabeth Catlett Cross, my maternal grandmother, who was born November 6, 1896 and died on November 24, 1973.

It is entirely fitting that Frampton dedicated the *Magellan Cycle* to a woman born just after the Lumières unveiled their cinematic apparatus, who raised her children during radio's youth, whose grandson came of age with television, and who died just before the advent of personal computing.

# DIANA THATER:
# CONSTRAINT DECREE

## Unique Activity

*Axiom:* Constraint is a principle, not a means.
*Jacques Roubaud*[1]

Georges Perec's novel *Life A User's Manual* tells the story of an English heir named Bartlebooth, expatriated to a Parisian apartment building from 1925 to 1975. During this half century, Bartlebooth dedicates his life to a single, arbitrarily constrained project. For the first decade, he learns to paint watercolors, adequately if not brilliantly. Through the following twenty years, he travels the world painting 500 seascapes of identical format; no matter where he is (or what his circumstances, even during the Second World War), he sends the paintings back to Paris to a specialized craftsman who glues them to wooden boards and cuts them into fantastically intricate jigsaw puzzles of exactly 750 pieces each. For the final two decades, Bartlebooth completes the puzzles in the order in which he painted them, one seascape a fortnight. When complete, he hands the puzzles over to a chemist in his employ who "retexturizes" their paper, eliminating the cuts, and then separates them from their wooden backings. These reconstituted watercolors are then dipped into a special solution, from which they emerge as unmarked sheets of Whatman paper. "Thus no trace would remain of an operation which would have been, throughout the period of fifty years, the sole motivation and unique activity of the author."[2]

## Space as Time, Time as Narrative

Diana Thater makes single channel videos, compositing clouds floating along in clear blue California skies with the Salt Flats in Utah (*Nature is a Language, can't you read?*, 1997); fashions installations of wintry imagescapes delineated by the red, green, and blue guns of the

The watch tower glows with a phosphorescence making it simultaneously a projection of ancient light magic and a wry comment on modern televisuality.

Diana Thater, *Broken Circle* (1997). Exterior view of the Buddenturm, Sculpture Project in Münster. Photo: Roman Mensing. Courtesy of the artist and David Zwirner Gallery, New York.

video projector (*The Bad Infinite*, 1993); and takes production stills shot on film (sequences that are themselves destined to be transferred to laserdisc), digitally manipulates the images and then outputs on a high resolution printer (*The Future Was an Illusion*, 1997). In other words, Thater works with film, video and digital media, the very art forms that—like Bartlebooth's self-erasing practice—are destined to leave little or no trace.[3]

The preservation of impermanent media art, however, is a question better left to conservators and institutions, which is why the second issue Bartlebooth's project raises—the way he so carefully restricts the field of his own work—is the more interesting, at least for Thater. Her art offers pleasures both immediate and intellectual—her painterly use of color on the one hand, the way she demonstrates a command over the syntax of the moving image not seen since the glory days of the structuralist cinema. Yet underlying all of this, lending both resonance and rigor, is the way she observes the constraints—inherited and self-imposed—of her chosen media.

Thater, to begin with, eschews what video artists routinely embrace: the black room fetish, the desire to transform portions of galleries, museums or found spaces into videothèques, darkened pseudo-cinemas for the contemplation of the video artwork. Instead, she has long held fast to the dictum that her work should be seen in ambient light, that it should function within the constraints of its space and flow plan and work within video's limited color palette. In this, she accepts the necessity of not making "cinema on tape," and further accepts a certain displacement of narrative, that follows from the understanding that the reception of video installations is profoundly different from the cinematic experience. Finally, by accepting that video's utopian moment has passed—both as technology and as an art movement—Thater paradoxically opens up a whole new range of possibilities.

*Broken Circle* (1997), her major statement to date, shows Thater embracing, transcending and subverting these three constraints simultaneously. Commissioned for the most recent *Sculpture Projects* in Münster, *Broken Circle* was installed in the Buddenturm, a twelfth-century tower that is the last remaining element of the city's medieval fortifications. Thater played up and off the structure's monumentality and history, filling five interior levels with six projection environments and a video monitor, as well as making her project visible from the outside by applying a series of colored films to the windows and lighting them from the inside. A rickety wooden staircase provided access to each level, and the journey first up and then down traces a circuit that in turn establishes a narrative. The Buddenturm was designed to function as a watch tower, and *Broken Circle* addresses both watching and being watched. The video footage was shot at a horse ranch in California, and like her well-known installation *China* (1995), which featured wolves, once again the animals in question are trained performers who work in Hollywood's film factory. Thater's "stars" were Woody and Ajax, two trick horses who rear and fall on command. To those who would protest Thater's imposition of a mythical, acculturated American West onto a provincial German town, remember the singular figure of Karl May, a turn-of-the-century pulp author who never visited America, but whose lurid cowboy and Indian yarns formed the cultural imaginary of the Wild West for generations of German schoolboys.

The heart of *Broken Circle*, however, was a 360° pan following the animal trainers as they stampeded a herd of 30 horses and mules in and out of a canyon. As the viewer journeyed up the Buddenturm, the stampede unfolded (a cinematic set piece rehearsed by everyone from John Ford to Akira Kurasawa), but this stock spectacle was shattered, the different levels of the tower breaking the circular camera motion into jagged but related intersecting parts. As is becoming a signature in her work, here Thater allowed the spatial to assume a temporal aspect and then ensured that the temporal took on a narrative charge: that the titles were on first floor and the credits on the fifth implied that the temporal was spatialized in *Broken Circle*, but the top floor was really the middle of the piece (people had to descend the stairs to emerge from the work), thus reminding viewers that putative endings are so often merely markers of continuity.

Thater's installations are less site-specific than site dependent, and the artist works this dependency into her pieces as one more constraint.[4] Colored window films are a recurring motif, used to strong effect in earlier work like *Abyss of Light* (1993), *Perspective is an Energy* (1995), and *Moluccan Cockatoo* (1995). During the day, these scrims

Thater's trick is to turn video into architecture, throwing the image up to play over the found space of her installations.

Diana Thater, *The Wicked Witch* (1996). Installation view, the Walker Art Center, Minneapolis. Courtesy of the artist and David Zwirner Gallery, New York.

bathed interiors in colored sunlight, creating the sense of being fully inside a projection while at the same time reducing the natural light enough to let the projection and monitor pieces have their effect. It is at night, though, that they are most startling, as in the way *Broken Circle* dominated Münster's Promenade ring, the watch tower glowing with a phosphorescence that made it simultaneously a projection of ancient light magic and a wry comment on modern televisuality. For the first time in *Broken Circle*, Thater used tertiary colors like lime, pink, orange, and turquoise, breaking with her exclusive use of the primary colors red, green and blue (which constitute the component colors of video monitors and three gun projectors).

These tertiary techno-colors reference the *Wizard of Oz*, a film which also subtends *Wicked Witch* (1996). *Wicked Witch* is a manipulated projection environment of a field of flowers, but unlike the field of poppies into which Dorothy and her companions are lured and almost lulled into sleep, this is a field of ranunculus. The poppy is an ancient flower, but the ranunculus is a hybridized anemone no more than fifty years old, a flower therefore contemporary with the film that immortalized Dorothy and the Wizard. *Wicked Witch*'s constraints are finely focused: a single laserdisk drives five or six projectors (depending on the size and configuration of the room), creating a 360° projection of the single image. The field of ranunculus was shot on film and then transferred to laserdisk, a hybrid procedure in and of itself. On the first wall, all the images are in focus and the colors perfectly registered—in other words, the "front" projection is organized and calibrated to mimic what we know as broadcast standard video. Yet each succeeding wall features images that are increasingly askew, and as the viewer takes in the wall opposite the first (which is generally the third wall), everything is totally out of registration: there are three separate images, green, red, and blue.

The title of her 1997 solo show at the Walker Art Center, "Orchids in the Land of Technology," draws from Walter Benjamin's comment that "the sight of immediate reality has become an orchid in the land of technology." There is, however, a danger to reading both the quote and the title too literally, and thereby seeing nature in Thater's work as the irreducible real that is always and forever mediated by and for culture: wolves trained to violate their nature by sitting still in *China*; chimpanzees at a rest home for retired performing animals in *Electric Mind* (1996); and even the Monument Valley landscapes of *Pape's Pumpkin* (1994), which viewers cannot help but see through the scrim of the epic Hollywood Westerns shot there. But Benjamin's original German alludes not to a generic orchid but rather to the poet Novalis's "blaue Blume," the "Blue Flower" the Romantics cherished as an ever-unrealizable goal.[5] In critiquing Char Davies' virtual reality installations in chapter 7, I discussed the Edenic fallacy, by which artists invested in technological practice choose to employ these technologies to reconnect their viewers with nature. It is to Thater's credit that she accepts the mediation of nature as yet another of the constraints of high-tech art practice, and that rather than "reconnecting" her audience with nature, posturing towards some sort of shamanistic ritual, she instead uses the tools at her disposal to construct ever more impossible flowers in the field of technology, fashioning divergent cyborganic media ecologies.

Take *Ginger Kittens* (1994), a hypersaturated imagescape of sunflowers in a field of green, shot in Provence. At the Walker, it was pressed into doing triple duty: as a room-sized projection, as a dynamic banner surmounting the entrance desk, and as a window installation visible to anyone passing the museum. *Ginger Kittens* explores both the possibilities and the limits of video's buzzing pixels and fuzzy colors, expanding upon the structuralist attention to the specifics of the video image in earlier pieces like *Oo Fifi, Five Days in Claude Monet's Garden* (1992) and *The Bad Infinite*.

In exploiting the constraints of the video image's potency, Thater opened up an exploration of video's painterly qualities, and critics have tended to concentrate on this as well as on her links to the avant-garde structuralist cinema.[6] What has been discussed far less often is the way Thater grafts video to architecture. Long regarded as the lesser cousin of the cinema, video has for the most part offered a domesticated imagescape, a technology capable of offering a window onto the world (think of McLuhan's Global Village), but never to be thought of in terms of the sublime; if, according to Kant, it is nature that offers access to the sublime, how can anything as *heimlich* as video hope to compete? Dealing as it does in scale designed to dwarf the body, architecture is the only art that can strive towards the sublime; Thater's trick is to turn video into architecture, throwing the image up to play over the found space of her installations. The combination of this hybridized media imagescape/architectural hardscape with the subject of acculturated nature—as in *Ginger Kittens*—creates not a simulation of the natural sublime but something entirely different, a techno-sublime.[7]

Thater's techno-sublime is particularly interesting in the way it deploys narrative. Her work comes along at a point when our culture has evacuated narrative from large swaths of mass media. Pornography, video games, and the dominant effects-driven, high-concept Hollywood spectaculars are all essentially narrative-free: a succession of money shots, twitch reflex action, and visceral thrills strung together in time without ever being unified by classic story structure. Thater

The spatial assumes a temporal aspect, and the temporal takes on a narrative charge.

Diana Thater, *Surface Effect* (1997). Courtesy of the artist and David Zwirner Gallery, New York.

slyly treats this environment as yet another constraint: her installations are not narrative in and of themselves; she displaces the narrative onto separate textual systems. In earlier projects she tended to make indices out of her research and use these oddly tortured addenda as the basis for the announcements for her shows, the textual apparatus being brought forward to entice the potential user into the system. In this, Thater showed herself very much a product of the technoculture, which has elevated the searchable database (which is what an index is, after all) into one of its highest art forms.

In *Electric Mind*, she plays even more directly with the whole concept of narrative. The video, shot at a ranch in California for performing animals and in Arizona's Painted Desert, juxtaposes a chimpanzee undergoing training with views of the desert shot from the highway. Fauna, flora, and even the aridity of the empty vista are all unified in the projection environment, but never quite narrativized though montage. The narrative is again displaced, here three times. First to a screenplay for a science-fiction film, also called "Electric Minds," which is in turn adapted from "Rachel in Love," a short story by Pat Murphy about a girl whose mind is transferred into the body of a chimpanzee; second to four monochromatic Iris prints which read "cat, a / is" "mouse, a / is" "cat, a / is" "chimp, a / is" "girl, a"; and finally, to two monitors sitting on the floor that flash these same words, meant to distill the screenplay's theme. The fragments forming the phrase "a mouse is a cat is a chimp is a girl" creates a non-narrativized loop about the interrelationship of all living beings that is almost shocking in its denial of the uniqueness of humankind.[8] In *Electric Mind*, as in all Thater's work, complexity is revealed, not explained.

In her catalogue essay for *The best animals are the flat animals—the best space is the deep space* (1998), Thater writes: "The project when plotted becomes an incomprehensible web of works, which may not ever all be seen together in the same place, but which are all intended to occupy the same temporal framework . . . [it] is committed to working with an idea of freeing space and time from the single artwork."[9] Consisting of eight works for installation constructed from twenty-seven different constituent parts, *The best animals are the flat animals animals—the best space is the deep space* can be arranged and rearranged from its many parts, mounted in different spaces in different cities

This multi-part, multi-venue series acknowledges its presence within a world where both space and time contract but manages to function without capitulating to telematic technologies.

Diana Thater, *The best animals are the flat animals* (1998), installation view. Photo: Fredrik Nilson. Courtesy of the artist.

simultaneously; there are individual titles for each piece and each show. Over a six month period bridging 1998 and 1999, Thater exhibited the work in five locations across North America.

At the Museum of Modern Art in New York, *The best animals are the flat animals* occupied a gallery just off the ground floor entrance. Projectors threw images onto walls, ceilings, and a free-standing wall. At Ohio's Allen Memorial Art Museum, *The best space is the deep space* consisted of projections onto a free-standing wall and a stack of five video monitors. At the MAK Center for Art and Architecture, Los Angeles, *The best animals are the flat animals—the best space is the deep space* had no free-standing wall and monitors sat on the floor of the

Schindler House, that shrine to early twentieth-century architectural modernism. The house's distinctive slit windows were covered over by Thater's signature gels, bathing the interior space in an even warmer glow than usual. Like the shows at the other venues, *The best sense is the non-sense* at Toronto's York University Art Gallery, mixed stacked monitor pieces and projections onto free-standing walls. *The best outside is the inside*, at the St. Louis Art Museum, was configured in a very similar way, but the show's content was reminiscent of Thater's earlier landscape studies as opposed to the animal pieces in the other venues, which were more animated.

No matter where the hardscape in real space, the imagescape was comprised of the same basic components: shots of a performing horse and its trainer, extreme close-ups of a herd of zebras, a tableau of plants shot within an arboretum, and so on. The installations themselves mixed the obviously representational with the abstract and the geometric, the prancing stallion situated incongruously in a static garden, the zebras' skins blown up into a quasi-cinematic, op-art imagescape. *The best animals are the flat animals—the best space is the deep space* acknowledges its presence within a world where both space and time contract but manages to function without capitulating to telematic technologies or pretending that art was somehow purer before their invention. In this project, Thater intentionally creates an irreconcilable tension. To appreciate the show they are looking at, viewers must understand the system as a whole. Yet the artist has constructed a dispersed network that simply cannot be seen in its totality by any single viewer; the distances are too vast. *The best animals are the flat animals—the best space is the deep space* thereby forces its audience to think about many spaces in one time, the opposite of the intent of a piece like *China*, which engages with many times in one space.

Thater claims that we see through technology and that her work is structured to examine "how technology sees through us."[10] It is to her credit, though, that she understands the impossibility of such a project at this point in time. Theoretically informed and formally rigorous work like *The best animals are the flat animals—the best space is the deep space* can simultaneously mime and critique a culture that has constructed a communication structure that none of us can any longer conceive of, much less "see through" in full.

Returning for a moment to *Life A User's Manual,* Perec was a member of OuLiPo, which took as its working premise that systems of constraints do not restrict artists so much as empower them. The Oulipean model—to "prove motion by walking," in the words of poet and founding member Raymond Queneau—offers hope to artists embracing video in its post-utopian phase.[11] In the 1960s and '70s, the portapack was supposed to offer access to the tools of production, transforming the population from spectators to creators and fabricating communities of the like-minded. The discourse of liberation through media technology is still being bandied about, but this time in relation to computer-driven interactive art, immersive virtual reality and the World Wide Web; in short, the utopian dream has moved from video to digital media. So what of an artist like Thater, who with contemporaries such as Douglas Gordon, Jennifer Steinkamp, and Steve McQueen does not define herself as a "video artist" so much as an artist using video? This is a more crucial distinction than might appear at first glance, because it shifts attention away from the technology of production (video as art) to the overall concerns of reception (art as art). Like Cindy Sherman and Richard Prince in the late 1970s, who were not photographers so much as artists using photography, and who in turn reconfigured the way photography was received by and disseminated through the art world, Thater and her peers are transforming the place of video. The constraint that video as a technology cannot save the world has in fact saved video as art.

# JENNIFER STEINKAMP:
# LIGHT IN SPACE

Enter a room. All is darkness, except for a luminous play of color on the floor. There is no way to resist walking into the light; the projection plays down like a sunset devised by a technologized god. Skin becomes a canvas, as your shadow is transformed into a pictorial element.
*Un-titled (1993)*

The sound of gagging penetrates the air, growing in volume as you ascend the staircase. Above, the skylight has been covered with an imagescape that swirls in tandem with the retching sounds, turning the space of the staircase into a disembodied throat.
*Gag (1993)*

Projected light moves from blue tones to red, as the airy heavens morph into fiery hells and back again. The projections, gridded and intertwined, take hold of the space, and the wall swells and deflates like a lung.
*Elbowroom (1994)*

After Einstein, we know that the speed of light is the constant that relates matter to energy and vice versa, and therefore that playing with light is far more than an aesthetic gesture: it is to intervene in our certainties about the materiality of matter and the flow of energy. Projecting complex and often interlacing animations onto surfaces that were formerly blank, Jennifer Steinkamp's computer-generated installations challenge our prejudices that architecture is stable while the projected image is not. Her riots of color, form, and light blur and reconfigure the place of bodies in space and the relationship of those bodies to the installation, the architectural environment, and one another.

Jennifer Steinkamp searches for architectural idiosyncrasies, for those spaces vulnerable to aesthetic fission.

Jennifer Steinkamp, *Balconette* (1994). Courtesy of the artist and ACME., Los Angeles.

Systems are often most vulnerable where they deviate from their systematicity. With this in mind, Steinkamp searches for architectural idiosyncrasies, for those spaces vulnerable to aesthetic fission. In one untitled piece from 1994, the rounded exterior walls of the theater of the California Museum of Photography serve as parabolic canvases on which Steinkamp creates a dynamized audio and imagescape with movement both elliptical and mirrored. What seems to be dead space carved out behind a specialized structure becomes a pulsing grid of black squares, between which can be glimpsed fleshy expanses of yellow and pink that both emphasize and transcend the site's curved lines.

*Balconette* (1994) made use of an otherwise anonymous detail at the Allen Memorial Art Museum in Ohio. High above the spectator, a balcony window that looks out onto an interior courtyard is replaced with an hallucinatory projection—black and white riddled through with flashes of intense color. Here, a sphere rushes out at the spectator, eventually fills the screen, and then retreats. The effect is of a field folding in on itself, advancing and then flattening again. Steinkamp's digital trompe l'oeil, her op art in motion, takes on added resonance as it plays off the romantic implications of an inaccessible portal.

Steinkamp has also built her own hybrid architectural environments, most successfully with *Swell* (1995) and *The TV Room* (1998). Like Christian Möller's *Interaktive Architektur* and Diana Thater's site-dependent installations, Steinkamp combines the hardscapes of built architecture with the dynamic imagescapes of her projections.[1] *Swell* is constructed in a light-proof room where projectors are situated on either side of a specially constructed wall, with a pass-through enabling the spectators to walk from one side to the other. The front projection extends only part of the way across the wall, and appended to the wall is a scrim of equal height but reduced width, which serves as the screen surface for the rear projection.[2] Both imagescapes are in essence the same—confetti-like bits of blue, yellow and white that appear to be blowing through a wind tunnel, like some slapstick meditation upon eternally dissolving matter; but the one on the scrim is shifted by ninety degrees—from the horizontal to the vertical—and is considerably smaller, though a similar aspect ratio is maintained. Coming into *Swell*, then, requires a series of adjustments: first from the quiet and the sun's glare outside the gallery to the controlled sound and light within; then to acknowledging the fact that what appear to be two distinct imagescapes are, in fact, rotations of one another; and finally that our faith in a single, wholly legible projection, cultivated by years of movie-going, has been ruptured by the use of second projector positioned opposite.

As spectators move from the front to the back, they intersect with the dual projections, their shadows becoming part of the piece itself. With this awareness comes the invitation to others to participate, to cross from spectator to element of the piece, to become involved in the piece as a social construction.

Like *Swell*, *A Sailor's Life Is the Life for Me* (1998), *Happy Happy* (1997), and *Double Take* (1996) encourage viewers to immerse themselves in the play of light by casting their own shadows into the artwork (this works especially well in the latter piece, *Double Take*, which derives its look, soundtrack, and psychological undertow from Alfred

As spectators move from the front to the back, they intersect with dual projections, their shadows becoming part of the piece itself.

Jennifer Steinkamp and Bryan Brown, *Swell* (1995). Photo: Joshua White. Courtesy of the artists and ACME., Los Angeles.

Hitchcock's *Vertigo*, itself a canny investigation of ego and desire). These pieces—or experiences, to be precise—play with the narcissism inherent in contemporary technologies. That is, so much of digital visual culture involves a feedback between the user and the machine: the fabled interactivity that is less open system than closed loop. Though Steinkamp's art doesn't involve this kind of interactivity, her installations are perforce interactive: viewers revel in the recognition of their own shadows and elevate the traces of their own bodies to the realm of art. Steinkamp has commented about the question of interaction in her work: "The projectors are often placed low so the viewer has no choice but to become part of the work. Children immediately understand that they are expected to play in the projection. . . . As the viewer internalizes the image in her mind, she also experiences it physically in real space as she sees her shadow."[3] But the very transience of the spectators's marks on the image field denotes the vanity of their efforts.

Just as thorny as Steinkamp's relationship to interactive art are attempts to craft a genealogy for her work. The default comparison is to
non-figurative painting, distilled here by critic David Pagel: "Without
paint or canvas, her abstractions fulfill many of the Abstract Expres-
sionists' intentions, simultaneously pushing painting into the fourth
dimension."[4] Art criticism routinely bows to these venerated masters
whenever abstraction enters the frame, but in her acute attention to
the fourth dimension of time, Steinkamp is at least as indebted to
structuralist filmmaking of the 1960s and 1970s as to AbEx canvases of
the 1950s. Like Diana Thater, and as noted in chapter 9, Steinkamp
has long been interested in Hollis Frampton, but many other avant-
garde and structuralist filmmakers have influenced her. Take Paul
Sharits's color flicker films, among them *Ray Gun Virus* (1966) and
*N:O:T:H:I:N:G* (1968), which create chromatic chords, assaulting the
sensorium with staccato bursts of light. Michael Snow's single
screen, dual-sided projection piece, *Two Sides to Every Story* (1974), for
another, forces spectators constantly to readjust their positions, dissolving the boundaries between two- and three-dimensional representation, and creating a unique kind of 2.5D space (precisely what
screen-based digital virtual environment strive to effect).

Yet while filmmakers like Sharits, Peter Kubelka and Tony Con-
rad worked within the controlled space of the theater—in darkness,
with the sole light source of the film projector—Steinkamp engages
with the diffusion of environmental light sculpture and works within
the constraints of a number of differing media. Interestingly, I almost
never think of her work in terms of video, though she uses video projectors and has created single channel tapes. Yes, she uses videodisks
and video projectors, but if she could go straight off a hard drive into a
hi-res data projector, she would. In other words, for all of her attention
to video's limited color palette and the specificities of using the technology within projection installations, her attention to video boils
down to an entirely pragmatic assessment: "whatever gets the job
done."

This attitude towards getting the job done betrays a particular
West Coast pragmatism, a willingness to engage with materials on
their own merits in the service of a series of concrete investigations. It
has been said of the metaphysical pragmatist Robert Irwin that the

more you look, the more you see, and the same applies to Steinkamp. But her relationship to Irwin is more pointed. A central figure of the 1960's "Light and Space" movement, Irwin created ephemeral interventions into architecture that challenged the viewer's perception of the environment and the play of light within that environment; subtlety and diaphanous materials—neon tubes, sheer scrims, highly determined lighting schemes—were the work's distinguishing characteristics. Irwin was also well known for his obsession with the automobile and the great flowering of California car culture in the 1960s (that last stand of aestheticized mechanization that Tom Wolfe summed up in his title *The Kandy-Kolored Tangerine-Flake Streamline Baby*). The mobilized gaze that the driver commands from behind the wheel, landscapes whizzing by at sixty miles per hour, the glimpses of architecture, the distance from the human pedestrian, all of these have helped to shape both the modern and the postmodern, from the Futurists to J. G. Ballard. It also fed into the finish fetish so typical of that era's art in Southern California. But what the customized hot-rod was to the '60s, the full-blown, RAM-hogging graphics engine is to the present. And it is precisely that sort of high-end equipment that Steinkamp uses to create her animations. Her works, like Irwin's, are self-conscious of their *luxe* and sheen. But they revel in the possibilities of technology without fetishizing the machines or even the processes of their production.

These processes are, admittedly, complex. From the earliest 3D modeling of the space of the exhibition, to the development of animations on high-end graphics engine hardware, to the melding of image and sound, Steinkamp is determined to situate the work precisely within its architectural context. She develops detailed three-dimensional computer schematics of the hardscape and then designs a series of renderings to plan for the deployment of the projectors and speakers. Once that is completed, she runs a series of simulations of the play of light within the space. Steinkamp has also been collaborating with sound artists to add an aural dimension to her work, and these explorations into expanded multimedia come together to transform silent, white spaces into rhythmic and extruded abstractions.[5]

A site-specific installation at the Santa Monica Museum of Art, *The TV Room* involves three distinct spaces unified only by sound.

From the earliest 3D modeling of the space of the exhibition, to the simulations of the play of light within the space, to the melding of image and sound, Jennifer Steinkamp is determined to situate the work precisely within its architectural context.

Jennifer Steinkamp, computer model for *Inney* (1995), at the Huntington Beach Art Center. Courtesy of the artist and ACME., Los Angeles.

Visual culture broadly rather than fine art strictly sets the context for this work.

Jennifer Steinkamp and Andrew Bucksbarg, installation shot of *The TV Room* (1998) at the Santa Monica Museum of Art. Photo: Alex Slade. Courtesy of the artists and ACME., Los Angeles.

Here, Steinkamp divides a rectangular gallery in half with three wall strips stretching horizontally across the room. These strips themselves comprise a space, adding a third environment to the now bifurcated gallery. Each strip has its own abstract animation projected on it, while the now inaccessible wall behind the strips has a full-scale animation thrown by a projector hidden behind one of the strips. This surface combines with the three strips to create the total viewing experience, one in which four projections interlace (much like the scan lines on a standard television monitor) and then separate again into discrete imagescapes.

Andrew Bucksbarg's quadraphonic sound environment creates a counterpart to this schizophrenic relationship between space and image. Two speakers positioned in the inaccessible space of the wall projection offer a fuller sound than the discontinuous tracks coming from the other two speakers, which are closer to the spectators. Steinkamp refers to the piece's effects as a "parallactic shift . . . between the viewer and the multiple image planes as the viewer moves through the room."[6] But in the end, only the sound penetrates all three zones of *The TV Room*, a reminder that television is at least as aural as it is visual.

As important as the sonic environments are to Steinkamp, her work does indeed privilege the visual, and in that she is much like her LA contemporaries Jorge Pardo and Pae White insofar as her environments are energized by commercial art's attention to surface. Thus, Steinkamp's work must be contextualized broadly within visual culture rather than strictly in terms of fine art. Obviously architecture is central to her work, but so are the design fields: graphics, computer imaging, and the three-dimensional arenas of industrial and product design. Steinkamp has worked for major production houses and teaches computer animation to a range of students, the majority of whom will not be working within the gallery/museum nexus. In 1997, she founded Blush, a boutique commercial animation house, and her first client was the band U2, which commissioned abstract animations for the massive video monitors of their "PopMart" world tour. In other words, Steinkamp creates work that demands an open field of inquiry aware of the present technological moment and informed by a raft of artistic and aesthetic discourses.[7]

This is not to say that, in embracing computer graphics and entertainment design, Steinkamp is abandoning conceptual rigor simply to revel in tech. Too much art that engages with technology mutates into "techno-art," a ghettoized form that begs to be admitted to the big table simply because of the fact that it is so hard to make or to make work. Techno-art can end up simulating Magic Eye picture displays in shopping malls, where a group gathers around, staring for ten or more minutes at an abstract pattern, until a three-dimensional horse finally pops out. Yes, the group has seen something, but was it worth the wait? Steinkamp's work is extremely exacting and difficult to produce, but that is hardly the point. Her insistence on acknowledging the body of the spectator and her resistance to the facile demands for a rote sort of interactivity lend her work a seriousness that her often playful titles belie (one of my favorites is 1995's *Inney*, which expands the notion of navel-gazing to absurdly cosmic proportions). She is interested in a fully phenomenological interactivity, one in which the body in space is acknowledged as an active subject, and where the choice to orient the body in relation to the work is seen as every bit as "contemporary" as the deployment of buttons and tiresome tree-structured interactions.

Hers is a curious kind of art, then, dependent upon technology, though resistant to anything but direct experience. Fully simulated before being installed, it must be engaged bodily to be understood and appreciated. It derives from, then, but is not *of* technology. Here, there is a constant modulation between the aesthetization of space and the spatialization of aesthetics. The wall becomes another space; the space becomes another image; the image becomes another wall.

# PERRY HOBERMAN/GARY HILL/ADAM ROSS:
## CLICK/FOCUS/DREAM

### Perry Hoberman: Click

There has to be that interval of neglect, there has to be discontinuity; it is religiously and artistically essential. That is what I mean when I refer to the necessity for ruins: ruins provide the incentive for restoration, and for a return to origins.

*J. B. Jackson*, The Necessity for Ruins[1]

A 35 millimeter projector starts up in the booth, and *The Big Easy*, a *policier* set in New Orleans, opens with daylight traveling shots through the Louisiana bayous. These accelerate and darken, culminating in a descent through the city's night skies into Charles Moore's classically inspired postmodern pastiche, the Piazza d'Italia. This being a crime movie, there's a corpse face down in the fountain.[2]

The first time I see this film, I know the Piazza d'Italia only through illustrations in architectural publications. But here, the Piazza—with its brilliantly lit faux columns, flowing "wetopes" (witty, dribbling metopes), and topographic map of the boot of Italy—has never looked more enticing. This is, after all, the movies, and people, places, and things are supposed to look better in the movies.[3]

Some years pass, and I am walking through downtown New Orleans for the first time. I happen upon a ruin. Neon tubes are missing or shattered, the water has been turned off for years, and the walls are cracked and peeling—a peculiar aspect of the "witty" construction that faced steel-framed construction with stone and now sees the two separating through the effects of time and vandalism. The Piazza d'Italia, no more than a decade and half after it was completed, doesn't need a body to resemble the scene of the crime. The discourse of contemporary architecture too often is over the day of the ribbon cutting. Perhaps it should revisit its showpieces as they adapt to their

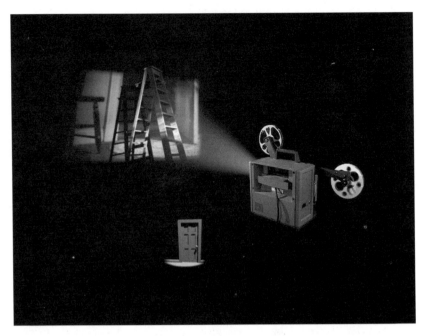

A calculated nostalgia engine, calibrated to our memories of an earlier media era, one of bright bulbs, photochemical emulsions, reflective surfaces, and dust motes that swirl into life, into light.

Perry Hoberman, *The Sub-Division of the Electric Light* (1996). © Perry Hoberman/ZKM, Karlsruhe.

environments, inhabitants, and unexpected uses—even to their unjust, sometimes ignominious fates.[4]

Still more years pass, and I'm back in New Orleans, looking at a prototype of Perry Hoberman's *The Sub-Division of the Electric Light*. I've come from Los Angeles, Hoberman from San Francisco, yet that odd triangulation that the tradeshow, conference, and lecture circuits work on geography has brought us together in the shadow of the Piazza d'Italia. This may be Hoberman's first project specifically for a CD-ROM, but it is in keeping with the artist's long held and keenly realized attention to the intertwinings of technology, images, and nostalgia. So, with the Piazza as context, the screen instantiates the imagescape as postmodern ruin.

Click. Antique projectors whir in an undifferentiated, phosphor-lit blankness. Click, and the projectors perform their destiny; they project. The images they throw across the virtual space of the monitor consist of home movies, found footage, family slides. The imagescape is a calculated nostalgia engine, calibrated to our memories of an earlier media era, one of bright bulbs, photochemical emulsions, reflective surfaces, and dust motes that swirl into life, into light. Hoberman subdivides our cultural memory of light in the service of media. On a monitor, he conjures projection to remind us of the ever-accelerating speed with which we consume and then dispose of media technologies—and that with every move there is a loss as well as a gain. At a moment when the computer market's most fervent dream can be summed up as "full-screen, full-motion video," Hoberman is an iconoclast, shattering and subdividing the monitor, playing with its spurious two-and-one-half dimensions of depth.

Click, and a scenario begins: an antique 8mm Bell and Howell projector whirs to life in one corner of the monitor, fulfilling the expectations for interaction. Click again, this time on the miniaturized moving image of a baby, cooing and gurgling on a screen situated at an oblique angle from the projector, and expectations are challenged. This click brings on the projectionist's nightmare: the image blurs, skips, freezes, and then burns from the inside to its edges. But we are afraid of system crashes now, not film jamming the gates and bursting into flames, which raises the question: Where do antique nightmares go when no one dreams them anymore?

Click, and one of the barely finished rooms is bathed in a projection. An immensely overscaled ball rolls by the wall, catching and ransforming the light, a reminder that the moving image should not always be measured in the diagonal increments of monitor models. Click, and the projection takes on the attributes of that onto which it is projected. Click, and be reminded of the great pleasures that were to be had in the interruption, manipulation, and scaling of projected light.

Playing with light is not simply an aesthetic gesture, it is also a manipulation of time, a result of the laws of relativity and the twentieth-century mantra that $E = mc^2$. *The Sub-Division of the Electric Light* is also about the parceling and reapportionment of time that dynamic media bring in their wake: Jean Luc Godard spoke of film as truth twenty-four times a second; video cassette recorders made time shift-

Where do antique nightmares go when no one dreams them anymore?

Perry Hoberman, *The Sub-Division of the Electric Light* (1996). © Perry Hoberman/ZKM, Karlsruhe.

ing a phenomenological commonplace; the grail of computer graphics is "real-time" applications; and the aesthetic of the World Wide Web is based at least as much on the wait between images as it is on the on-line imagescapes themselves.

Hoberman plays off this interrelationship between the visual and the temporal. Click, and each *mise-en-scène* manifests its singularity (or gimmick, as it were), either with another click or with a movement of the mouse: the film runs in reverse, light sources shift, objects rotate or deform; and in one, the screen moves closer or farther away, creating a time slider in space. Click, and time is spatialized. Click, and space is temporalized. In reference to this project, Hoberman has written, "I want to make something where time never stops completely—but not something where you are trapped in an automated clockwork of time—where the user can play with time, where time is something malleable—however not something where the user controls time (which would be impossible anyway)."[5]

This quotation is likewise a description of memory, that slippery somewhere where "time is something malleable." And memory is central to *The Sub-Division of the Electric Light*. There are forgotten memories: Edison's electric lightbulb as the refutation of the commonly held nineteenth-century belief that the small-scale domestication of artificial illumination was impossible.[6] There are dim memories: management information systems engineers dismissing desktop computing as a hobbyist's pursuit, one that posed no threat to the mainframe's mandarin caste system. There are personal memories of the distant past: relatives hauling out obscure machinery to show their home movies and the slide shows of their travels. There are professional memories: machines (the Apple II), platforms (the Amiga), hardware (the dot matrix printer), software (Wordstar), storage systems (the 5-1/4″ floppy)—once central to computing, now hand-me-downs to poor relatives or entirely abandoned.

And so, back to architecture and the postmodern ruin of the Piazza d'Italia. We can see most electronic art sharing the fate, sooner rather than later, of Moore's monument—the silver oxide that flakes off 1″ videotape; the pioneering audio and visual work done on computer systems that no longer have manuals or spare parts; even the CD-ROM itself, a delivery system referred to as transitional since its very inception. Thus it is that Perry Hoberman, whose works have so often been performance-based, may indeed be an emblematic artist for the CD-ROM. It may be a mistake to regard *The Sub-Division of the Electric Light* as an art object, for that implies a certain permanence and stability that the work and its medium do not offer. Better to think of it as performance, for performances, unlike monuments, don't leave ruins; they leave memories.

## Gary Hill: Focus

A forty-yard meander through Los Angeles's Museum of Jurassic Technology (MJT) is a more interactive experience than a week spent navigating through all but the rarest new media projects. But, like a newcomer to *<jodi.org>*, prepare to be confused. Moving from the Misch/Webster Gallery's display of real letters addressed to the Mt.

A series of dissimilar objects come into focus, only to fade out as the focal plane of the camera shifts, revealing yet another object, which blurs in turn.

Gary Hill, *Site Recite (a prologue)* (1989). Detail and production stills. Photo: Gary Hill. Courtesy of Donald Young Gallery, Chicago.

Wilson Observatory to the explication of Geoffrey Sonnabend's highly implausible "Cone of Obliscence" (a mad theory of memory) in the Delani/Sonnabend Halls, and then to the impossible diorama of the Deprong Mori, a bat that can vibrate through lead walls, is to "interact" with truth value, a full range of sensory input, and the nagging sense of doubt that is the only residue we can ever take with us after engaging with a full sense of wonder. The MJT is more than a museum, as one regular notes. It is "a museum, a critique of museums, and a celebration of museums—all rolled up into one."[7]

The MJT is conceptual artist David Wilson's deadpan take on the tradition of the *Kunst- und Wunderkammern*, those sixteenth- through nineteenth-century collections where the wonders of nature were displayed cheek by jowl with art works and a variety of ephemera, apocrypha and just plain nonsense that slots into neither category, or both. These *Wunderkammern*, or wonder chambers, were the foundation of both the "scientific museum" and what we now think of as its antithesis, the roadside freak show. The *Wunderkammern*'s galleries were chockablock with contemporary paintings, fragments from Noah's Ark, late Renaissance forgeries of imperial Roman copies of classical Greek statuary (presented as authentic relics of Atlantis), cloth from Africa, mementos from the New World, and all manner of other objects of interest and fancy, collected by scholars and aristocrats, enthusiasts and obsessives of all stripes. These collections both predated and survived the Enlightenment concept of the museum as the repository of the real, serving as a place where "attractions" of all kind were gathered.[8]

In the introduction I discussed the way that digital media still remain for the most part "media of attractions." Too much of new media aesthetic practice apes the market, using the art object as the excuse to demo the system, software, or network of the moment. Indeed, the new media art world too often resembles a huge *Wunderkammern* that thinks it is a museum, filled with novelties it mistakes for meaning. Gary Hill's videotape *Site Recite (a prologue)* (1989) is one of the great correctives to the kind of aesthetic practice that insists on being accorded notice because it is an interactive, immersive, networked or some other such technologized *Wunder*. *Site Recite* is an exercise in focus, a four-minute simulacrum of a continuous movement through a dataspace.

Beginning in darkness, a resonant voice reads from the artist's text: "Nothing seems to have ever been moved. There is something of every description which can only be a trap."[9] The first of a long series of dissimilar objects then comes into focus, only to fade out as the focal plane of the camera shifts, revealing yet another object, which blurs in turn. The effect somehow mimics the experience of sitting through an eye exam as the optometrist fiddles with the lenses and abruptly transforms the eye's ability to focus. It is not just the focal distance that recalibrates, as the camera moves continuously and fluidly through this darkly indeterminate space. So deft is the camerawork that the spectator experiences an almost bodily sense of movement through the dataspace.

In time, the viewer is confronted with animal skulls, jawbones, broken egg shells, butterfly wings, fragments of sea shells, and little scraps of typewritten paper that fade into and out of view too quickly to decipher. On one level, *Site Recite* is Hill's mediated *vanitas*, that staple of art history which, by concentrating on skulls, bones and other *momento mori* confront us with our own mortality. But this video is many other things as well, including, as John Hanhardt notes, a *Wunderkammern* "filled with lost and remembered objects."[10] In its conceptual clarity and technical mastery, *Site Recite*—like the Museum of Jurassic Technology—offers a damning critique of the paltriness of tree-structured interactivity. By this I mean interactive media's mechanistic myth of choice: up/down, left/right, fight/flight. This is the brute interactivity of the database: options are arrayed, choices expected to be made. Yes, there is interaction, but to what point beyond demonstrating that interaction itself is possible?

Hill made *Site Recite* to simulate a single pass through a never realized "interactive" videodisc which the artist had planned to title *Which tree*.[11] The videotape, which serves as a record of a single reading/writing/navigating of the dataspace, is intended specifically to "mark this word interactive with its tendency to attract an optimism of infinite possibilities, contrary to the fact that it is not only delimited by if/then scenarios, but thoroughly collapses when the viewer finds him/her self forced to make decisions inscribed by "multiple choice."[12] David Wilson commented on the Entertainment-Industrial complex: "Face it, in that kind of work you can count the themes you engage on the fingers of one hand, even if you don't have any arms."[13] For all the discourse and marketing hype around new media, the themes—as well as the paradigms—for creating truly interactive multimedia experiences responsive to user input have been few and far between.

Hill's seamless long take, with its constant fluctuations between and among the depth of the objects, is reminiscent of Alfred Hitchcock's narrative feature *Rope* (1948), which adapted a play of the same name into a seemingly continuous, real-time, 90-minute-long take, with the camera serving as the equivalent of the eyes of a spectator at one of those live "interactive" and "immersive" murder mysteries like *Tamara* that became popular live performances over the last two decades.[14] But no 35mm camera of Hitchcock's time had a magazine with 90 minutes' worth of film in it, and no major studio would ever have released a single take film from anybody, even a director as meticulous as Hitchcock. *Rope*, however, is not a single take; it just looks like one, as Hitchcock spliced together a series of ten-minute takes, cutting on tight shots of clothing, furniture, and architectural details (which could be completely immobilized and matched) to create the fiction of continuity.[15]

In a like maneuver, what seems in *Site Recite* to be one long, fluid and incredible take is in fact the stitching together of hundreds of smaller shots, each cut to the other at the moment of blur between focus. The comparison between this short video and Hitchcock's narrative feature is doubly apt because *Site Recite* is itself a mystery, one complete with a denouement. Like one of Agatha Christie's *Ten Little Indians* who discovers why she is on a deserted island only at the end of the novel, we encounter the solution to the mystery in the video's closing frames. Yet Hill is sly: his ending, which shows—in crystal-clear focus—the table and those eccentric objects that have thus far eluded our vision, would be anyone else's point of departure. Here, that is, what in cinema is referred to as the "establishing shot" is recast as a conclusion of sorts. Another circle, then, is created—a non-narrative loop.

But *Site Recite* is not just a mystery, it is also a thriller, with a last, unexpected shock. Hill's text resonates: "I must become a warrior of self-consciousness and move my body to move my mind to move the words to move my mouth to spin the spur of the moment. Imagining the brain closer than the eyes."[16] The last sentence is spoken by a mouth that we see made animate, from inside that mouth itself. This sequence was composed of still photographs of the inside of Hill's mouth and the surface of his tongue captured using dental mirrors. These stills were then texture-mapped onto a computer-graphic animation to create the illusion of speech captured from the point of view of the speaking subject's cortex, a witty, rather shocking comment on the search for a truly grounded subject position.

Hill is one of the most important and theoretically sophisticated figures to emerge from the genre of video art and the great body of his work has been engaged with the issue of how to build and describe an *"electronic linguistic."*[17] While *Site Recite* is obviously an investigation of

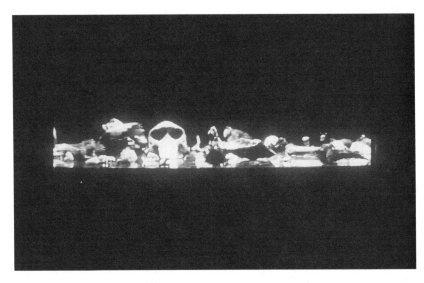

What in cinema is referred to as the establishing shot is here recast as a conclusion.

Gary Hill, *Site Recite (a prologue)* (1989). Detail and production stills. Photo: Gary Hill. Courtesy of Donald Young Gallery, Chicago.

the cinematographic and videographic technique of the "focus pull," it offers a template for other, more specific explorations of digital hyperaesthetics. Hill's electronic linguistic engages with language as an embodied technology, with language as a virtual system, with language as a visual object. Interactivity may be a chimera right now, but if artists ever hope to make more of it than a *Wunder*, they would do well to emulate *Site Recite*.

## Adam Ross: Dream

Of all the doxa generated by the psychoanalytic faith, my favorite is the dream-day residue. This is the notion that each night's dream is built at least in part from fragments gleaned during the dream-day.[18] This direct linkage between the sunlit experience of our conscious waking and the unconscious dream-work of condensing, displacing, and revising that raw material is one of the strongest arguments for art, in all its forms. For if by consciously seeking out aesthetic experiences that are challenging and/or beautiful, perverse and/or sublime, stimulating

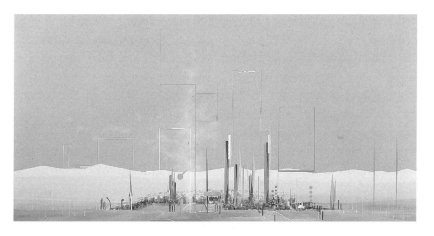

A technological imaginary, a realm of both conscious calculation and unconscious reverie.

Adam Ross, *Untitled (AT 7)* (1998). Courtesy of Shoshana Wayne Gallery, Santa Monica.

and/or peaceful we can impact even our dreams, who can argue against the power of art?

But it has been the impact of the digital on our lives—both conscious and unconscious—that has been the purview of this book. How then are we to assess the import of the computer-inflected as well as the computer generated for this particular cultural moment? Since both are so ubiquitous, why not appropriate the digital as a frame? Why not discuss an oil painting on wood as a digital artwork? There are indeed many digital paintings, and innumerable ways of relating painting to digital input. In *Powerbook* (1996), Miltos Manetas paints hardware, fuzzing the focus on a laptop computer until the canvas begins to resemble a Robert Ryman abstract swath of gray, with a small, warm blob in the lower center (the ubiquitous bitten Apple icon reduced to an image trace). Monique Prieto takes another tack, plotting out the deflated balloon shapes of non-representational paintings like *Pedestrian* (1998) on the computer's screen and then transferring these designs to canvas so that she can more fully concentrate on the treatment of color, having already "solved" the form-making digitally. But what of paintings that bear no trace of technology beyond the artist's brush: can these too be computer-inflected?

Adam Ross's *Untitled (AT 7)* (1998) is a painting of a technological imaginary, a realm of both conscious calculation and unconscious reverie. The rectangular wood surface, six feet long and three feet high, is divided into four major elements. The first is the gray ground that stretches off into the horizon, its topography taking up the bottom quarter of the painting, surmounted by a slightly jagged horizon line, suggesting either hills close by or vast mountains unimaginably far from the viewer's vantage point. Taking up three quarters of the painting above the horizon line is a green sky, but one whose particular density of color refamiliarizes it; this green sky somehow captures the same depth and weight as our blue sky, creating an atmosphere disturbing and yet somehow reassuring. On the one hand, this painting can be read as representational, the landscape as an architectural rendering: out of the gray plane a cityscape emerges, one composed of smaller structures gridded out rationally, as we expect of every Radiant City since Le Corbusier. Complementing this reading are vast vertical forms rising above the grid, scraping the green sky, surpassing the wildest dreams of Southeast Asian autarks (for they seem to be the only ones still in thrall to the twentieth century's obsession with tower as phallus).

But the techno-sublime reading of this painting as a representational rendering of a fantastic urban plan is skewed by the overlay of a grid of ghostly perpendicular yellow and blue lines coming up from the gray plane and floating in the green ether. These are neither precisely abstract, nor, truth be told, completely non-representational. I cannot help but read these forms as floating windows, interfaces somehow blown up beyond the scope even of architecture. Like the single beam shooting into space from the apex of the pyramid hotel that announces the Luxor Casino even to tourists flying over Las Vegas, perhaps these are simply advertisements, for *Windows*® *2295* or some other such soon to be outmoded product. But they may be more. Perhaps they are structures in their own rights, or even a delicate, as yet unimaginable art form.

The painting has a crispness and playfulness that appeals to anyone who has ever thought about what it would be like to build in an environment in which the rules of gravity and the behaviors of building materials either do not hold or can be willfully ignored. The "AT"

Abstract forms as floating windows, interfaces blown up beyond even the scope of architecture.

Adam Ross, *Untitled (AT 7)* (1998), detail. Courtesy of Shoshana Wayne Gallery, Santa Monica.

in the title stands for the overall title of the series from which it comes, "Architecture and Time," and *Untitled (AT 7)* encourages the viewer to suspend disbelief, to posit a different kind of space-time, and in so doing, a different kind of life. But this is not a wholehearted embrace of the future, either. For all of the brightness of tone, the world depicted is cool. The structures do not read as particularly habitable (or even designed for humans), and a spectre of loneliness hangs heavy in the green air. Is this painting related to the tradition of architectural photography, which prizes above all else the shot of the building just before people step into it? Or is it instead an archaeological rendering, with the city's inhabitants long dead, the structures just excavated? In other words, is the city sleeping or is it dead?

This painting may be ambiguous, but it is not ironic. In standing against irony, the painting participates in an ongoing critique of postmodernism that defines the post-'89 generation, perhaps even questioning the appropriateness of the very notion of the "post"-modern. Ross explicitly positions his *Untitled (AT 7)* in a continuum that embraces the pre-modern, the high modern (it is a painting, after all), as well as the postmodern and even post-postmodern phases. In this expansiveness, Ross battles the nihilistic truism inherited from postmodernism, that neither life nor art are as interesting as they once were, and that all that remains is to rework the past in an endless series of appropriations, metacritical commentaries, and nostalgic references. This is not to say that Ross's painting is naïve; far from it, in fact. The references in this body of work extend far beyond the science-fictional imaginary to include what can be called an illusionistic Surrealism of the kind practiced by painters Matta and Yves Tanguy in the '50s, the speculative pavilions of Britain's Archigram group in the '60s, comic artist Moebius's vertiginous cityscapes of the '70s, the paper architecture of Lebbeus Wood's floating cities in the '80s, and Frank Gehry's curved and folded design of the Guggenheim Bilbao at the close of the century.[19]

What Ross shares with all of these artists is a sense that good or bad, the present is now, the past is gone and we have some say about the way the future will look and feel. We need work like *Untitled (AT 7)* to contribute to our dream-day residue, for how else are we to escape a sense of permanent present?

# Appendix:
# Terms and Conditions

*The Alexandrine Dream:* The desire to collect the whole of human cultural production under one roof. This impulse runs directly from the classical Library of Alexandria to hypertext pioneer Ted Nelson's forever unfinished project Xanadu.

*Camera Rasa:* In the discourse of virtuality, the imagination confronts a *camera rasa*—a blank room, the erased slate of the *tabula rasa* extruded into three dimensions—and renders into it all manners of wonders.

*Commodity Camaraderie:* The primary cohesive force binding electronic artists, less a shared sense of artistic destiny than the common use of similar tools.

*Demo or Die:* The demonstration, or demo, is the defining moment of the digital artist's practice at the turn of the millennium. The failure to demo leads to the end of financial and/or critical support, hence "Demo or Die."

*Dialectical Immaterialism:* A vapor theory of ruminations unsupported by material underpinnings.

*Digital Dialectic:* A method to ground the insights of theory in the constraints of practice, combining critical investigations of contemporary culture with the hands-on analysis of the possibilities (and limitations) of new technologies.

*Dynamic Non-Conscious:* Higher-order computer mediated communication brings about a relationship between the human user's split psyche—both conscious and unconscious—and the non- but pseudo-consciousness of the computer. The dynamic non-conscious, then, is the machine part of the human computer interface.

*The Edenic Fallacy:* A never-ending idyllicization of nature in the service of a feel-good eco-aesthetic practiced by too many of the artists who employ vastly expensive technologies to create their work. A puzzling tendency to create simplistic critiques of machine culture using systems dependent on the latest hardware and software.

*The Electronic Corpse:* One of the default settings of net.art. The digital era's take on the Surrealists' Exquisite Corpse, the Electronic Corpse ships images over the net and around the globe, in the hopes of creating a truly collaborative art form. The usual result is rasterbated murk.

*Electronic Semiotics:* A mutated science of signs that confronts the truth value of digital photography. The computer's photo-graphic brings about a return to the aesthetic of the pre-photographic era, to a signscape that is reduced to the dichotomy between the word and the image, though both are now merely different outputs of the same binary code.

*Future/Present:* In an era of technological hyperobsolescence, the present is no longer sufficient; we have need of a future/present, a phenomenological equivalent to the future perfect tense.

*Gesamtkunstmedium:* Since the nineteenth century, artists have invested certain art works with the hopes of inducing radical synesthesia—the prime example being Richard Wagner's vision of the *gesamtkunstwerk*. For the past few decades, artists have searched not simply for the "total work of art," but also for the *gesamtkunstmedium,* a conceptual space for collaboration between disciplines. Although the cinema at first appeared to fulfill these dreams, the interest has shifted to the computer.

*Hardscape:* The built structures that house or hold the visual screens constituting hybrid architecture's imagescapes.

*Hybrid Architecture:* Architectural systems that combine the built hardscapes with mutable imagescapes.

*Hype Cycle:* A technology develops in obscurity, then a breakthrough either real or imagined thrusts it into the glare of the mediasphere. Claims are made, then exaggerated by those who do not fully understand what they are promoting. The inability of these technologies to deliver what they never promised finally brings on a long, dark winter of media avoidance.

*Hyperaesthetics:* A dynamic aesthetics applied to dynamic arts. Hyperaesthetics requires theorization in real-time.

*Imagescapes:* The mutable visual technologies embedded within and/or covering the built hardscapes of conventional architecture.

*Media of Attractions:* Artifacts of digital culture whose appeal is essentially their perceived novelty. They attract less for what they mean than for the fact that they are.

*Nano-thoughts:* Ideas, metaphors, and images processed down to their smallest units, and then repeated *ad nauseam* throughout digital databases.

*Neologorrhea:* The compulsive, almost hysterical need to neologize, to create new words to describe and confront new situations. Neologorrhea is pandemic within the technoculture.

*Nostalgia for the Future:* The condition that allows us the mental space to confront the ever redoubling speed of digital technologies that renders them obsolete memories in the blink of an eye.

*The Paradox of Unfolding:* The quality of virtual architecture in which users approach objects in cyberspace, moving towards them only to have them transform, or unfold, into new objects. It is a spatialization of the mathematical concept of infinite regression.

*Permanent Present:* The sense that, for all the technological innovations of the past two decades, our visual culture remains trapped in a relentless now, idly circling itself as if waiting for inspiration it doesn't expect to come. The situation of being unable to imagine a future more interesting, viable, or beautiful than the moment in which we live now.

*Photo-graphic:* In a digital environment, the discrete photograph is transformed into the essentially unbounded graphic. The formerly "unique" photograph has been merged, even submerged, into the computer's overall visual environment.

*Post-'89 Theory:* The year the Berlin Wall fell and the Cold War ended, 1989, has replaced 1968 as the defining moment for contemporary theory. Post-'89 theories self-consciously live in, with, and through new communication technologies; reject the notion that every instance of cultural consumption should be read in reverse as an act of resistance to consumerism; and acknowledge market forces without necessarily embracing them.

*Science-fictionalized Discourse:* An ever-escalating cycle of conjecture and unsubstantiated speculation that generally sorts out into odd combinations of utopian longings, dystopian warnings, and technomysticism.

*TechnoVolksgeist:* As digital artists and other groups heavily invested in the creative use of technology extend their commodity camaraderie from software to platform to network, they transform the idea of a geographically specific Bohemia into a broader concept of the user group as proto-social formation.

*Unitary Virtuality (UV):* The quest for fully immersive virtual reality systems that are completely mutable, controllable environments. VR unwittingly inherited this synesthetic fantasy from such 1960s groups as the Situationist International and Archigram.

*Vapor Theory:* Dialectical immaterialism, critical discussions about technology untethered to the constraints of production. Vapor theory often mutates into technomysticism, and can lead even exceptionally able thinkers into a hype-driven discourse that dates instantly.

# Notes

## Introduction

1. *Miracleman* #16, Eclipse Comics (December, 1989), p. 2.

2. Martin Heidegger, "The Question Concerning Technology," in *The Question Concerning Technology and Other Essays*, trans. William Lovitt (New York: Harper Torchbooks, 1977), p. 4.

3. Christian Metz, *The Imaginary Signifier: Psychoanalysis and the Cinema* (Bloomington: Indiana University Press, 1982), pp. 15–16, Susan Sontag, *Against Interpretation* (New York: Dell, 1981).

4. "The cinema of attractions, rather than telling stories, bases itself on film's ability to show something . . . this is an exhibitionistic cinema, a cinema that displays its visibility." Tom Gunning, *D.W. Griffith and the Origins of American Narrative Film: The Early Years at Biograph* (Urbana: University of Illinois Press, 1991), p. 41. Also see Charles Musser, *The Emergence of Cinema: The American Screen to 1907*, Vol. 1 of *A History of the American Cinema*, ed. Charles Harpole (New York: Charles Scribner's Sons, 1990).

5. David Bordwell, Janet Staiger, and Kristin Thompson call this the Classical Hollywood style, date it from 1917 to 1960, and refer to it as "an aesthetic system" that "functioned historically as a set of norms." *The Classical Hollywood Cinema: Film Style and Mode of Production to 1960*, (New York: Columbia University Press, 1985), p. 5.

6. Thomas Elsaesser makes a direct link between the cinema of attraction and contemporary digital media in "Louis Lumière—the Cinema's First Virtualist" in Thomas Elsaesser and Kay Hoffman, eds., *Cinema Futures: Cain, Abel or Cable?: The Screen Arts in the Digital Age* (Amsterdam: Amsterdam University Press, 1998), pp. 45–61.

7. Lord Byron (Baron George Gordon Byron), *Don Juan*, c. 12, v. 69 (London: John Lane; New York: Dodd, Mead and Company, 1926), p. 300.

8. Arthur Kroker contrasts Marshall McLuhan's and Roland Barthes's divergent approaches to the relationship between art and technology. McLuhan "suggested the image of art as a probe which serves as an early warning system of coming changes in technological society," while Barthes sees "not art as a

metaphor for key transformations in the field of technological change, but technology as a critical probe of coming transitions in the field of art." Arthur Kroker, *The Possessed Individual: Technology and the French Postmodern* (New York: St. Martin's Press, 1992), p. 99.

9. Simon Reynolds and Kodwo Eshun, "The Natural Laws of Music," *frieze* 46 (May 1999): p. 52.

10. Liam Gillick, *Erasmus is Late* (London: Book Works, 1995).

## Chapter 1

1. My choice of gender here is deliberate: in the early 1980s, the IBM PC was designed for, and marketed to, males.

2. Immanuel Kant, "Critique of Aesthetic Judgment," in *Critique of Judgement*, trans. Werner S. Pluhar (Indianapolis: Hackett Publishing Company, 1987), p. 175.

3. Some critics have taken the notion of the author's death rather too literally. As a corrective, one only has to read Michel Foucault's seminal articles on the subject to see how he saw this "death" not as an end, but rather as a fascinating beginning.

It is obviously insufficient to repeat empty slogans: the author has disappeared; God and man died a common death. Rather, we should reexamine the empty space left by the author's disappearance; we should attentively examine, along its gaps and fault lines, its new demarcations, and the reapportionment of this void; we should await the fluid functions released by this disappearance" (p. 121).

Michel Foucault, "What is an Author?" in *Language, Counter-Memory, Practice*, translated by Donald F. Bouchard and Sherry Simon, edited by Donald F. Bouchard (Ithaca: Cornell University Press, 1977), pp. 113–138. For more of the originating discourse, see Roland Barthes, "The Death of the Author," in *Image-Music-Text*, trans. Stephen Heath (New York: Hill and Wang, 1977), pp. 142–148; to relate these concepts to digital media, see George P. Landow, *Hypertext 2.0: The Convergence of Contemporary Critical Theory and Technology* (Baltimore: Johns Hopkins University Press, 1997).

4. As an example of this kind of discourse, look to Gabriel-Désiré Laverdant, a minor Fouieriste, who in 1845 created the template for all the future claims of the avant-garde in his book *De la mission de l'art et du rôle des artistes*. "Art, the expression of society, manifests, in its highest soaring, the most advanced social tendencies: it is to be the forerunner and the revealer. Therefore, to know whether art worthily fulfills its proper mission as initiator, whether the artist is truly of the avant-garde, one must know where human-

ity is going, know what the destiny of the human race is." Cited in Renato Poggioli, *The Theory of the Avant-Garde*, trans. Gerald Fitzgerald (Cambridge, MA: Harvard University Press, 1968), p. 9.

5. Karl Marx, "The Fetishism of Commodities and the Secret Thereof," in *Capital: A Critique of Political Economy*, trans. Samuel Moore and Edward Aveling (New York: Modern Library, 1936), p. 83.

6. Ibid., p. 84.

7. See David Harvey's discussion of Fordist production vs. Just-in-time production, as well as the flexible accumulation model of postmodern capitalism. Harvey's interpretations impel us to see software production as a harbinger of an emerging, more fully flexible mode of production/consumption. David Harvey, *The Condition of Postmodernity: An Inquiry into the Origins of Cultural Change* (Cambridge, MA: Blackwell Publishers, 1989), pp. 177–179.

8. Marx, "The Fetishism of Commodities and the Secret Thereof," p. 87.

9. For an analysis of the gift economy as it relates to open source coding and specifically to the development of the Linux operating system after hacker Linus Torvalds released its code in the early 1990s, see Eric S. Raymond, "Homesteading the Noosphere" (April 1998), <tuxedo.org/~esr/writings/homesteading/homesteading.txt>. For an anthropological and historical overview, see David Cheal, *The Gift Economy* (New York: Routledge, 1988).

10. Although the abstraction as developed here applies to software, with some changes it is also relevant to the manufacture of hardware as well.

11. For histories of these communities as they evolved through the 1990s, see Constance Penley and Andrew Ross, eds., *Technoculture* (Minneapolis: University of Minnesota, 1991); Rudy Rucker, R.U. Sirius, and Queen Mu, eds., *Mondo 2000: A User's Guide to the New Edge* (New York: HarperPerennial, 1992); and Mark Dery, *Escape Velocity: Cyberculture at the End of the Century* (New York: Grove Press, 1996).

12. Isaiah Berlin, "Return of the Volksgeist," *New Perspectives Quarterly* 8, no. 4 (Fall 1991): 8.

13. Isaiah Berlin, *Vico and Herder: Two Studies in the History of Ideas* (New York: Viking, 1976).

14. From *The Origin of Language* [V, 134–147], excerpted in *Herder on Social and Political Culture*, F. M. Barnard, ed. (Cambridge: Cambridge University Press, 1969), p. 160.

15. For examples of how the TechnoVolksgeist slides too easily into libertarianism and the neo-liberal economic hyperbole of the so-called "New Economy," see Kevin Kelly, *New Rules for the New Economy: 10 Radical Strategies for a Connected World* (New York: Viking Penguin, 1998) and cyber-pundit

George Gilder's "Telecosm" columns in *Forbes ASAP, Microcosm: The Quantum Revolution in Economics and Technology* (New York: Simon and Schuster, 1989) and *Life After Television* (New York: W.W. Norton & Company, 1992).

16. Paul Virilio, *Speed and Politics: An Essay on Dromology*, trans. Mark Polizzoti (New York: Semiotext(e), 1986), especially Part Three, "Dromocratic Society," pp. 61–132.

17. The responses to the events of 1989 are so varied and vast that it would be pointless to summarize them here. As a start, I offer three distinct and highly ambiguous vantage points: a history, a film, and an exhibition. Andreas Huyssen, *Twilight Memories, Marking Time in a Culture of Amnesia* (New York: Routledge, 1995) filters Germany's own narratives of reunification through a reading of their experience of division. Jean-Luc Godard's *Germany Year 90 Nine Zero* (1991) is a multi-layered commentary making reference to Roberto Rossellini's post-war, neo-realist masterpiece *Germany Year Zero* (1946), Godard's own deadpan Orwellian fable *Alphaville* (1965), and the intertwined emotions of optimism and caution that the rest of Europe felt watching events unfold in Berlin. *Documenta* is the hugely important international art exhibition held regularly since 1955 in Kassel, a small town in the former West Germany, close to its then eastern border. By the tenth mounting of the show in 1997, Kassel was no longer a border town, it was in the center of the reunified nation. *documenta X* (the lowercase "d" was intentional) was for the first time under the direction of a non-German curator, in this case Catherine David from France. David's show was much excoriated by both press and public and offered an exercise in cultural nostalgia, reading the events of 1989 through the aesthetic politics of the generation of '68. Even there, *documenta X*'s highly theoretical companion volume specifically closed its periodization of cultural production since World War II with "the end of 'real communism' in 1989." *Politics-Poetics documenta X—the book*, Documenta and Museum Fridericianum, eds., Catherine David and Jean-François Chevrier, idea and conception (Stuttgart: Cantz Verlag, 1997), p. 26.

18. The French theorist Pierre Lévy goes much further than I am willing to when he claims that digital technologies were in fact a root cause of the implosion of the former Soviet Union and its satellites. "Totalitarianism collapsed in the face of new forms of mobile and cooperative labor [brought about by telematic technologies]. *It was incapable of collective intelligence*" [emphasis in the original]. Pierre Lévy, *Collective Intelligence: Mankind's Emerging World in Cyberspace*, trans. Robert Bononno (New York: Plenum Press, 1997), p. 3. In a more measured tone, the third volume of Manuel Castells's series on the Information Age is predicated on an analysis of the breakdown of the

Soviet Union and attempts to answer the question, "Why was statism structurally incapable of proceeding with the necessary restructuring to adapt to informationalism?" Manuel Castells, *End of Millennium. The Information Age: Economy, Society, and Culture,* vol. 3 (Cambridge: Blackwell, 1998).

19. Susan Sontag, "Why Are We in Kosovo?," *New York Times Sunday Magazine* (May 2, 1999): 53.

20. Meaghan Morris, "Banality in Cultural Studies," *Discourse* 10:2 (Spring/Summer, 1988): 3–29, has had an obvious impact on my thinking here. Lawrence Grossberg, Cary Nelson, Paula A. Treichler, eds., *Cultural Studies* (New York: Routledge, 1992) remains a central document to explore the impact of post–'68 thinking on the then emerging discipline of cultural studies.

21. Marcelin Pleynet, "For an Approach to Abstract Expressionism," in Michael Auping, ed., *Abstract Expression: The Critical Developments* (New York: Harry N. Abrams, Inc. 1987), p. 36.

## Chapter 2

1. In this chapter there are various neologisms, including words such as "demoing." These are becoming standard usages, following the corporate linguistic convention that "there is no noun which can't be verbed." For more on the urge to neologize, see chapter 3.

2. One reason why design as a profession seems to hold such sway in the entire arena of contemporary visual culture is its inextricable linkage to the market. Design is, after all, still commonly referred to as commercial art.

3. Quite contrary to the techno-libertarian fantasies of certain Silicon Valley demagogues, government money was integral to the development of everything from the integrated circuit to the Internet.

4. Deutsche Telecom made a big splash in 1996 sponsoring a major show titled "Mediascape," but not without the Guggenheim Museum SoHo enduring some criticism for letting corporate funding drive its curatorial initiative, the sternest of which came from Rosalind Kraus and Hal Foster, "Introduction," *October* 77 (Summer, 1996): 3–4. Interestingly, however, no further jointly sponsored shows materialized after "Mediascape," and within three years a museum spokesperson noted discreetly that "the relationship between the Guggenheim and Deutsche Telecom ended amicably and has not been renewed." Cited in Eleanor Heartney, "Growing Pains," *Art in America* (June 1999): 47.

5. The company was Lyon Lamb Video Animation Systems of Burbank, CA.

6. Critics and theorists have also found themselves entranced, not simply by the demos themselves but also by the appeal of giving them. In fact, it is difficult

for critics and theorists to discuss this arena of cultural production, and virtually impossible to teach it, without giving demos themselves.

7. This stability has been ruptured before, of course. When artists and designers began to work with audiovisual, time-based media, they faced difficulties similar to those brought on by computer-based presentations. With film, format was a major issue, as was display. 8mm, Super 8, 16mm, Super 16, mono audio tracks, stereo delivery, combinations of the above, and the inevitable difficulty of getting the loop right in the projector all contributed to a heightened sense of anxiety. The earlier eras of video also had their format wars, with the move from open-reel 1" systems to cassettes—1", ¾", and ½". Yet the passage of time itself has imposed its own default: the ½" VHS tape is pretty much guaranteed to work. Whatever the source, however—film or video or even still image—VHS tape delivery systems are almost completely idiot-proof, and thereby do not generally engender the techno-anxiety that computer imaging brings in its wake.

8. See Douglas Engelbart, "Letter to Vannevar Bush and Program on Human Effectiveness," in James M. Nyce and Paul Kahn, eds., *From Memex to Hypertext: Vannevar Bush and the Mind's Machine* (Boston: Academic Press, 1991), pp. 235–244.

9. Howard Rheingold, *Virtual Reality* (New York: Summit Books, 1991), p. 84.

10. Steven Levy characterizes Jobs as negotiating the borderlands between "chutzpah and hubris." Steven Levy, *Insanely Great: The Life and Times of Macintosh, the Computer That Changed Everything* (New York: Penguin Books, 1995), p. 17.

11. John Markoff, "Masters of High-Tech Demo Spin Their Magic," *New York Times*, March 11, 1996.

12. On Billups see Paula Parisi, "The New Hollywood Silicon Stars," *Wired* 3.12 (December, 1995): 142–145, 202–210. On Backes, see Burr Snider's cover story, "Rocket Science," *Wired* 2.11 (November, 1994): 108–113, 159–162.

13. Stewart Brand, *The Media Lab: Inventing the Future at MIT* (New York: Viking, 1987).

14. Howard Singerman, *Art Subjects: Making Artists in the American University* (Berkeley: University of California Press, 1999), offers an extended historical and theoretical investigation of art pedagogy and the crit, especially chapter 6, "Professing Postmodernism," pp. 155–186.

15. Stelarc characterizes *Stomach Sculpture* as "the most dangerous performance" he ever attempted. Paulo Atzori and Kirk Woolford, "Extended Body: An Interview with Stelarc," in Arthur Kroker and Marilouise Kroker, eds., *Digital Delirium* (New York: St. Martin's Press, 1997), p. 199.

16. Sigmund Freud, *The Problem of Anxiety*, trans. Henry Alden Bunker (New York: The Psychoanalytic Quarterly Press and W. W. Norton & Company, Inc., 1936 [orig. 1926]).

17. Donna Haraway, "A Cyborg Manifesto: Science, Technology and Techno-Feminism in the Late Twentieth Century," in *Simians, Cyborgs, and Women: The Reinvention of Nature* (New York: Routledge, 1991), pp. 149–181. This seems to have surpassed Laura Mulvey's 1977 essay "Visual Pleasure in the Narrative Cinema" (collected in *Visual and Other Pleasures* [Bloomington: Indiana University Press, 1989]) as the most cited reference in contemporary feminist literature on visual culture.

18. J. G. Ballard, *Crash* (New York: Noonday, 1995 [orig. 1973]), p. 68.

19. Brenda Laurel, *Computers as Theatre* (Reading, MA: Addison-Wesley, 1991).

20. Annette Wagner and Maria Capucciati, "Demo or Die: User Interface as Marketing Theatre," in Ralf Bilger, Steve Guest, and Michael J. Tauber, eds. *CHI 96—Electronic Proceedings*, <www.acm.org/sigs/sigchi/chi96/proceedings/desbrief/Wagner/aw_txt.htm>.

21. I would like to thank Vivian Sobchack for her close reading and editing of an earlier version of this chapter, and also note the influence of Lorne Falk and Heidi Gilpin's article, "The Demo Aesthetic," in *Convergence: The Journal of Research into New Media Technologies* 2, no. 2 (Autumn, 1995): 127–139.

## Chapter 3

1. Jérôme Sans, "Interview with Paul Virilio," *Flash Art* 138 (Jan/Feb, 1988): p. 57.

2. Georges Duhamel, *America: The Menace, Scenes of the Life of the Future*, trans. Charles M. Thompson (Boston: Houghton Mifflin, 1931), p. xii.

3. Jerry Mander, *In the Absence of the Sacred: The Failure of Technology & the Survival of the Indian Nations* (San Francisco: Sierra Club Books, 1991), p. 43.

4. Allucquère Rosanne Stone, "Will the Real Body Please Stand Up," in Michael Benedikt, ed., *Cyberspace: First Steps* (Cambridge: MIT Press, 1991), pp. 81–118. Also see her *The War between Technology and Desire at the End of the Twentieth Century* (Cambridge: MIT Press, 1995).

5. Manuel De Landa, *War in the Age of Intelligent Machines* (New York: Zone Books, 1991); Les Levidow and Kevin Robins, eds., *Cyborg Worlds: The Military Information Society* (London: Free Association Books, 1989); Paul N. Edwards, *The Closed World: Computers and the Politics of Discourse in Cold War America* (Cambridge, MA: MIT Press, 1996).

6. Kirkpatrick Sale offers a partisan history, with a contemporary moral, in *Rebels against the Future: The Luddites and Their War on the Industrial Revolution: Lessons for the Computer Age* (Reading, MA: Addison-Wesley, 1995). Other works of note include Theodore Roszak, *The Cult of Information: A Neo-*

*Luddite Treatise on High Tech, Artificial Intelligence, and the True Art of Thinking*, 2nd ed. (Berkeley: University of California Press, 1994); Clifford Stoll, *Silicon Snake Oil: Second Thoughts on the Information Highway* (New York: Doubleday, 1995); and Sven Birkerts, *The Gutenberg Elegies: The Fate of Reading in an Electronic Age* (Boston: Farber and Faber, 1994).

7. The Luddites have long appealed to science-fiction authors. In the classic eco-dynastic saga *Dune*, Frank Herbert created the Butlerian Jihad—a crusade far in the future against computers and thinking machines that spawns the commandment "Thou shalt not make a machine in the image of the human mind." Frank Herbert, *Dune* (New York: Ace Books, 1987, orig. 1965), p. 521. There is even more explicit reference to Ned Ludd in William Gibson and Bruce Sterling's *The Difference Engine* (New York: Bantam Books, 1991). *The Difference Engine* is a prime example of "steampunk" science fiction, a movement that aims to create alternate, fictionalized histories for the 19th century's Industrial Revolution. "The Luddites are dead as cold ashes. Oh, we marched and ranted for the rights of labor and such. . . . But Lord Charles Babbage made blueprints while we made pamphlets. And his blueprints built this world" (p. 22). The other historical reference in this passage is to Charles Babbage, a polymath nineteenth-century inventor who created calculating machines, including the programmable "Difference Engine." He is considered a great ancestral figure of computing.

8. Langdon Winner, "Artifacts/Ideas and Political Culture," *Whole Earth Review* 73 (Winter 1991): 18.

9. Chris Carlsson, ed., *Bad Attitude: The Processed World Anthology* (New York: Verso, 1990).

10. Andrew Ross, *Strange Weather: Culture, Science and Technology in the Age of Limits* (New York: Verso, 1991), p. 99.

11. William Irwin Thompson, *The American Replacement of Nature* (New York: Doubleday, 1991), p. 31.

12. Douglas Coupland, *Generation X: Tales for an Accelerated Culture* (New York: St. Martin's Press, 1991), pp. 80, 139.

13. "Jargon Watch," *Wired* 2.04 (April, 1994): 31. This word's root is the computer's display technology of the "raster grid."

14. Eric Raymond, ed., *The New Hacker's Dictionary* (Cambridge: MIT Press, 1991), p. 2. For an analysis of the spread of these new words outwards from the laboratory to the general culture, see John A. Barry, *Technobabble* (Cambridge, MA: MIT Press, 1991).

15. Mark Dery, ed., *Flame Wars: The Discourses of Cyberculture*, a special issue of the *South Atlantic Quarterly* 92, no. 4 (Fall, 1993). This issue was later packaged

as a book: Mark Dery, ed. *Flame Wars: The Discourse of Cyberculture* (Durham, NC: Duke University Press, 1994).

16. I am hardly preaching from a position of grace: after all, this book has an appendix titled "Terms and Conditions."

17. Jefferson's comment is the motto of *The Barnhart Dictionary Companion: A Quarterly of New Words*, an idiosyncratic and fascinating resource published by Merriam-Webster, Inc.

18. This demonization is by no means restricted to North America. See Luther Blissett, *Lasciate che i bimbi. Pedofilia: Pretesto per la caccia alle streghe* (Rome: Castelvecchi Edizioni, 1997), portions of which, including a discussion of Italian anti-child pornography laws and Internet censorship, have been translated into English as "Let The Children . . . Pedophilia as a Pretext for a Witch Hunt" and are available on-line at <c8.com/datacide/text/children.html>.

19. Mark C. Taylor and Esa Saarinen, *Imagologies: Media Philosophy* (New York: Routledge, 1994), p. 20 [emphasis in the original].

20. R.L. Rutsky, *High Techne: Art and Technology from the Machine Aesthetic to the Posthuman* (Minneapolis: University of Minnesota Press, 1999) and Donna Haraway, "A Cyborg Manifesto: Science, Technology and Techno-Feminism in the Late Twentieth Century," in *Simians, Cyborgs, and Women: The Reinvention of Nature* (New York: Routledge, 1991), pp. 149–181.

21. Max Dublin, *Future Hype: The Tyranny of Prophecy* (New York: Plume/Penguin, 1992), p. 101.

22. Timothy Druckrey, "Feedback to Immersion: Machine Culture to Neuromachines/Modernity to Postmodernity," in *Computer Graphics: Visual Proceedings*, Annual Conference Series (New York: The Association for Computing Machinery, Inc., 1993), p. 127.

23. N. Katherine Hayles, *How We Became Posthuman: Virtual Bodies in Cybernetics, Literature, and Informatics* (Chicago: University of Chicago Press, 1999).

24. "Virtual reality is two-way, interactive. It allows for interspecial, cybernetic, intergendered interactions: you can be a Weimaraner, a vacuum cleaner, a trumpet, a table. Previous 'identity bound' positions of race, class, ethnicity, age, and gender can be technologically transmuted. In virtual reality . . . men can be women, women can be men, and so forth." Anne Friedberg, *Window Shopping: Cinema and the Postmodern* (Berkeley: University of California Press, 1993), p. 145.

25. "The myth of spirit ends in the gathering of conscious life into unified being; that word we know today as Web. In the inevitable collision of these endpoints, a new teleology emerges, where being and doing collapse into a unified expression of will. For, at the end of time, all forces must converge."

Mark Pesce, "*Ontos* and *Techne*" (1997), <www.hyperreal.org/~mpesce/
oant.html>.

26. Pierre Lévy, *Collective Intelligence: Mankind's Emerging World in Cyberspace*,
p. 250. For more of this Teilhardian strain of vapor theory, see Jennifer J.
Cobb, *CyberGrace: The Search for God in the Digital World* (New York:
Crown, 1998).

27. Erik Davis, *Techgnosis: Myth, Magic, and Mysticism in the Age of Information*
(New York: Harmony Books, 1998), pp. 297–298.

28. Northrup Frye, *The Anatomy of Criticism: Four Essays* (New York: Athenaeum,
1970), p. 88.

29. These are generalities, of course, as academic presses do regularly publish
timely and free-flowing work on new media and magazines such as *Mute* and
*Artbyte* do offer sustained, if not entirely systematic, readings of digital
cultures.

30. Kevin Kelly and Gary Wolf, "Kill Your Browser," *Wired* 5.03 (March, 1997):
12–23. For an autopsy of the object of their enthusiasm, see Greg Miller,
"Cyberspace: When 'Push' Technology Came to Shove, Mailing Lists
Emerged as the Winner," *Los Angeles Times*, May 31, 1999: C4.

31. Howard Rheingold, *The Virtual Community: Homesteading on the Electronic
Frontier* (New York: HarperPerennial, 1993), p. 264.

32. Subscription information is available at each list's Web site/archive:
<www.nettime.org>, <www.thing.net>, <www.rhizome.org>.

33. Jordan Crandall, "Hot List," *Artforum* XXXVI, no. 7 (March, 1998): 20.

34. One episode saw false postings attributed to hypertext author Mark Amerika,
critic Tim Druckrey and artist Peter Weibel. See Matthew Mirapaul, "arts@
large: War of the Words: Ersatz E-Mail Tilts at Art," *CyberTimes: The New
York Times on the Web* (January 29, 1998), <www.nytimes.com/library/
cyber/mirapaul/010898mirapaul.html>.

35. Media activists Geert Lovink from Holland and Pit Schultz from Germany
founded <nettime> as "an attempt to formulate an international, networked
discourse, which promotes neither the dominant euphoria (in order to sell
some product), nor to continue the cynical pessimism, spread by journalists
and intellectuals working in the 'old' media, who can still make general
statements without any deeper knowledge on the specific communication
aspects of the so-called 'new' media." From the nettime archive home page,
<www.nettime.org>.

36. This correspondence can be found at <www.nettime.org>.

37. The question of the repurposing of Net discourse is very much an open one.
The nettime ZKP collections on newsprint have captured the list's spirit
quite well, as has the collection group-authored by nettime, *ReadMe! ASCII*

*Culture and the Revenge of Knowledge* (Brooklyn: Autonomedia, 1999). Another good volume collects Re:Wired posts, and is edited by moderator David Hudson, in association with eLine Productions: *Rewired: A Brief (and Opinionated) Net History* (Indianapolis, IN: Macmillan Technical Publishing, 1997). S. Paige Baty, *e-male trouble: love & addiction @ the matrix* (Austin University of Texas Press, 1999) is an intriguing book of theory in electronic epistolary form. On the other hand, as noted earlier, the transcriptions of Taylor and Saarinen's e-mail correspondence in *Imagologies* did not work.

## Chapter 4

1. Theodor Holm Nelson, *Literary Machines* [version 90.1] (Sausalito, CA: Mindful Press, 1990), p. 0/2.

2. Although the critical literature on hypertext, both in print and in electronic journals like *Postmodern Culture*, is now too vast to list adequately here, three comprehensive studies with extensive bibliographies are: George P. Landow, *Hypertext 2.0: The Convergence of Contemporary Critical Theory and Technology.* (Baltimore: Johns Hopkins University Press, 1997); Jay David Bolter, *Writing Space: The Computer, Hypertext, and the History of Writing* (Hillsdale, NJ: Lawrence Erlbaum, 1991); and Richard A. Lanham, *The Electronic Word: Democracy, Technology, and the Arts* (Chicago: University of Chicago Press, 1994).

3. See Roland Barthes, *S/Z* (New York: Hill and Wang, 1974).

4. David Kippen, "We Have Seen the Future and It Beeps," *Los Angeles Times Book Review*, August 29, 1993; Robert Coover, "Hyperfiction: Novels for the Computer," *New York Times Book Review*, August 29, 1993.

5. Stuart Moulthrop, *Victory Garden*, introduction by Michael Joyce and J. Yellowlees Douglas (Watertown, MA: Eastgate Systems, 1993).

6. Peter Schwenger, "*Agrippa*, or the Apocalyptic Book," in Mark Dery, ed., *Flame Wars: The Discourse of Cyberculture* (Durham, NC: Duke University Press, 1994), p. 61.

7. Cited in Matthew Mirapaul, "arts@large: Hypertext Fiction on the Web: Unbound From Convention," *CyberTimes: The New York Times on the Web* (June 26, 1997), <www.nytimes.com/library/cyber/mirapaul/062697mirapaul.html>.

8. Marshall McLuhan, *The Gutenberg Galaxy: The Making of Typographic Man* (Toronto: University of Toronto Press, 1986 [orig. 1962]), p. 22.

9. My comments here do not concern the culture of business, in which the text of the memo and the spreadsheet, either on paper and on screen, reigns supreme.

10. "In watching a film, the spectator submits to a programmed temporal form. Under normal viewing circumstances, the film absolutely controls the order, frequency, and duration of the presentation of events. You cannot skip a dull spot or linger over a rich one, jump back to an earlier passage or start at the end of the film and work forward." David Bordwell, *Narration and the Fiction Film* (Madison: University of Wisconsin Press, 1985), p. 74. There are, of course, the transitional technologies of video and the video cassette recorder, and even more so the instantly accessible storage and playback capabilities of the laserdisc and the DVD. I will not take up these issues here, though I can suggest Sean Cubbitt, *Time Shift: On Video Culture* (London: Routledge, 1991) as a place to begin such an investigation.

11. Information design guru Edward Tufte does not hide his preference: "the printed page allows *readers* to control the order and pace of the flow of information . . . unlike the fixed one-dimensional ordering imposed by the rush of voice with video" [emphasis in the original]. Edward Tufte, *Visual Explanations: Images and Quantities, Evidence and Narrative* (Cheshire, CT: Graphics Press, 1997), p. 145.

12. Just about the only legible text added to NTSC broadcast signals have been in entirely separate fields: closed captioning for the deaf and translations into languages other than that on the soundtrack. These appear in offset boxes and very large fonts. Their user populations had been woefully underserved before this technology filled that gap, efficiently if not elegantly. Although I concentrate here on NTSC, PAL and SECAM (the other two major world standards) are not appreciably better in regard to text delivery. The manufacturers of high-definition television (HDTV) promise far better text quality, but the manufacturers of HDTV promise many, many things, few of which have yet materialized.

13. A. Michael Noll offers solid explanations of all the technical issues covered so briefly here in *Television Technology: Fundamentals and Future Prospects* (Norwood, MA: Artech House, 1988). He discusses the failures of videotext in *Highway of Dreams: A Critical View Along the Information Superhighway* (Mahwah, NJ: Erlbaum, 1997).

14. The development of WebTV and other Internet set-top-box service providers that use the television monitor as their delivery mechanism has begun to effect convergence between the two technologies, but few users would deny that it is still far preferable to read on a computer monitor.

15. This movement from the page to the screen has not been without its concomitant translation problems.

The incursion into the trade of engineers and computer scientists has aggravated what was already a situation of uncertainty and imprecision. For example, the term "font" (or "fount") has a long history of use in letterpress printing, denoting a set of types at a definite size, for a definite purpose and for the founder's type—measured by weight. In its transfer to the new technologies and its appropriation by those outside the old trade, "font" has come to refer rather to the style of letterform, without regard to size. In the dematerialization of typography, "leading" has lost its sense of "strips of lead" (precisely measured) and come to mean—very vaguely—the space between rows of words.

Robin Kinross, *Modern Typography: An Essay in Critical History* (London: Hyphen Press, 1992), p. 141.

16. The closest the piano can mimic the continuity of string instruments is with a glissando, a sliding effect achieved by sounding a series of adjacent tones in rapid succession.

17. Niels Bohr, "On the Constitution of Atoms and Molecules," in *Collected Works: Volume 2: Works on Atomic Physics (1912–1917)*, Leon Rosenfeld, general ed., Ulrich Hoyer, ed. (Amsterdam: North-Holland Publishing Company, 1996), pp. 159–234. P. A. M. Dirac, "The Quantum Theory of the Electron, Part II," in *The Collected Works of P.A.M. Dirac, 1924–1948*, R. H. Dalitz, ed. (Cambridge: Cambridge University Press, 1995), p. 323.

18. In *Hypertext 2.0*, George Landow offers a typology of linkages, useful to both hypertext authors and users. His categories include "Lexia to Lexia Unidirectional," "Lexia to Lexia Bidirectional," "String (word or phrase) to Lexia," "String to String," "One-to-Many," "Many-to-One Linking," and "Typed Links," pp. 11–20.

19. Susan Stewart, *On Longing: Narratives of the Miniature, the Gigantic, the Souvenir, the Collection* (Durham: Duke University Press, 1993), p. 43.

20. Marshall McLuhan, cited by Eric McLuhan, "Aphorisms," in Paul Benedetti and Nancy DeHart, eds., *On McLuhan: Forward through the Rearview Mirror* (Cambridge, MA: MIT Press, 1997), p. 45. The younger McLuhan's comments on his father's style are worth quoting in depth:

My father decided in the sixties that he would try as much as he could to present his ideas in an aphoristic style. Aphorisms, as Francis Bacon said, are incomplete, a bit like cartoons. They are not filled-out essay writing that is highly compressed. The aphorism is a poetic form that calls for a lot of participation on the part of the reader. You have to chew on an aphorism and work with it for a while before you understand it fully. A good aphorism could keep you busy for a week—kicking it around, playing with it, exploring it, taking it apart to see what you can get out of it . . . the aphoristic style gives you the opportunity to get a dialogue going, to engage people in the process of discovery.

21. Gregory Ulmer, "Grammatology Hypermedia," *Postmodern Culture*, 1, n. 2 (January, 1991), <jefferson.village.virginia.edu/pmc/text-only/issue.191/ulmer. 191>. The definitive monograph on the *mise en abyme* is Lucien Dällenbach, *The Mirror in the Text*, trans. Jeremy Whiteley with Emma Hughes (Chicago: University of Chicago Press, 1989).

22. Michael Heim, *Electronic Language: A Philosophical Study of Word Processing*, second edition, with a foreword by David Gelernter (New Haven: Yale University Press, 1999), p. 224.

## Chapter 5

1. Luciano Canfora, *The Vanished Library: A Wonder of the Ancient World*, trans. Martin Ryle (Berkeley: University of California Press, 1990), p. 20.

2. On writing as a technology of textual reproduction, see Walter Ong, *Orality and Literacy: The Technologizing of the Word* (New York: Routledge, 1982), p. 82.

3. La Croix du Main, *Les Cents Buffets pour dresser une bibliotheque parfaite* (1583), cited in Michel Foucault, *The Order of Things: An Archaeology of the Human Sciences* (New York: Vintage, 1970), p. 38.

4. "Caverns Measureless to Man: An Interview with Xanadu Founder Ted Nelson by John Perry Barlow," *Mondo 2000* 4 (1991): 138. In a more measured moment, Nelson defined Xanadu as a "distributed repository scheme for worldwide electronic publishing." Theodor Holm Nelson, "Summary of the Xanadu™ Hypertext System," in Victor J. Vitanza, ed., *CyberReader* (Boston: Allyn and Bacon, 1996), pp. 295–298. For his early thinking on these issues, see the 1972 paper, "As We Will Think," reprinted in James M. Nyce and Paul Kahn, eds., *From Memex to Hypertext: Vannevar Bush and the Mind's Machine*, pp. 245–260.

5. Oliver Wendell Holmes, "Stereoscopy and the Stereograph" [orig. 1859], excerpted in Vicki Goldberg, ed., *Photography in Print: Writings from 1816 to the Present* (New York: Touchstone, 1981), p. 113.

6. Donald Preziosi, *Rethinking Art History: Meditations on a Coy Science* (New Haven: Yale University Press, 1989), p. 209, n. 83. This triumph of the representation over the object is not restricted to the profession of art history, as noted in chapter 2. Any painter, sculptor, or even photographer who has been forced to submit slides to a call for work can attest to the primacy of the representation.

7. Remember that the "photorealistic" graphic and the digital photograph are compositionally indistinguishable from each other, as they are at base simply representations of binary pairs: yes/no, 0/1, on/off.

8. As Douglas Crimp points out, this contextualization of photography within art history is in and of itself a recent phenomenon. "Photography was invented in 1839, but it was only *discovered* in the 1960s and 1970s—photography that is as an essence, photography *itself*" [emphasis in the original]. Douglas Crimp, "The Museum's Old, the Library's New Subject," in *On the Museum's Ruins* (Cambridge: MIT Press, 1993), p. 74.

9. This is not, of course, to intimate that this is the first time such a theorization has been called for. In the keynote address to the 1978 National Conference of the Society for Photographic Education, A. D. Coleman demanded that those interested in the theorization of photography come to grips with what he then saw as its inevitable transformation in the electronic age. "Since much of the tradition of photography—in educational, historical, and critical terms—is based upon the silver negative and the silver print, extensive revision of our premises in these regards will be necessary, as will the development of comparable understandings of such likely replacements as magnetic and/or electronic films and paper." A. D. Coleman, "No Future for You? Speculations on the Next Decade in Photography Education," in *Light Readings: A Photographic Critic's Writings 1968–1978* (New York: Oxford University Press, 1979), p. 272

10. "A science that studies the signs within society is conceivable; it would be a part of social psychology and consequently of general psychology; I call it semiology (from the Greek semion 'sign'). Semiology would show what constitutes signs, what laws govern them. Since the science does not yet exist, no one can say what it would be; but it has a right to existence, a place staked out in advance." Ferdinand de Saussure, *Course on General Linguistics*, trans. Wade Baskin (New York: McGraw Hill, 1966 [orig. 1915]), p. 16.

11. Roland Barthes, "The Photographic Image," in *Image, Music, Text*, trans. Stephen Heath (New York: Hill and Wang, 1977), p. 16.

12. Ibid., p. 17.

13. Rick Altman, *The American Film Musical* (Bloomington: University of Indiana Press, 1987), p. 10.

14. William J. Mitchell, *The Reconfigured Eye: Visual Truth in the Post-Photographic Era* (Cambridge: MIT Press, 1992), p. 4.

15. Ibid., p. 5.

16. Peter Wollen, *Signs and Meanings in the Cinema* (Bloomington: Indiana University Press, 1972), p. 120.

17. *The Collected Papers of Charles Saunders Peirce: Volume II*, Charles Hartshorne and Paul Weiss, eds. (Cambridge: Harvard University Press, 1931), p. 159.

18. While I here point to the debt that the discourse of semiotics bears to photography, Victor Burgin stresses the importance of a science of signs to a theory of photography. Structuralist semiotics "demonstrated that there is no single signifying system upon which all photographs depend (in the sense in which all texts in English ultimately depend upon the English language); there is, rather, a heterogeneous complex of codes upon which photography may draw." Victor Burgin, "Re-reading *Camera Lucida*," in *The End of Art Theory: Criticism and Postmodernity* (Atlantic Highlands, NJ: Humanities Press International, 1986), p. 72.

19. Hollis Frampton, "Digressions on the Photographic Agony," in *Circles of Confusion: Film, Photography, Video: Texts 1968–1980* (Rochester: Visual Studies Workshop Press, 1983), p. 190.

20. Gisèle Freund, *Photography & Society* (Boston: David R. Godine, 1980), p. 178.

21. Ibid.

22. Walter Benjamin, "The Work of Art in the Age of Mechanical Reproduction," in *Illuminations*, Hannah Arendt, ed., trans. Harry Zohn. (New York: Schocken, 1969), pp. 217–251, pp. 220–221.

23. Douglas Crimp, "The Photographic Activity of Postmodernism," in *On the Museum's Ruins* p. 124.

24. Abigail Solomon-Godeau, "Photography after Art Photography," in *Photography at the Dock: Essays on Photographic History, Institutions, and Practices* (Minneapolis: University of Minnesota Press, 1991), p. 113.

25. Abigail Solomon-Godeau, "Playing in the Fields of the Image," in *Photography at the Dock: Essays on Photographic History, Institutions, and Practices* (Minneapolis: University of Minnesota Press, 1991), p. 87.

26. Holmes, "Stereoscopy and the Stereograph," p. 101.

27. Jonathan Crary, *Techniques of the Observer: On Vision and Modernity in the Nineteenth Century* (Cambridge: MIT Press, 1990), p. 13.

28. This determination brings with it the corollary question: If one of the effects of photography was the development of semiotics, will electronic imaging bring about an equivalent theoretical shift?

29. In a short study of the film, Scott Bukatman observes that *Blade Runner* is "all about vision." Scott Bukatman, *Blade Runner* (London: British Film Institute, 1997), p. 7. *Blade Runner*'s visual style has prompted critics to acknowledge it as an exemplary postmodern object of study. See Guiliana Bruno, "Ramble City: Postmodernism and *Blade Runner*," *October* 41 (Summer 1987): 61–74.

30. Two articles in *Camera Obscura* 27 (September, 1991), offer psychoanalytic readings of this scene. Elsa Marder, "*Blade Runner*'s Moving Still": 89–107; Kaja Silverman, "Back to the Future": 109–132.

31. Legrady has since repurposed the work as a CD-ROM project. The CD-ROM was included, along with an artist's statement. The quotation is taken from George Legrady, "Slippery Traces: Three Lines of Pursuit," in *Artintact* 3, Astrid Sommer, ed. (Karhlsruhe: Zentrum für Kunst und Medientechnologie, 1996), p. 101.

32. Although there are production notes referring to the Esper, it was never identified as such in the original release print. See "The Esper" in Paul M. Sammon, *Future Noir: The Making of Blade Runner* (New York: HarperCollins, 1996), pp. 145–147. In this fantasy of omniscience, the Esper can almost be read as director Scott's homage to Michelangelo Antonioni's *Blowup* (1966), a film in which the protagonist repeatedly enlarges a single negative that impossibly maintains enough detail to identify a possible crime.

## Chapter 6

1. Beastie Boys, "Get It Together," from the album *Ill Communication* (Los Angeles: Capitol Records, 1994).

2. Martin Heidegger, "The Origin of the Work of Art," in *Poetry, Language, Thought*, trans. Albert Hofsteadter (New York: Harper and Row, 1975), p. 33.

3. The nostalgia for the future discussed in chapter 3 impels me to note that as cable modems and other high speed connections from the home to the Internet proliferate, the dial tone's aural reminder of the Web's debt to telephony will fade away.

4. See Gregory Ulmer, *Teletheory: Grammatology in the Age of Video* (New York: Routledge, 1989), pp. 15–16, and *Heuretics: The Logic of Invention* (Baltimore: Johns Hopkins, 1994). For a discussion on the euretics/heuretics methodology, see the series of Re/Inter/Views between Victor J. Vitanza and Greg Ulmer archived at the Pretext Site: <jefferson.village.virginia.edu/~spoons/pretext/reinvw.html>.

5. An extensive database of historical information about the World Wide Web, its history, and its development is maintained at <www.w3.org/pub/WWW/>. Brian Winston, *Media, Technology and Society: A History: From the Telegraph to the Internet* (London: Routledge, 1998), challenges the rhetoric of "revolution" invoked in most discussions of the Web by contextualizing its development in a larger narrative history of more than a century of communications media.

6. That egalitarianism of text is a proposition not without its detractors, of course, for text-only or text-heavy environments tends to favor native speakers and those with a gift for writing (an obvious advantage). With the Internet's international community often forced to use a single language, and with that single language being English for the most part, the text environment can be seen as yet another facet of Anglo-American digital hegemony.

7. Portions of this section were taken from an earlier text co-written with Ken Goldberg.

8. Edmund White, *Marcel Proust* (New York: Viking, 1999), p. 111.

9. Carolyn Marvin, *When Old Technologies Were New: Thinking About Communications in the Late Nineteenth Century* (New York: Oxford University Press, 1988), pp. 209–231.

10. "Painting was treated as a functional task and the good painter was recognised, for instance, by the fact that he ordered his works from a carpenter, giving his specifications on the phone." Alexander Partens, "Dada Art," in Richard Huelsenbeck, ed., *The Dada Almanac*, trans. Malcolm Green (London: Atlas Press, 1993 [orig. 1920]). p. 95. *N.B.* "Alexander Partens" was a pseudonym for Tristan Tzara, Hans Arp, and Walter Serner.

11. Lázló Moholy-Nagy, *The New Vision and Abstract of an Artist* (New York: Wittenborn, 1947), p. 79. It is uncertain whether or not Moholy-Nagy, who was in Berlin in 1920, read Partens's "Dada Art" in Huelsenbeck's *Almanac*. There is also a dispute whether Moholy-Nagy did ever actually call in the *Telephonbilder*. Lucia Moholy claims that they are, in fact, apocryphal. Lucia Moholy, *Marginalien zu Moholy-Nagy—Moholy-Nagy Marginal Notes* (Krefeld, 1972), p. 76. An attempt to syncretize the various claims and denials is found in Louis Kaplan, "The Telephone Paintings: Hanging Up Moholy," *Leonardo* 26, no. 2 (April 1993): 165–168.

12. See "Art by Telephone," record-catalogue of the show, Museum of Contemporary Art, Chicago, 1969. I gleaned much from Eduardo Kac, "Aspects of the Aesthetics of Telecommunications," in John Grimes and Gray Lorig, eds., *SIGGRAPH Visual Proceedings* (New York: ACM, 1992), pp. 47–57, <ekac.org/Telecom.Paper.Siggrap.html>. Also see Derrick De Kerckhove, "Communication Arts for a New Spatial Sensibility (Technological Extensions of Our Minds via Radio, Telephone and Computers)," *Leonardo* 24, no. 2 (April 1991): 131–5. In that same issue of *Leonardo*, Carl Eugene Loeffler and Roy Ascott offer a useful "Chronology and Working Survey of Select Telecommunications Activity": 236–240.

13. Maurice Tuchman, *A Report on the Art and Technology Program of the Los Angeles County Museum of Art* (Los Angeles: Los Angeles County Museum of Art, 1971), p. 56.

14. For an example, see Allen S. Bridge, *Apology Magazine: The National Confession* 2 (October 1995).

15. As for other telecommunications media art, there is On Kawara's series of "I am still alive" telegrams, which he has sent out on and off since 1970. The fax brought on its own art projects, like 1982's *The World in 24 Hours* and pARTiciFAX in 1984. Further hybrids between point-to-point communications and visualization technologies include the closed-circuit television happenings of the '60s and early '70s that Nam June Paik participated in, video letters between artists, and Kit Galloway and Sherry Rabinowitz's famed *Hole in Space* project between New York and Los Angeles in 1979 (which established the still extant Electronic Cafe International).

16. The piece itself was titled *Objects of the Dealer (with Speakers)*; see David Pagel, "Musical Chairs," *frieze* 25 (November-December, 1995): 42–43.

17. Ian Pollock and Janet Silk's "Local 411" ran from January 20 to February 17, 1997 in San Francisco.

18. Michael Coughlan and Jory Felice, *Telephone*, catalogue for the show of the same name (Los Angeles: Works on Paper, 1998), np.

19. The linkages between film and art practice are simply too numerous to list here. One place to start is the catalogue of the show *Hall of Mirrors: Art and Film Since 1945*, organized by Kerry Brougher at the Museum of Contemporary Art, Los Angeles, in 1996, edited by Russell Ferguson and published by the museum and the Monacelli Press, New York. On radio, see Douglas Kahn and Gregory Whitehead, eds., *Wireless Imagination: Sound, Radio, and the Avant-Garde* (Cambridge: MIT Press, 1992). Michael Renov and Erika Suderburg, eds., *Resolutions: Contemporary Video Practice* (Minneapolis: University of Minnesota Press, 1996) is a collection on the intersections of video technologies and art practice. The linkages between art and television are less compellingly argued but present nonetheless. Recent manifestations include Joshua Decter, "Deliver Me into Reality? (Or It's All There on TV, Theoretically)," *art/text* 54 (May, 1996): 42–43 and the decidedly minor Bernard Welt, *Mythomania: Fantasies, Fables, and Sheer Lies in Contemporary American Popular Art* (Los Angeles: Art issues. Press, 1996).

20. See chapter 9 for more on the *gesamtkunstwerk*.

21. Ray Johnson's mail art of the 1950s and '60s is obviously a derivative of the Exquisite Corpse, as was Craig Ede's *Exquisite Fax* of the 1980s. A comic book based on the theme was edited by Art Speigelman and R. Sikoryak, *The Narrative Corpse: A Chain Story by 69 Artists* (New York and Richmond, VA: Raw Books and Gates of Heck, 1995); The Drawing Center in New York organized a major show of collaborative work entitled *The Return of the Cadavre Exquis* in 1993. Finally, there is a Web site directly titled *Exquisite*

*Corpse Artsite*, organized by Jager Di Paola Kemp design, <www.jdk.com/corpse/corpsefra.htm >.

22. <math240.lehman.cuny.edu/art>.

23. André Breton, "Against the Liquidators," in *What Is Surrealism? Selected Writings*, edited and introduced by Franklin Rosemont (New York: Monad Press, 1978), p. 352. Breton is, of course, recasting Lautréamont's maxim: "Poetry must be made by all, not by one."

24. <ziris.syr.edu/ChainReaction/public_html/chainReaction.html>.

25. See, for example, the now defunct Collaborative Internet Art Online (CIAO) project formerly housed at <www.dcs.qmw.ac.uk/~andrewn/pages/research/ciao.htm>, which similarly left its precepts almost entirely unexamined.

26. <www.diacenter.org/km>.

27. See *Painting by Numbers: Komar and Melamid's Scientific Guide to Art*, JoAnn Wypijewski, ed. (New York: Farrar Straus Giroux, 1997). *Most Wanted* began in 1994 as an off-line project. The artists hired the Nation Institute, an opinion polling firm, to conduct a professional survey, the results of which Komar and Melamid used for the first paintings. The Dia Foundation then invited the artists to move the project onto the Web. As Andrew Ross noted of the offline version, in this post–Cold War, one-worldist survey, both the American and the Russian results are strikingly similar, with a contemplative Jesus taking the place of the heroic Washington in the Russian version. Andrew Ross, "Poll Stars," *Artforum* XXXIII, no. 5 (January 1995): 72–77, 109.

28. See Peter Wollen, "Morbid Symptoms: Komar and Melamid," in *Raiding the Icebox: Reflections on Twentieth Century Culture* (Bloomington: Indiana University Press, 1993), pp. 176–189.

29. The *Cybervato* site was set up in conjunction with "The Shame Man and El Mexican't Meet the Cybervato," a performance/installation by Guillermo Gómez-Peña, Roberto Sifuentes, and James Luna at the Satellite Gallery of the Rice University Art Gallery in 1995: *<www.ruf.rice.edu/~ruag/95F/CyberVato/>*. The text accompanying the Techno-Ethno-Graphic Profile reads as follows:

The following questionnaire, conducted by experimental Chicano anthropologists, attempts to survey the inter cultural [sic] desires and artistic concerns of the Internet users. The results will be utilized as source of inspiration for a series of performances and 'living dioramas' currently taking place at 'DiverseWorks,' Houston. Please answer the questions as fully as possible, and if you prefer not to identify yourself it's fine. Carnales, we are looking for innovative ways to utilize this technology.

30. The artist has informed me that Tebroc's comments refer to an earlier version of project, entitled *Virtual Concrete*, and that she has since solved the rendering issues about which he complains. Victoria Vesna, *Bodies© INCorporated* <www.arts.ucsb.edu/bodiesinc>.

31. Sol LeWitt, "Sentences on Conceptual Art," in Ellen H. Johnson, ed., *American Artists on American Art: From 1940 to 1980* (New York: Harper & Row, 1982), p. 126. August Sander,

32. *August Sander: Citizens of the Twentieth Century: Portrait Photographs, 1892–1952*, Gunther Sander, ed., text by Ulrich Keller, trans. Linda Keller (Cambridge, MA: MIT Press, 1986). Douglas Huebler, *Crocodile Tears: (Brief Fictions Re-Sounding from the Proposal in Variable Piece #70:1971 "To Photographically Document the Existence of Everyone Alive")* (Buffalo, NY: Albright-Knox Art Gallery; CEPA Gallery, 1985).

33. "Ljubljana interview with Heath Bunting," posted by Josephine Bosma to <nettime>, June 11, 1998. <www.nettime.org>.

34. The activities of the Fluxus movement in the 1960s and the concurrent development of mail art can be seen as precursors to net.art, as these earlier movements shared an interest in communication and creativity across national borders and continental divides. See Andreas Huyssen, "Back to the Future: Fluxus in Context," in the catalogue *In the Spirit of Fluxus*, Janet Jenkins, ed. (Minneapolis: Walker Art Center, 1993), pp. 142–151.

35. I discuss the evanescent, performative qualities of digital media in "Screen Grabs: The Digital Dialectic and New Media Theory," in *The Digital Dialectic: New Essays on New Media*, pp. xiv–xxi.

36. Susan Kandel, "jodi.org," in Gilda Williams, ed., *Cream: Contemporary Art in Culture* (London: Phaidon, 1998), p. 209.

37. The Web's visible coding is different from that of the cinema, in which the frames are not visible when the film is running, and from that of video, in which the analog signal on the tape is never visible through the same equipment as the sound-image matrix.

## Chapter 7

1. Hollis Frampton, "Digressions on the Photographic Agony," *Circles of Confusion: Film, Photography, Video: Texts 1968–1980* (Rochester, NY: Visual Studies Workshop Press, 1983), p. 179.

2. Sherry Turkle, *Psychoanalytic Politics: Jacques Lacan and Freud's French Revolution* (New York: The Guilford Press, 1992), p. xxvi. See also her *Life on the Screen: Identity in the Age of the Internet* (New York: Simon & Schuster, 1995) and *The Second Self: Computers and the Human Spirit* (New York: Simon & Schuster, 1984).

3. My thinking here has been greatly influenced by Susan Kandel's analysis of "theoreticism," the pejorative adjective hurled by certain high theorists at those they saw as encroaching on their own, sacred grounds. See "Theory as Phantom Text: Plundering Smithson's Non-Sites," in Alex Coles and Richard Bentley, eds., *de-, dis-, ex-*, Volume 1 (London: BACKless Books, 1996), pp. 84–92.

4. Brenda Laurel, *Computers as Theater* (Reading, MA: Addison-Wesley, 1991), p. 161. Like so many other imaging technologies, the military was the father of VR, and it were not at all driven to develop these systems for ludic reasons. Thus it was that flight simulators were the earliest influential VR systems. These simulators combined the replication of an actual space, that of the cockpit, with the graphic simulation on large screens of the exterior phenomena of the take-off and landings. This mix of real and virtual space has been superseded by systems that create a more seamless sense of computer-generated "cyberspace" by cutting the user off from real space.

5. The Hollywood treatment of VR, from *Lawnmower Man* (Brett Leonard, 1992) to *The Matrix* (Larry and Andrew Wachowski, 1999), tends to use some flavor of the HMD and the body suit as icons of virtuality, and though these particular interfaces to virtual systems are not the only ones, nor even necessarily always the most efficient, this configuration is nonetheless the best known and, at risk of oversimplifying, I will concentrate my analyses on them. Also, under the constraints of (publishing) space, I have not included a discussion of aural interfaces in VR, though the developing virtual 3D audio systems deserve attention in their own right.

6. Regina Cornwall, "Where Is the Window: Virtual Reality Technologies Now," *Artscribe* 85 (January-February 1991): 56–59; Howard Rheingold, "The Wildest Dreams of Virtual Reality," *M* (March 1992): 84–89, p. 87.

7. Chitra Shriram claimed that participants at high-end techno-gatherings maintained the credo, "We are the chosen ones," as they waited for the messiah of VR. "Nano-Sex and Virtual Seduction" Panel, ACM-SIGGRAPH, 1993.

8. John Locke, *An Essay Concerning Human Understanding* Volume 2. J.W. Yolton, ed. (New York: Dutton, 1964), p. 2.

9. Chris Miller, "Change All," *Frame-Work: The Journal of Images and Culture* 6, no. 2 (Spring 1993): p. 20.

10. For a critical discussion of sexually oriented film and video, see Linda Williams, *Hardcore: Power, Pleasure, and the "Frenzy of the Visible"* (Berkeley: University of California Press, 1989).

11. Raymond Kurzweil, *The Age of Spiritual Machines: When Computers Exceed Human Intelligence* (New York: Viking, 1999), p. 147.

12. "The Cybersex 2 System," *Future Sex* 2 (1992): 28–31. Credits were listed as follows. Concept/Article: Mike Saenz; Graphic Design: Ken Holewczynski; 3D Modeling and Graphics: Mike Saenz and Norm Dwyer; Photos: Bill Weiss; Human Models: Hans and Madison.

13. Lisa Palac, "The Sugardaddy of Sexware," *Future Sex* 2 (1992): 22–26. In her autobiography, the editor gives the history this way: "In the spirit of parody, Saenz suggested we create our own phony VR sex gear and publish it in *Future Sex*. Give the people what they want!" Lisa Palac, *The Edge of the Bed: How Dirty Pictures Changed My Life* (Boston, MA: Little, Brown, 1998), p. 94.

14. Philip K. Dick, *The Divine Invasion*, in *The Valis Trilogy* (New York: BOMC, 1990, orig. 1981), p. 163.

15. Just as reassurance that *Future Sex*, a low-budget startup that barely lasted two years, was not alone, the international fashion magazine *Elle* assigned their first piece on VR to Susie Bright, a Tantric guru for women of all preferences, who wrote with great and unexamined verve about the promise of teledildonics. Susie Bright, "Sex in the Computer Age," *Elle* (February 1992): 56–62. Never one to miss out on a zeitgeist, Bright moved into the *camera rasa*, setting up a little booth in the corner with *Susie Bright's Sexual Reality: A Virtual Sex World Reader* (Pittsburgh, PA: Cleis Press, 1992).

16. Gaston Bachelard, *The Poetics of Space*, trans. Maria Jolas, with a new foreword by John R. Stilgoe (Boston: Beacon, 1994 [orig. 1958]), pp. 150, 161, 184, and 212.

17. Alton J. DeLong, "Phenomenological Space Time: Towards an Experiential Relativity," *Science* 213, no. 4508 (7 August 1981): 681–683.

18. See the chapter titled "Time-space Compression and the Postmodern Condition," in David Harvey, *The Condition of Postmodernity: An Enquiry into the Origins of Cultural Change* (Cambridge: Blackwell, 1989), pp. 284–307.

19. For a description of the environment, see Marcos Novak, "Dancing with the Virtual Dervish: Worlds in Progress," in Mary Anne Moser and Douglas MacLeod, eds. *Immersed in Technology: Art and Virtual Environments* (Cambridge, MA: MIT Press, 1996), pp. 303–308. Novak commented on Heim's experiences during the discussion that followed his presentation, "Transarchitecture," at ***mediawork*** 9, Special Focus on "Architecture & Imaging," MAK Center for Art and Architecture, Los Angeles, 1996.

## Chapter 8

1. TED 2, Monterey, CA, 1986.

2. While "user" is a descriptor taken from the discourses of computing in this context, it can serve to a subsume both the terms "inhabitant," with its connota-

tions of a stable relationship to a stable space, and "spectator," which implies too close a correspondence to the usual engagements with the televisual and cinematic.

3. See Werner Herzog's film *Fitzcarraldo* (1982) for the recreation of this act, and Les Blank's documentary *Burden of Dreams* (1982) for a study of Herzog's obsession to mimic the film's protagonist no matter what the odds.

4. Karen D. Stein, "Virtual Reality: D.E. Shaw & Co.'s Offices in New York City," *Architectural Record*, vol. 180 (June 1992): p. 116.

5. Steve Holl, "Locus Soulless," in *The End of Architecture?: Documents and Manifestos*, ed. Peter Noever (Munich: Prestel-Verlag, 1992), p. 39.

6. "The Center for Art and Media Technology," in Jacques Lucan, *OMA—Rem Koolhaas: Architecture 1970–1990* (New York: Princeton Architectural Press, 1991), p. 141.

7. *OMA—Rem Koolhaas Living, Vivre, Leben* (Berlin: Birkhauser, 1998), p. 92.

8. Ibid., p. 62.

9. Kristin Spense, "Electrotechture," *Wired* 1.4 (September/October 1993): 61. Also see Steven Perrella, ed., *Hypersurface Architecture, Architectural Design* 68, no. 5/6 (May-June 1998).

10. Yve-Alain Bois, "Painting: The Task of Mourning," in *Endgame: Reference and Simulation in Recent Painting and Sculpture*, David Joselit and Elizabeth Sussman, eds. (Cambridge, MA: MIT Press and the Institute of Contemporary Art, Boston, 1986), p. 29.

11. Lev Manovich, "Avantgarde, Cyberspace und die Architektur der Zukunft," in Stefan Iglhaut, Armin Medosch, and Florian Rötzer, eds., *Stadt am Netz. Ansichten von Telepolis* (Bollman Verlag, 1996), pp. 39–40. Manovich provided the original English manuscript, "Avant-Garde, Cyberspace, and Architecture of a Future," from which this quotation was taken.

12. Even architects are speaking this way. "General interest in tangible, three dimensional architectural creations is steadily decreasing. . . . Virtual space is becoming the sphere of activity for the life of the mind." Coop Himmelb(l)au, "The End of Architecture," in *The End of Architecture?: Documents and Manifestos*, ed. Peter Noever (Munich: Prestel-Verlag, 1992), p. 18.

13. The OED defines "scape" as a back formation from "landscape," meaning "a view of scenery of any kind."

14. See John Cheever's *Bullet Park: A Novel* (New York: Knopf, 1969) and *The Stories of John Cheever* (New York: Knopf, 1978); Richard Ford, *The Sportswriter* (New York: Vintage Books, 1986) and *Independence Day* (New York: A.A. Knopf, 1995).

15. In 1999 the Museum of Modern Art mounted "The Un-Private House," its first significant exploration of residential architecture since 1934. The exhibition showcased how contemporary architects like Stephen Holl, OMA-Rem Koolhaas, Shigeru Ban, and Diller + Scofidio are reconfiguring the home as a locus for both work and pleasure. Many of the projects were notable for their hybrid hardscapes and imagescapes, the result of the architects' engagement with digital technologies. Terence Riley, *The Un-Private House* (New York: Harry N. Abrams, 1999).

16. Patricia Leigh Brown, "Virtual Beach House: Sand, No Grit," *New York Times*, August 13, 1998.

17. K.C. Cole, "Mind Over Matter: From a Field of Metaphors, a Crop of Ideas May Sprout," *Los Angeles Times*, December 5, 1996: B2.

18. <www.fnal.gov/pub/top95/top95_tennis_balls.html>.

19. I have here condensed the racecourse argument, related in Aristotle's *Physics* 239b11–13, and the Achilles, related in Aristotle's *Physics* 239b15–18. This reflects the general conflation of these two into the rather fuzzily understood "Zeno's paradox" of popular imagination. For more on this literature, see Gregory Vlastos, "Zeno's Race Course," *Journal of the History of Philosophy* 4 (1966): 95–108, which includes an appendix on the Achilles.

20. William Gibson, *Neuromancer* (New York: Ace Books, 1984), p. 63.

21. Michael Benedikt, "Cyberspace: Some Proposals," in Michael Benedikt, ed., *Cyberspace: First Steps* (Cambridge, MA: MIT Press, 1991), p. 144.

22. Real numbers include rationals (integers and fractions) and irrationals (those numbers, like $\pi$, which cannot be represented as fractions).

23. *Powers of Ten* has served as an introduction to the notion of scale and exponentiality in science museums, classrooms and public television for years, and was remade in 1977 with the assistance of Philip Morrison. See Pat Kirkham, *Charles and Ray Eames: Designers of the Twentieth Century* (Cambridge, MA: MIT Press, 1995), pp. 350–354.

24. Fractal geometry, concepts of singularity, and the new sciences of complexity are obviously key issues here. For a model that accounts for these kinds of approaches, see the discussion of fractals, self-reflexivity, and the nature of scale as it applies to literary works in Peter Stoicheff, "The Chaos of Metafiction," in N. Katherine Hayles, ed., *Chaos and Order: Complex Dynamics in Literature and Science* (Chicago: University of Chicago Press, 1991), pp. 85–99. For an overview of the field, see N. Katherine Hayles, *Chaos Bound: Orderly Disorder in Contemporary Literature and Science* (Ithaca: Cornell University Press, 1990).

25. Myron Krueger, *Artificial Reality II* (Reading, MA: Addison-Wesley, 1991), p. 252.

26. As early as 1969 Krueger was working on interactive spaces like "Glowflow," at the Memorial Union Galley at the University of Wisconsin—a "kinetic environmental sculpture." Benjamin Wooley, *Virtual Worlds: A Journey in Hype and Hyperreality* (Cambridge: Blackwell, 1992), p. 141.

27. The SI was one of those pivotal avant-garde movements that inspired intense passions at the moment and devoted partisanship in those who have tried to interpret its legacy. In other words, nothing that anyone says about the SI is ever fully accepted, much less supported, by everyone interested in it.

28. Guy Debord, *The Society of the Spectacle*, trans. Donald Nicholson-Smith (New York: Zone Books, 1994), p. 24.

29. Greil Marcus, *Lipstick Traces: A Secret History of the Twentieth Century* (Cambridge, MA: Harvard University Press, 1989), p. 99.

30. Debord wrote his 1988 volume, *Comments on the Society of the Spectacle*, in defense against the accusation that he had invented the theory of the spectacle "out of thin air." In other words, Debord defended himself from the critique of indulging in the kind of science-fictionalized discourse discussed in chapter 3; "Real-Time Theory." He maintained that the quarter-century following the first volume had only proven his point. Guy Debord, *Comments on the Society of the Spectacle*, trans. Malcolm Imrie (New York: Verso, 1990), p. 3.

31. Thomas F. McDonough, "Situationist Space," *October* 67 (Winter 1994): 77.

32. "Definitions," in *Situationist International Anthology*, ed. and trans. Ken Knabb (Berkeley: Bureau of Public Secrets, 1981), pp. 45–46. The SI maintained that UU was first proposed in the Italian tract "Manifeste a favore dell'Urbanismo Unitario," which has been reprinted in Mirella, Bandini, *L'estetico il politico: Da Cobra all'Internationazionale situazionista, 1948–1957* (Rome: Officina Edizioni, 1977), p. 274. The SI's interest in UU was an outgrowth of the influences of Elisée Reclus's researches into "social geography." Reclus felt geography is best understood as "history in space" and that geography is "not an immutable thing. It is made, it is remade every day, at each instant, it is modified by men's actions." The SI followed these ideas through in their conception and propagation of UU. See McDonough, "Situationist Space," p. 66.

33. "Report on the Construction of Situations and on the International Situationist Tendency's Conditions of Organization and Action," [excerpts] in *Situationist International Anthology*, p. 23. Peter Wollen defines unitary urbanism as "the design of an experimental utopian city with changing zones for free play, whose nomadic inhabitants could collectively choose their own climate, sensory environment, organization of space, and so on," explicitly focusing on the speculative aspects of UU. Peter Wollen, "Bitter Victory:

The Art and Politics of the Situationist International," in Elisabeth Sussman, ed., *On the Passage of a Few People Through a Rather Brief Moment in Time: The Situationist International 1957–1972* (Cambridge, MA: MIT Press, 1989), p. 25.

34. Quoted in "The Seven Wired Wonders," *Wired* 1.6 (December 1993): p. 107.

35. As the earliest virtual systems were flight simulators that combined projections, hydraulics, and physical recreations of airplane cockpits, the retreat from the rarefied realms of disembodied cyberspace to the hybrid hardscape and digital facings is in some ways a return to the roots of virtuality. In 1953, VR pioneer Morton Helig theorized a cinema of the future that acknowledged this hybridity—including olfactory, taste, and tactile inputs as well as a wraparound screen with a visual aspect ratio greater than that of the human eye. This screen is described as curving "past the spectator's ears on both sides and beyond his sphere of vision above and below." Morton Helig, "El Cine del Futuro: The Cinema of the Future," *Presence* 1, no. 3 (Summer, 1992): 279–294. Helig first published the article in 1955 in *Espacio*, a Mexican architectural magazine.

36. Attila Kotányi and Raoul Vaneigem, "Elementary Program of the Bureau of Unitary Urbanism" (1961), in *Situationist International Anthology*, p. 66.

37. Little that is coming out of contemporary studios goes much further than the never materialized—a word already quaint to the ears—designs of Britain's Archigram. Ron Herron's collaged mock-up of "Instant City" (1969), with its integrated electronic messaging boards, large-screen displays and happy, energetic people surrounded by happy energetic phrases like "variable shelters, self pace, information screen, and urban servicing," offers up an appealing dream of a pop architecture that never was. See Dennis Crompton, ed., *A Guide to Archigram, 1961–74* (London: Academy Editions, 1994).

38. The titles and dates of the Christian Möller pieces discussed in this paragraph are as follows: *The Sound of Grass Growing* (1991), *Kinotoskop* (1991), and *Kinetic Light Sculpture of the Zeilgalerie* (1992).

39. Christian Möller, *Levels of Variable Visibility—Electronic Mirror I* (1993).

## Chapter 9

1. Raymond Bellour, "The Double Helix," in *Passages de l'image* (Barcelona: Fundació Caixa de Pensions, 1991), p. 58. Catalogue of the show of the same title curated by Raymond Bellour, Catherine David and Christine Van Assche. "The Double Helix" has been reprinted in Timothy Druckrey, ed., *Electronic Culture: Technology and Visual Representation* (New York: Aperture, 1996), pp. 173–199.

2. There is an obvious resonance with Frampton's pre-filmic photography here. For more on his photographic work of the early 1960s, and for a discussion of his continuing involvement with the medium even as he took up the cinema, see *Hollis Frampton: Recollections/Recreations*, Bruce Jenkins and Susan Krane, eds. (Cambridge, MA: MIT Press, 1984).

3. Also on the 1992 program were *Dino Tours Pilot* (Deborah Devgan), *Batman Returns Visual Effects* (Richard Hollander) and *MandelSplat* (Booker C. Bense). Every year, the Electronic Theater offers up new versions of these same old clichés.

4. Even those theorists who disavow the idea of the *gesamtkunstwerk* cannot help but invoke it in their discussions of experimental cinema. "[T]he avant-garde made itself felt late in the cinema and it is still very marginal, in comparison with painting or music or even writing. Yet, in a way, the cinema offers more opportunities than any other art—the cross-fertilization, so striking of those early decades, the reciprocal interlocking and input between painting, writing, music, theatre, could take place within the field of cinema itself. This is not a plea for a great harmony, a synesthetic *gesamtkunstwerk* in the Wagnerian sense. But cinema, because it is a multiple system, could develop and elaborate the semiotic shifts that marked the origins of the avant-garde in a uniquely complex way, a dialectical montage within and between a complex of codes." Peter Wollen, "The Two Avant-Gardes," in *Readings and Writings* (London: Verso, 1982), p. 104.

5. See, for example, the elegy David James offers for alternative cinematic practices when he speaks of "the termination of film's social urgency" by the 1980s in the "Afterword" to his book *Allegories of Cinema: American Film in the Sixties* (Princeton: Princeton University Press, 1989), p. 348.

6. How experimental video relates to digital media is obviously relevant to these questions, but I have chosen to concentrate on film in this chapter. For more on the relationship between video and digital media, see Michael Nash, "Vision After Television: Technocultural Convergence, Hypermedia, and the New Media Arts Field," in Michael Renov and Erika Suderburg, eds., *Resolutions: Contemporary Video Practices* (Minneapolis: University of Minnesota Press, 1996), pp. 382–399.

7. Gene Youngblood, *Expanded Cinema*, with an introduction by R. Buckminster Fuller (New York: E.P. Dutton & Co., 1970). Edward S. Small attempts to unify a notion of the avant-garde moving image matrix across media and platforms using the term "Experimental Film/Video" as an overarching category. Small's sub-categories include the European Avant-Garde, the American Avant-Garde, American Underground, Expanded Cinema (where he creates a sub-sub category for "Computer-generated Work") and Mini-

malist Structuralist. Edward S. Small, *Direct Theory: Experimental Film/Video as Major Genre* (Carbondale: Southern Illinois University UP, 1994), p. 81, fig. 5.1.

8. The classic collection is P. Adams Sitney, ed., *The Avant-Garde Film: A Reader of Theory and Criticism*, Anthology Film Archives Series: #3 (New York: New York University Press, 1978).

9. The best known of these interventions is no doubt Gregory Markopolous's demand to have the chapter on his work dropped from the second edition of P. Adams Sitney's comparative study *Visionary Film: The American Avant-Garde 1943–1978* (New York: Oxford University Press, 1979). See the "Preface to the Second Edition," pp. x–xi.

10. J. Hoberman, "After Avant-Garde Film," in Hal Wallis, ed., *Art After Modernism: Rethinking Representation* (Boston: David R. Godine, 1984), p. 66.

11. Harold Bloom, *A Map of Misreading* (New York: Oxford University Press, 1975).

12. Having garnered a public with books like *Junkie* [originally published under the pen-name William Lee and spelled as *Junky* (New York: Ace Books, 1953)] and *Naked Lunch* (New York: Grove Press, 1959), by the time Burroughs published *The Wild Boys: A Book of the Dead* (New York: Grove Press, 1971), he was considered past his prime.

13. See the catalogue of the first major show on Burroughs' contribution to and legacy within the visual arts, Robert A. Sobieszek, ed., *Ports of Entry: William S. Burroughs and the Arts* (Los Angeles: Los Angeles County Museum of Art and Thames and Hudson, 1996). There is a discussion (albeit partially inaccurate) of the Nova Convention in Ted Morgan, *Literary Outlaw: The Life and Times of William S. Burroughs* (New York: Henry Holt, 1988). My thanks to Sylvère Lotringer and Chris Kraus for setting the record straight for me in personal conversation.

14. Norman Klein, *The History of Forgetting: The Erasure of Memory in Los Angeles* (New York: Verso, 1997), p. 7.

15. The attention this chapter gives to the *Magellan* is atypical, as this cycle has never had the same kind of attention as earlier works like *Zorns Lemma* (1970) or *nostalgia* (1971). Scott MacDonald's dismissal is typical: "for all their visual and structural elegance, many of [*Magellan*'s] films seem somehow empty of the personal passion that, deflected or reconstituted, gives Frampton's best early work its power." Scott MacDonald, "Hollis Frampton," in *A Critical Cinema: Interviews with Independent Filmmakers* (Berkeley: University of California Press, 1988), pp. 21–77.

16. "Unfinished Business," in Peter Lunenfeld, ed., *The Digital Dialectic: New Essays on New Media* (Cambridge: MIT Press, 1999).

17. Cited in Brian Henderson, "Propositions for the Explorations of Frampton's *Magellan*," *October* 32 (Spring 1985): 131.
18. Coined by Intel founder Gordon Moore, the law posits that computer processing speeds will double every 18 months or less (and that the price/power ratio will follow suit).
19. This is not to ignore the fact that there are indeed debates within film studies about what constitutes the "proper" text nor to discount the proliferation of letter-boxed video versions, filmic restorations and director's cuts. I simply note that digital media push this debate to its limits.
20. There is no ur-text of the *Magellan Cycle;* there are differing schedules, orders and ways of viewing it. I can comment definitively only on the cycle as I saw it in Los Angeles in the summer of 1997 as programmed by filmmaker Thom Andersen. Andersen broke the cycle into six distinct programs, screened over succeeding weeks to give a sense of the duration for which Frampton had planned. Yet Andersen freely admits that there innumerable other ways to present the cycle. The *Magellan Cycle* as Andersen programmed it follows:

**First Program**
*The Birth of Magellan:*
   *Cadenzas I* (1977–80, 6 min)
   *Mindfall I* (1977–80, 21 min)
   *Matrix [First Dream]* (1977–79, 28 min)
   *Mindfall VII* (1977–80, 21 min)
   *Cadenzas XIV* (1977–80, 6 min)

**Second Program**
   *Palindrome [Second Dream]* (1969, 22 min)
   *Public Domain* (1972, 14 min)
   *Noctiluca [Magellan's Toys No. 1]* (1974, 3 1/2 min)
   *Straits of Magellan: Drafts and Fragments [Panopticons]* (51 min)

**Third Program**
   *Solariumagelani: Summer Solstice* (1974, 32 min)
   *Ingenium Nobis Ipsa Puella Fecit* (formerly *Vernal Equinox*) (1974, 62 min)

**Fourth Program**
   *Solariumagelani: Autumn Equinox* (1974, 27 min)
   *Solariumagelani: Winter Solstice* (1974, 33 min)

**Fifth Program**
> *Magellan at the Gates of Death:*
> *The Red Gate* (1976, 54 min)
> *The Green Gate* (1976, 52 min)

**Sixth Program**
Films from the Final Day of the Cycle and Studies for Magellan:
> *A&B in Ontario* (1967/84, 16 min)
> *Pas de Trois* (1975, 5 min)
> *Apparatus Sum [Studies for Magellan #1]* (1972, 3 min)
> *Procession* (1976, 4 min)
> *Otherwise Unexplained Fires [Memoranda Magelani]* (1976, 14 min)
> *Yellow Springs [Magellan: Vanishing Point: #1] [Pares Magelani]* (1972, 5 min)
> *Quarternion [Pares Magelani]* (1978, 4 min)
> *For Georgia O'Keeffe [Pares Magelani]* (1976, 4 min)
> *More than Meets the Eye [Tempora Magelani]* (1979, 8 min)
> *Not the First Time [Tempora Magelani]* (1976, 5 min)
> *Tiger Balm [Memoranda Magelani: #1]* (1972, 10 min)
> *Gloria!* (1979, 10 min)

21. See Warren F. Motte, Jr., ed. and trans., *Oulipo: A Primer of Potential Literature* (Lincoln: University of Nebraska Press, 1986). OuLiPo counted among its members the prolific palindromist George Perec, best known as the author of the constraint-driven novels, *Life A User's Manual*, trans. David Bellos (Boston: David R. Godine, 1987 [orig. 1978]) and *A Void*, trans. Gilbert Adair (London: Harvill, 1994 [orig. 1969]). I discuss OuLiPo at greater length in discussing Diana Thater's work in chapter 10, "Constraint Decree."

22. Hollis Frampton, "A Pentagram for Conjuring the Narrative," in *Circles of Confusion: Film, Photography, Video: Texts 1968–1980* (Rochester: New York: Visual Studies Workshop Press, 1983), p. 64.

23. Frampton's achievement is all the more impressive when it is compared to the surface shock and emotional emptiness of the grotesque tableaux created by contemporary photographer Joel-Peter Witkin. Witkin too uses cadavers and body parts, but his deadened aesthetic strips even the vestiges of humanity and life from his raw materials, creating a voyeuristic jolt that fades to self-loathing almost immediately. See Joel-Peter Witkin, *Gods of Earth and Heaven* (Pasadena, CA: Twelvetrees Press, 1989).

24. Graham Harwood, *A Rehearsal of Memory* (London: ARTEC and Book Works, 1996).

25. When phrased this way, the mouse seems less a technological metaphor than an atavistic holdover from the Victorian madhouses in Bram Stoker's *Dracula* and his visual interpreters from Carl Theodor Dreyer to Francis Coppola.

26. Graham Harwood, text for the *Next 5 Minutes Conference Web Site* (n.d.), <www.dds.nl/~n5m/texts/graham.html>.

27. For more on Shaw's work, see Anne-Marie Duguet, Heinrich Klotz, and Peter Weibel, *Jeffrey Shaw: A User's Manual, From Expanded Cinema to Virtual Reality* (Cantz: Edition ZKM, 1997).

28. Hollis Frampton, unpublished grant application for the Magellan Cycle, cited in James Peterson, *Dreams of Chaos, Visions of Order: Understanding the American Avant-Garde Cinema* (Detroit: Wayne State University Press, 1994), p. 112. See Scott MacDonald, "Michael Snow," in *A Critical Cinema 2: Interviews with Independent Filmmakers* (Berkeley: UC Press, 1992), pp. 74–75 for a discussion on the importance of written text to the filmmaking of Frampton, Snow, Marcel Duchamp and Su Friedrich.

29. A lemma is a proposition that is proved, or assumed to be true, and is then used in proving a theorem. In referring to the film's title, Frampton offers a fairly dense explanation. Like Kurt Gödel, Max Zorn tried to determine whether mathematics could be internally self-proving. Zorn's work was "concerned with the question of whether it was possible to make exact statements about the amount and kind of order that was to be found within sets, including the set of all propositions and proofs that constitutes mathematics itself. The result was Zorn's lemma." Scott MacDonald, "Hollis Frampton," in *A Critical Cinema*, pp. 21–77, p. 51.

30. Hollis Frampton, "Film in the House of the Word," in *Circles of Confusion*, pp. 81–85, pp. 84–85. This text is inextricably bound up with Eisenstein's own essay, "Word and Image," in *Film Sense*, trans. Jay Leyda (New York: Harcourt Brace Jovanovich, 1975 [orig. 1947]), pp. 3–65.

31. McLuhan opens *War and Peace in the Global Village* with a direct discussion of the *Wake*'s importance to his own work: "The frequent marginal quotes from *Finnegans Wake* serve a variety of functions. James Joyce's book is about the electrical retribalization of the West. . . . Joyce was probably the only man ever to discover that all social changes are the effects of new technologies." Marshall McLuhan and Quentin Fiore, *War and Peace in the Global Village* (San Francisco: HardWired, 1997 [orig. 1968]), pp. 4–5. Donald F. Theall, *James Joyce's Techno Poetics* (Toronto: University of Toronto Press, 1997).

32. Other filmmakers were aware of Frampton's growing interest in computers. James Benning made *Pascal's Lemma* (1985), a computer-generated piece, at least in part as homage to Frampton and *Zorns Lemma*. "There's a general reference to Hollis [Frampton] because of his interest in computers . . ." Scott MacDonald, "James Benning," in *A Critical Cinema 2*, p. 246.

33. Henderson, "Propositions for the Explorations of Frampton's *Magellan*," p. 150.

34. Lev Manovich, "What Is Digital Cinema?," in Lunenfeld, *The Digital Dialectic*, pp. 172–192.

35. Henderson, "Propositions for the Explorations of Frampton's *Magellan*," p. 136.

36. "For a Metahistory of Film: Commonplace Notes and Hypotheses," in *Circles of Confusion*, p. 114.

37. Bruce Jenkins, "The 'Other' Cinema: American Avant-Garde Film of the 1960s," in the catalogue *Hall of Mirrors: Art and Film Since 1945*, organized by Kerry Brougher, edited by Russell Ferguson (The Museum of Contemporary Art, Los Angeles and The Monacelli Press, New York, 1996), p. 215.

## Chapter 10

1. Jacques Roubaud, "Mathematics in the Method of Raymond Queneau," in Warren F. Motte, Jr., ed. and trans., *Oulipo: A Primer of Potential Literature* (Lincoln: University of Nebraska Press, 1986), p. 87.

2. Georges Perec, *Life A User's Manual*, trans. David Bellos (Boston: David R. Godine, 1987), p. 119.

3. The twentieth century's obsession with the machine has created a situation in which a huge swath of our artists find themselves—willingly or not—to be Bartlebooths. Artists working in dynamic forms like film, video and digital media confront not simply the questions of access (to funding, to the technologies of production themselves, to institutions that still remain chary of anything they can't nail to a wall or stand on a pedestal) but also of maintenance. From the pleas of film preservationists that "nitrate can't wait" to video archivists who confront storerooms of flaking, unplayable 1" tapes, to the realization that digital media obsolesce within the span of business quarters, as a culture we are only now coming to grips with the fact that most of the works created using technological media will not, cannot survive.

4. Roni Horn describes her own work as site-dependent, and Thater employed this distinction in comments during an interview with the author, Glendale, 1998.

5. Walter Benjamin, "The Work of Art in the Age of Mechanical Reproduction," in *Illuminations*, Hannah Arendt, ed., trans. Harry Zohn (New York:

Schocken, 1969), pp. 217–251. On the issue of Zohn's translation, see Miriam Hansen, "Benjamin, Cinema and Experience: 'The Blue Flower in the Land of Technology,'" *New German Critique* 40 (Winter 1987): 179–224.

6. Jan Avgikos, "Sense Surround: Diana Thater's Screen Scenes," *Artforum* (May 1996): 74–118, and David Pagel, "Into the Light," *frieze* 17 (June-July-August 1994): 22–25.

7. On video art and the techno-sublime see Jeremy Gilbert-Rolfe, "Cabbages, Raspberries, and Video's Thin Brightness," in David Moos, ed., *Painting in the Age of Artificial Intelligence*, *Art & Design* Profile No. 48 (London: Academy Group, 1996), pp. 14–23.

8. Diana Thater, *Electric Mind* (Ghent, Belgium: Imschoot, 1996), contains her screenplay as well as Murphy's story "Rachel in Love."

9. Diana Thater, "Skin deep," in Peter Noever, ed., *The best animals are the flat animals—the best space is the deep space* (Los Angeles: MAK Center for Art and Architecture, LA, 1998), pp. 32–33.

10. Douglas Fogle, "Diana Thater: Being Inside a Work of Art," *Flash Art* 31, no. 198 (January-February 1998): p. 89.

11. Raymond Queneau, "Potential Literature," in Motte, *Oulipo*, p. 51. Queneau, a poet, and the mathematician François Le Lionnais founded OuLiPo in 1960, and its history since that time offers a marvelous counter-fable to the usual teleological march from structuralist to poststructuralist and then on to postmodern practice and theory.

## Chapter 11

1. See chapter 8, "Hardscapes and Imagescapes," and chapter 10, "Constraint Decree."

2. The use of scrims seems to be increasingly important in projection work. The third portion of Bill Viola's piece at the 1995 Venice Biennale was comprised of a series of hanging scrims with projections on either side, leading to the images eventually melting into each other. As mentioned in chapter 7, Char Davies's VR installation *Osmose* (1996) used a backlit scrim to incorporate the figure and movements of her "immersants" for those who watched the show without the benefit of the head-mounted display.

3. Holly Willis, "A Conversation with Jennifer Steinkamp," *Artweek* (October 1998): 16.

4. David Pagel, "High Tech Abstractions," *Los Angeles Times*, December 7, 1995, p. F3. Also see David Greene's comment, "at its core her art's closest analogue is still abstract painting," in his review "Jennifer Steinkamp: ACME, Santa Monica," *frieze* 27 (March/April 1996): 72.

5. Though fully integrating aural elements into the installations remains a challenge (she refers to sound as "a real beast"), Steinkamp has worked with Jimmy Johnson on *Feel Purple, Taste Green* (1994), Brian Brown on *Swell*, and with techno-sound artists Grain on a series of projects including *Orange Six Point Sea* (1995), *Smoke Screen* (1995), *Naysplatter* (1996), *Double Take, Happy Happy*, and *Blue Blow*.

6. Jennifer Steinkamp, "My Only Sunshine," in Judy Malloy, ed., *Women, Art and Technology* (Cambridge, MA: MIT Press, forthcoming). This text and others can be found at the artist's Web site <jsteinkamp.com>.

7. Steinkamp's practice flies in the face of recent attempts to control the emerging discourses of "visual culture." The journal *October*'s special issue on the subject offered the editorial board's ponderous defenses of the disciplinary boundaries of art history and a questionnaire on visual culture that generated such gems as Emily Apter's completely hysterical definition of all things cyber: "Mobilizing ghostly, derealized selves within a dirty realist, sleaze, or pulp tradition (a tradition drawing visually on sci-fi, cartoons, comics, graffiti, porn, fanzines, slash and snuff movies, film noir, flight simulation, surveillance cameras, and technical imaging), cyber operates through a combination of ontological *projection* and ethical *subjection*," October 77 (Summer 1996): 26.

## Chapter 12

1. J. B. Jackson, *The Necessity for Ruins* (Cambridge, MA: MIT Press, 1980), p. 101.

2. *The Big Easy* (Jim McBride, 1987).

3. The Piazza d'Italia (1975–1978) is one of the best known works of American architect Charles W. Moore (1925–1993). Heinrich Klotz describes the Piazza d'Italia as "the most telling example of postmodern architecture" in his encyclopedic *The History of Postmodern Architecture*, trans. Radka Donnell (Cambridge, MA: MIT Press, 1988 [orig. 1984]), p. 130.

4. Stewart Brand is particularly informative on this lapse in architectural discourse in *How Buildings Learn: What Happens After They're Built* (New York: Viking, 1994).

5. From the artist's e-mail correspondence with Lorne Falk, June 27, 1996.

6. The artist shared his sources for the title of the piece.

In 1877 Fontaine, an eminent French engineer and scientist, wrote a book on the incandescent light in which he announced his fixed conclusion that the sub-division of the electric light, that is, the development of small illuminating units of electric light analogous to the illuminating units of gas distribution, was impossible. . . . William H. Preece, in a lecture given on February 15, 1879, before the Royal United Service

Institution, said: 'It is however easily shown (and that is by the application of perfectly definite and well-known scientific laws) that in a circuit where the electro-motive force is constant, and we insert additional lamps, then, when these lamps are joined up in one circuit, i.e., in series, the light varies inversely as the square of the number of lamps in circuit, and that joined up in multiple arc the light diminishes as the cube of the number inserted. Hence a sub-division of the electric light is an absolute *ignis fatuus.'*

Francis Jehl, *Menlo Park Reminiscences,* Volume One (Dearborn, MI: The Edison Institute, 1937), p. 197.

7. Marcia Tucker, then director of the New Museum in New York City, cited in Lawrence Weschler, *Mr. Wilson's Cabinet of Wonder; Pronged Ants, Horned Humans, Mice on Toast and Other Marvels of Jurassic Technology* (New York: Pantheon Books, 1995), p. 40.

8. The MJT promotes itself in its distinctive, almost courtly mode of discourse as

an educational institution dedicated to the advancement of knowledge and the public appreciation of the Lower Jurassic. Like a coat of two colors, the Museum serves dual functions. On the one hand the Museum provides the academic community with a specialized repository of relics and artifacts from the Lower Jurassic, with an emphasis on those that demonstrate unusual or curious technological qualities. On the other hand the Museum serves the general public by providing the visitor a hands-on experience of 'life in the Jurassic.'

From the Museum's promotional materials available on their Web site: <www.mjt.org>.

9. Gary Hill, "Site Re:cite," *Camera Obscura* 24 (September 1990): p. 128.

10. John G. Hanhardt, "Between Language and the Moving Image: The Art of Gary Hill," in *Gary Hill* (Seattle: Henry Art Gallery, 1994), p. 62.

11. The impulse behind *Which tree* can be seen to have migrated into *Withershins,* an interactive sound installation with video projections that premiered at the Venice Biennale in 1995.

12. Hill, "Site Re:cite," p. 135.

13. Weschler, *Mr. Wilson's Cabinet of Wonder,* p. 50. To tie this discussion back to *The Sub-Division of the Electric Light,* Erkki Huhtamo considers that Perry Hoberman's interactive project "might also be read as [a] mock museum of media art," akin to the MJT. Erkki Huhtamo, "Beams of Light in a Virtual Void," *Artbyte: The Magazine of Digital Arts* 1, no. 1 (April–May 1998): p. 60.

14. John Krizanc, *Tamara: A Play You Experience from Room to Room* (Toronto: Stoddart, 1989).

15. Robin Wood, *Hitchcock's Films Revisited* (New York: Columbia University Press, 1989), p. 78.

16. Hill, "Site Re:cite," p. 128.

17. Ibid., p. 125.

18. See "The Dream of the Botanical Monograph" in Sigmund Freud, *The Interpretation of Dreams*, James Stachey, ed. and trans. (New York: Avon, 1965), pp. 316–319.

19. For two reviews that discuss the range of influences, see Tom McDonough, "Adam Ross at Caren Golden," *Art in America* 86, no. 7 (July 1998): 99–100, and David Pagel, "Comes the Dawn: Adam Ross at Shoshana Wayne," *Los Angeles Times*, July 3, 1998: F26.

# Index